D1722453

Praise for *Enabling Next Generation Legacies*

Peter Jaskiewicz and Sabine Rau have compiled a brilliant collection of essays from practitioners and family members on topics that will be of value to enterprising families around the world—all from the perspective of the rising generation! It is a must-read for all families of wealth and their advisors.

> — **Tom McCullough**, Chairman and CEO, Northwood Family Office; Adjunct Professor, Rotman School of Management, University of Toronto; Co-author, *Wealth of Wisdom: The Top 50 Questions Wealthy Families Ask* (Canada)

Enabling Next Generation Legacies is an outstanding offering to the growing appetite for knowledge on how to sustain thriving family enterprises. This concise volume bridges the gap between scholarly expertise and practical wisdom on ensuring family business success and longevity. Peter Jaskiewicz and Sabine Rau have deployed an engaging narrative style that breaks the complexity of family enterprise success into its core constituent elements and presents a wealth of information organized around thirty-five fundamental questions. The book is a timely and wonderfully accessible resource for academics, professionals, and managers seeking a comprehensive guide to family enterprises.

> — **Roy Suddaby**, Professor of Management and Entrepreneurship, Peter B. Gustavson School of Business, University of Victoria (Canada); Carson College of Business, Washington State University (United States)

For a family member to become a professional owner takes continuous learning. It starts with the parental education and continues with professional learnings.

> — **Franz Haniel**, Chairman, Franz Haniel & Cie. GmbH (Germany)

This comprehensive summary of most important questions will support the next as well as current generation of family business leaders to redefine their legacy, manage generational transition, and foster intergenerational collaboration. Congratulations to Sabine, Peter, and all contributors!

> — **Peter English**, Partner, Global Family Business and Europe, Middle East and Africa; Entrepreneurial and Private Business Leader, PricewaterhouseCoopers (Germany)

I am glad future next generations won't have to do it all by themselves. This book has many insights and helpful information together with real NxG [Next Gen] experiences.

— **Alessandra Nishimura**, Third-Generation Board Member, Jacto Group; Co-founder, Arvore da Cidadania; Board Member, Instituto de Desenvolvimento Familiar, Family Business Network (Brazil)

Jaskiewicz and Rau focus on an emergent and fascinating body of research. They succeed in harnessing it into pearls of evidence-based wisdom and advice for next generation members striving to succeed within and beyond their family enterprise.

— **Stéphane Brutus**, Dean, Telfer School of Management, University of Ottawa (Canada)

Profound leadership requires the fearless pursuit of uncomfortable conversations. Without a path, map, or guide, the family context makes such discussions incendiary. Jaskiewicz and Rau have elegantly crafted a much-needed game plan for conversations between generations and self-reflection. This volume should be read by business owners who will benefit from gaining perspective, next generation leaders who need some insight into the problems and challenges they may face, and scholars looking to have closer connections with business-owning families.

— **Joe Astrachan**, Director of nine corporate boards in the U.S. and Europe; Emeritus Professor, Management Kennesaw State University (United States)

Enabling Next Generation Legacies is a family business must-read that we have all been waiting for. Tackling topics ranging from family, to ownership, business, and wealth, the book provides both academic and real-life approaches to the most pressing questions faced by NxGs in enterprising families.

— **Valentine Barbier-Mueller**, Board Member, SPG-Rytz; Board Member, Family Business Network (FBN); Vice President, FBN's NxG leadership program (Switzerland)

Covering the most central topics for the success of next generation members in enterprising families, this book is a MUST-read! It beautifully bridges the worlds of research and practice and offers game-changing guidance and immensely valuable food for thought.

— **Hanoof Abokhodair**, Senior Adviser, National Center for Family Businesses (Saudi Arabia)

Focusing on the next generation, this publication takes on an urgent, fresh perspective that often gets neglected. It presents a comprehensive how-to guide for the Next Gen to evaluate their approach of integration into the family business. For a future-oriented family business, this is an essential angle to highlight. I hope the decision strategies outlined will practically impact businesses, as much as they will create food for thought for the current and the Next Gen; both can benefit greatly from the insights given here.

> — **Albert Behler**, Chairman, CEO, and President, Paramount Group, Inc. (United States)

This book offers an all-encompassing yet easy access for Next Gens to understand the complexity of family business.

> — **Bernhard Simon**, Chairman of the Supervisory Board, DACHSER Group SE & Co. KG (Germany)

The authors—distinguished scholars with a profound understanding of family business practice—discuss thirty-five often-asked-yet-rarely-answered questions of business families worldwide. Their constructive discussions with other leading scholars, practitioners, and family owners offer wise and timely advice that will be of vast help to generations of business families from the West and East, including China.

> — **Chen Ling**, Professor, Family Business and Business History, School of Management, Zhejiang University; Director, Institute for Entrepreneurs, SOM-ZJU; Director, Institute of Family Business, ZJU (China)

From the various families that I've been fortunate to interact with, I've generally seen that responsible family businesses also have responsible next generations. They strive to make decisions that are based on deep thinking and take decisions that are impactful for communities, industries, and the environment. More than anything, this is the result of asking meaningful questions. Sabine and Peter's book looks into one of the most crucial aspects of how family businesses are nurtured over generations.

> — **Arjun Chogule**, Fourth-Generation Member, Executive Director, Chowgule & Company; Board Member, Family Business Network; President, FBN NxG Leadership Team (India)

This book sheds light on the challenges surrounding successful business succession in all its facets. My recommendation: It should be at hand in every family business. Very worth reading!

> — **Reinhold von Eben-Worlée**, CEO, Worlée; President, Die Familienunternehmer [The Family Business Owners] (Germany)

Readable. Insightful. Global. Relevant and very relatable. Jaskiewicz and Rau's Enabling Next Generation Legacies brings us a collection of thirty-five questions that Next Generation members of enterprising families ask. Each question is answered with deliberation, depth, and very naturally. Each answer is accompanied by thoughtful commentary. Not just for next generation leaders, Enabling Next Generation Legacies is a critical read for all members of enterprising families. And their advisors. Future focused, Jaskiewicz and Rau pose great questions and gathered great, provocative answers.

> — **Jeff Noble**, CMC, FEA; Director, Business and Wealth Transition,
> Private Client Services, BDO Canada LLP (Canada)

Full of keen insights from leading family enterprise scholars. Enabling next generation legacies is a valuable addition to any family business educator's bookshelf.

> — **Michael Carney**, Professor, Strategy and Entrepreneurship,
> Concordia University Montréal, Québec (Canada)

Coming from collectivist or individualistic societies, we constantly struggle to keep our families together. This book is a must-read. Real-life experiences, researchers' analysis, and questions to help you preserve and grow your family firms and wealth for generations to come. I recommend it to all family members, whatever their role.

> — **Lama AlSulaiman**, Board member of Rolaco Holdings;
> Shareholder of the AAS Group (Saudi Arabia)

The older one gets the more one realises that family is everything. The same applies to family businesses, where real focus is required to manage the transition to NxG. This book can only help bring clarity to this challenge.

> — **Andrew Wates**, OBE; Ex-Chairman, Wates Group (United
> Kingdom)

ENABLING NEXT GENERATION LEGACIES

35 Questions that
Next Generation Members
in Enterprising Families Ask

PETER JASKIEWICZ &
SABINE B. RAU

FAMILY ENTERPRISE KNOWLEDGE HUB PUBLISHING

Enabling Next Generation Legacies:
35 Questions that Next Generation Members in Enterprising Families Ask
© 2021, Peter Jaskiewicz & Sabine B. Rau. All rights reserved.

Published by Family Enterprise Knowledge Hub Publishing,
Ottawa, Ontario, Canada

ISBN: 978-1-7778063-1-6 (ebook)
ISBN: 978-1-7778063-0-9 (hardcover)

For more information on the book, the contributors, and for additional
resources, please visit: https://www.35questions.com/

Publisher's Cataloging-In-Publication Data

(Prepared by The Donohue Group, Inc.)

Names: Jaskiewicz, Peter, author. | Rau, Sabine B., author.

Title: Enabling next generation legacies : 35 questions that next generation members in
enterprising families ask / Peter Jaskiewicz & Sabine B. Rau.

Description: Ottawa, Ontario, Canada : Family Enterprise Knowledge Hub Publishing,
[2021] | Includes index.

Identifiers: ISBN 9781777806309 (hardcover) | ISBN 9781777806316 (ebook)

Subjects: LCSH: Family-owned business enterprises--Succession. | Family-owned
business enterprises--Management. | Success in business.

Classification: LCC HD62.25 .J37 2021 (print) | LCC HD62.25 (ebook) | DDC
658.04--dc23

Publishing services provided by AuthorImprints.com

Peter dedicates this book to Anna, Leon and Lidiane, Katrin, Jürgen and Christine, and their families: Thank you for being who you are. You give me meaning and inspiration and make a tremendous difference to my life.

Sabine dedicates this book to her late father Ulrich Rau, to Constantin, Renate, Diana, their families, and her close friends and soul mates. Thank you for giving purpose to my life, for your ongoing support and love.

Peter and Sabine have chosen to pay forward the Telfer School of Management's investment in this project by donating their book royalties to a Telfer fund, helping students in need.

TABLE OF CONTENTS

FOREWORD

**Alexis du Roy de Blicquy, CEO,
Family Business Network (FBN)**

When Sabine and Peter approached me about this book, the timing couldn't have been better. The Family Business Network (FBN; www.fbn-i.org) was going to celebrate the twentieth anniversary of its Next Gen community (www.fbn-i.org/communities/next-generation), a vibrant and dynamic group of 6,000-plus young and dedicated members in more than sixty countries. More than ever, Next Gens have the capacity to shape their family business and make an impact as they take up responsibilities as managers and/or (future) owners. Their collective impact can make a huge difference. Indeed, worldwide, family businesses account for two-thirds of businesses, employ 60 percent of the work force and contribute over 70 percent to global GDP. Given this predominance, they have the potential to lead responsible capitalism and be a force for good as our economic and societal systems face enormous and accelerating changes.

At FBN, we challenge the Friedman "shareholder-only" model of business and affirm that the purpose of business is to deliver for *all* stakeholders. We commit to champion a business model that will enable flourishing for people, community, the environment—for generations to come. To deliver on this commitment, FBN partnered with the United Nations Conference on Trade and Development (UNCTAD) to jointly develop the Family Business for Sustainable Development (FBSD) initiative, a first-of-its-kind partnership between the United Nations and the global family business community. Its ambitious package of deliverables aims at mobilizing business families to embed sustainability into their business strategies, thereby committing to concrete, measurable contributions toward the Sustainable Development Goals (SDGs; https://sdgs.un.org/). Key components of the nFBSD Initiative include the Family Business Sustainability Pledge (https://fbsd.unctad.org/pledge/), which is a global call to action to build sustainable family businesses and adopt transparent core sustainability indicators for reporting. Through the positive impacts we create, we can redefine success in business, for society, and across generations. This book will significantly contribute to these best practices and empower Next Gens to make their mark and redefine success based on their own value system. Many of them have contributed to building these practices into the book. Yet, this is much more than a book. It is a useful and practical guide, asking relevant questions and providing concrete tips on how to tackle difficult issues that Next Gens face daily as they increasingly find their place in the family and business organizations.

Business families understand that business is a marathon, not a sprint. By marrying the expertise of an enterprise with the soul of a family, we build values-based businesses across generations, that strive to deliver inclusive growth, better manage risk, and foster resilience.

Alexis du Roy de Blicquy is the CEO of the Family Business Network (FBN; www.fbn-i.org), the world's leading network bringing together over 4,000 business-owning families—17,000 individual members including 6,400 Next Generation members—in thirty-two chapters covering sixty-five countries. Prior to FBN, Alexis held senior positions, including at Lhoist, Verlinvest, Armonea, and IFC (World Bank Group). For six years, he was chairman of the board of ToolBox, supporting NGOs by offering professional consultancy (https://www.toolbox.be/en/). He is a member of the board of Trusted Family, the leading platform for family and shareholder governance (https://trustedfamily.com/), of the Advisory Council of AITIA Institute in Singapore (https://www.aitiainstitute.org), and of various cultural organizations. A Belgian and Swiss citizen, Alexis holds a master's degree in Management Science from Solvay Business School and is an INSEAD IEP and IMD HPL Graduate.

Bill Brushett, President and CEO, Family Enterprise Canada (FEC)

It is generally well-known and accepted that family-owned businesses are the engine of economies around the world. In Canada, they are the most prevalent form of business model and are, without a doubt, critical to our future success and prosperity. While we generally use the term "family business" in referring to this type of business model, the real drivers are the enterprising business families. Businesses may rise and fall over time; however, dynamic enterprising families endure and have been the foundation of the economy for hundreds of years, even millennia. If you believe as I do that enterprising business families really matter to our economic and social well-being, then it follows logically that the Next Gen leaders of those families are key to the future. Demographics and aging will soon guarantee that this next generation steps into leadership and ownership roles within their families. They will assume responsibility as stewards of the enterprise and the family legacy. Investing in the Next Gens and helping them prepare for their future roles is of utmost importance for every business family.

For all Next Gens thinking of getting involved in their family enterprise, I would encourage you to commit to investing in yourself. Transition is not just a matter of passing the torch from one generation to another, or simply stepping into the shoes of your parents. You will need to be innovative and entrepreneurial to ensure success and continuity as you create the next chapter of your family legacy. And you will need the knowledge and skills to help lead the family as well as the business. My advice is to be purposeful in what you do—preparing to take on a leadership role is a journey that requires focus and intentional development.

At **Family Enterprise Canada** (FamilyEnterprise.ca), in pursuing our stated purpose of ensuring the well-being, success, and continuity of business families and their family enterprises across generations, we believe in empowering the next generation by providing them with a dynamic peer community, access to global best resources, and excellent learning opportunities. Connecting with peers and sharing knowledge and experiences is both valuable and impactful for Next Gens who are preparing for leadership roles.

With this book, *Enabling Next Generation Legacies*, Peter and Sabine have created a great resource for Next Gens. With its thought-provoking questions, the book delivers wonderful insights and knowledge on some important topics, and it will serve as a great guide on your family enterprise journey. Enjoy!

Bill Brushett, FCPA, FCA, FEA is the president and CEO of Family Enterprise Canada (http://www.familyenterprise.ca/) and the associated Family Enterprise Foundation (https://familyenterprisefoundation.org/). Reporting to the board of directors, he is responsible for providing strategic and operational leadership and championing the pursuit of its vision, mission, and goals. Family Enterprise Canada is a dynamic community for enterprising families and designated Family Enterprise Advisors (FEAs; http://www.

familyenterprise.ca/) that provides a unique platform for members to learn, grow, share, and connect. Our ecosystem includes business families, designated FEAs, academics, researchers, Family Business Centres, and other entities, all of whom recognize the important role of family enterprise in driving sustainable economic prosperity.

Olivier de Richoufftz, General Secretary, Family Enterprise Foundation (FEF)

When individual projects are more prevalent than group or family projects, Next Gens care even more about making a mark and engaging in a fulfilling cause. The question then becomes: "Where can I best support society while satisfying myself?" If the fundamentals—indeed the purpose—of the company are sound, then bringing my perspective and skills to allow the project (the business's continuity) to endure is the best use I can make of my life. This means I might always come last . . . after our employees, our stakeholders, my immediate family, and family members at large. Empathy, humility, altruism, perseverance, and ethics are the qualities needed by family leaders to protect and strengthen their moral compass. A strong understanding that learning is a lifelong process, not limited to hard skills, and that working on improving soft skills—most needed in family firms—creates a daily struggle to help the company and the community thrive. A sense of effort and fairness as well as a good work-life balance are prerequisites. Every Next Gen should ask: "What can I bring to the project?" In the early stages, there are "my" elements and issues: my ideas, my energy, my talent, my appetite for calculated risks, my compassion. These "my" issues reveal how to be actively involved in a family project and why it is important. The one thing Next Gens should do before deciding to join a project (whatever it may be and whatever their role may be) is what I call a coherence or consistency check: "Do my convictions/aspirations/beliefs reconcile with my actions/attitudes/behaviors? Do they match the family's broader project(s)? Will I be able to deploy these aspects effectively by joining a new project and achieve something bigger than me?" This book is a fount of rare knowledge accumulated by families and experts since the beginning of family enterprise studies, just one generation ago. The next chapter is yours to write!

Olivier de Richoufftz is secretary-general of Family Enterprise Foundation (FEF; https://familyenterprisefoundation.org/), which provides educational resources to entrepreneurial families and promotes the family-owned business model worldwide. A forward-thinker, Olivier avidly supports initiatives that help families adapt for the betterment of their businesses, communities, and their family members. As such, Olivier's oversight of the FEF's Intrapreneurial program has helped shift thinking from the limits of succession planning to active business diversification. Beyond his career, Olivier is involved in humanitarian missions in Asia and Africa and sits on NGO boards of directors. A dual Swiss and French national, Olivier holds an MBA from HEC in Paris. He is married with four children.

Judy Green, President, Family Firm Institute (FFI)

Contemporary conversations about a Next Gens' involvement in a multigenerational family enterprise are complicated. Increasing life spans, evolving concepts of family, marriage, and gender, the future of work, the intersection of philanthropy with investment and impact goals and ideas on equality, and the responsibility of wealthy families in local and global economics are just a few of the topics that influence Next Gens' discussions. Moreover, current conceptual models are under scrutiny, sometimes forcing conversations into frameworks no longer viable, if they ever were. Even what constitutes a "generation" is up for debate when we live in an era in which 70 year olds having children is not something to be remarked upon. So, one could ask, what is the purpose of a book like this? As the editors well know, this was the first question that came to my mind when I was invited to write this brief introduction. Having ruminated on that question for several months, here are some of my thoughts. A book like this:

- Captures a moment in time—a matter of record of what the contributors thought about these topics during a global pandemic.
- Creates an opportunity to pursue the ever-elusive goal of bringing research and practice together in the family enterprise field.
- Serves as a series of conversations starters.

Of these three, my favorite is to think of the book as a point of departure for new and increasingly modern insights and discussions on the topics raised and written about by the contributors—topics for which there is never really "an end in sight." Enjoy!

Judy Green is the president of the Family Firm Institute (FFI), an international professional association of individuals and organizations that advise and study multigenerational family enterprises. She holds a PhD in aesthetics and education from Marquette University. More information on FFI and its educational programs can be found at www.ffi.org and www.ffigen.org. FFI is also the owner of the academic journal *Family Business Review*.

The views expressed in this introduction are her own and are not intended to represent the views of FFI or its members.

ACKNOWLEDGMENTS

T his little book would not exist without the shared efforts of a global community. First and foremost, we would like to thank our families. Peter would like to thank his wife Lidiane Cunha for her patience and unconditional support and the many good discussions they had while he worked on this project. Sabine is grateful to her children Constantin, Renate, and Diana, and their families for their patience while she worked on the book and even more so for their listening to the many stories that accompanied the work on this book.

Moreover, we are deeply indebted to our ninety-one contributing authors from twenty-seven countries who, during the COVID-19 pandemic joined us on our mission to make a difference to Next Gens worldwide. During challenging times, they found the time to write and rewrite their chapters and commentaries and for that, we thank them! We would like to mention a few contributors who went far above our expectations by helping beyond their respective contributions (in alphabetical order): Alexis du Roy de Blicquy, Christine Blondel, Bill Brushett, Marleen Dieleman, Gaia Marchisio, Nava Michael-Tsabari, Jennifer Myatt Pendergast, Olivier de Richoufftz, Kirby Rosplock, Carlo Salvato, Patricia Saputo, Dianne H.B. Welsh, Maximilian Werksmüller, and Marta Widz. We are also indebted to the many families that have, over the years, shared their questions and insights with us and participated in our research projects.

Next, this book project would not exist without the vision, leadership, and support of the previous dean of the Telfer School of Management, François Julien, who provided exemplary support in terms of personal leadership and seed funding to build a knowledge hub and training ground for family enterprises at the Telfer School of Management. It was François Julien who did not hesitate to support this project when Peter brought it to him and found the necessary financial resources to fund it. Thank you for all you have done for the field of family enterprise at Telfer, François!

This project would also not be possible without the many colleagues at the Telfer School of Management and the University of Ottawa who have, in their respective functions, chipped in many times to remove hurdles, resolve problems, and make things happen. Merci a tous et toutes (in alphabetical order): Marc Albert, Marielle Brabant, Stéphane Brutus, Jules Carrière, Roxanne Chénier, Carla De Ciccio, Louise Desjardins, Stéphanie Desnoyers, Shantanu Dutta, Benoit Gagnon, Nadine Guervin, Idil Hachi, Martine Lagacé, Lara Mainville, Wojtek Michalowski, Glen Orsak, James Price, Brianna Rennie, Gregory Richards, and Jonathan Simon.

We are also indebted to outstanding friendly feedback on early drafts from two team members—James Combs, professor of management at the University of Central Florida and visiting professor at the Telfer School of Management, and Elizabeth Tetzlaff, PhD candidate, at the Telfer School of Management. Moreover, we are indebted to Hanoof Abokhodair, Thomas Clark, and Emma O'Dwyer, who have made important suggestions.

Finally, we would not have succeeded in the execution of this book without the pro bono legal support of Ron Prehogan from Brazeau Seller LLP. We are also grateful to David Wogahn, Leslie Schwartz, and Katie Barry from AuthorImprints. David has mentored us on this journey and was of tremendous help. We also want to thank his team, who have done an amazing job in helping us to publish this book.

Thank you all for your patience, understanding, and support from its humble inception as an idea to the printing press.

MOTIVATION

by Peter Jaskiewicz and Sabine B. Rau

Family Enterprises

Family enterprises involve at least two committed family members. Most offer products or services, though there are other forms of family enterprises such as family foundations and family offices. In fact, many families pursue multiple enterprises. They might, for example, own a multigenerational family business, support several family-member start-ups, invest their financial wealth through a family office, and serve various communities and causes through a family foundation. Whatever their type, shape, and size, family enterprises are the most common type of organization around the world.[1] Additionally, despite frequent criticisms, succinctly told in the old adage, "From shirtsleeves to shirtsleeves in three generations," the number of family enterprises is not declining but *growing* in many parts of the world.[2] This growth is not to say that family enterprises do not face challenges; any enterprise—family or not—faces challenges. Family enterprises, however, have the added complexity of the *family* as part of the enterprise. The addition of the family to the enterprise has inspired many publications that provide important insights about how senior generation members (Senior Gens), in charge of the enterprise, should manage the additional complexity stemming from family dynamics, family ownership, family leadership, or family wealth. This book is different from published works because it addresses the intricacies of family enterprises from the perspective of next generation members (Next Gens) who might become in charge of the enterprise in the future. By Next Gens, we mean those who are more than eighteen years old and have grown up in families that pursue at least one enterprise. The answers and behaviors of Next Gens will decide the success of the next generation of family enterprises. The Next Gens are the future of their families and their enterprises. Their questions guide this book. This book is also written with the aid of Next Gens.

Working with and for Next Gens

Over the last five years, we have collected more than 150 formal and informal interviews with families who pursue various enterprises around the world. Building on our initial scribbles in margins and on Post-it notes, we quickly realized that the challenges and questions raised by Next Gens differed from those expressed by Senior Gens. Realizing there was a need to consider the Next Gens' perspective more actively, we systematically collected questions posed by Next Gens, which led to our initial list of questions. In spring of 2020, we asked more than sixty Next Gens in North America, Europe, and Asia to review and comment on our initial list. Their responses were a tremendous help, allowing us to revise our list and formulate thirty-five of their most pressing questions. Many of the Next Gens asked us to compile the answers to the thirty-five questions we shared with them. When asked about the best way to go about it, their responses were insightful:

- Share best practices that are based on evidence.
- Don't use academic language and offer brief responses
- Provide additional resources that I can peruse.
- Involve the leading academics and practitioners out there.
- Please do not sell me stuff.
- Connect me with others.
- Provide answers by families that had relevant experiences.
- Involve Next Gens in the answers.
- Make sure that I can read each chapter on its own.

A Modest Step Forward

Equipped with the Next Gens' suggestions, we compiled the answers to these questions in a format that suits their needs. We looked for the leading academics around the globe who have built both academic knowledge on a topic and practical knowledge working with family enterprises. In other words, most of these individuals are as familiar with hardcore academic methods as they are with real life around boardrooms and kitchen tables. This twofold perspective allows these academics to make a difference for enterprising families by sharing their knowledge—for which we are grateful. After we received their replies, we closed the loop by going back to enterprising families for commentaries. The outcome of this process is a list of thirty-five questions, thirty-five responses from specialized academics, and thirty-five commentaries from members of enterprising families. The questions, commentaries, and responses are grouped into four parts: (1) Family, (2) Ownership, (3) Business, and (4) Wealth.

Every Next Gen is a family member—whether or not they like it. However, their involvement with their family, their family's ownership, business, and wealth will vary across and within families over time. Some Next Gens might decide to work in the family business, while others may focus solely on ownership and board roles. Other Next Gens may choose not to enter the family business and instead manage the family's wealth, start their own venture, or pursue another vocation. Whatever role Next Gens will want or assume, this book provides some initial answers to their pressing questions. Our sincere hope is that the collective effort that has gone into creating this book will empower Next Gens to make a difference as family members, owners, employees, stewards of family wealth, community builders, and societal leaders. The time will come to hand over the power and resources to Next Gens, so that they can build their legacies.

FRAMEWORK

by Peter Jaskiewicz and Sabine B. Rau

Addressing the Questions of Those Whose Future is at Stake—Next Gens

Despite vast cultural, societal, and historical differences, many questions that burden Next Gens seem universal. Although each response and commentary in this book only provide limited insight about how to deal with the thirty-five questions presented, we hope that these insights will serve as a good starting point for Next Gens and their families. Exploring these questions is essential because Next Gens will, metaphorically speaking, sit behind the steering wheel sooner rather than later, and we have a responsibility to help them get ready for their ride. Unfortunately, for decades, Next Gens have been neglected. Compared to nonfamily firms, enterprising families have been perceived by skeptics to be incompetent, outdated, and inferior. The underlying opinion that Next Gens often do worse than Senior Gens has been so pervasive that euphemisms have developed that speak to the founder creating the business, their children maintaining it, and their grandchildren losing it. However, this perception of Next Gens is flawed. Enterprising families have repeatedly and continually proven that they can skillfully curate transgenerational capital, enabling each succeeding generation to be more robust and better prepared to make a difference than the previous. However, the skeptics' beliefs are not entirely unfounded: many other enterprising families decline. Why, then, do some enterprising families fare relatively well while many others fare poorly?

Research shows that enterprising families can be more successful *if* they understand how to both manage their family's complexity and its connection with their enterprise. Conversely, families are likely to be less successful in any enterprise if they are unaware of how to manage the complexity of their family.

Using the Three Circle Model to Understand the Complexity of Family Enterprises

To enable Next Gens to understand the complexity of their families and how to deal with enterprise entanglements, we need a framework. The best-known and most frequently used framework is the Three Circle Model developed by David Tagiuri and John Davis. As depicted below, this model highlights seven different roles that individuals may occupy at the intersection of the family, the business, and ownership.[3] The model is popular because it quickly illustrates that the root cause of common conflicts in enterprising families is individuals' different roles. For example, the family owner who does not work in the business (i.e., role #4) favors higher dividend payouts from the business. Conversely, a family member who works in the business but is not an owner (i.e., role #6) typically favors reinvesting profits in the family business.

The model is also of value for individuals occupying multiple roles—those juggling competing norms. For example, how can the principal family owner dismiss the underperforming CEO who happens to be her brother? In this example, common family norms (e.g., unlimited support and love) collide with common business norms (e.g., merit and performance). Evidence shows how important it is to be aware of overlapping roles and address their underlying norms separately. If the family owner was aware of the overlapping roles, she could tell her brother that in her role as his sister, she loves and respects him dearly and will do anything she can to support him. However, in her role as the principal owner of the business responsible for overseeing the company's leadership, she would communicate to him that unfortunately, because of his underperformance, she must dismiss him. Properly separating entangled roles enables the family owner to comply with the different underlying norms, avoid role confusion, and explain the owner decision clearly, making it more digestible for her brother while preserving their family tie.

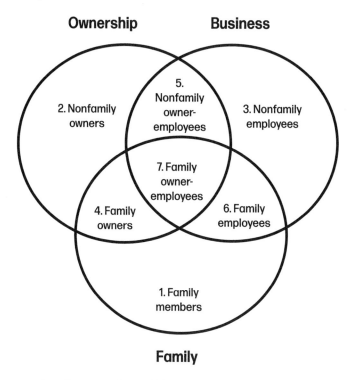

Figure 1: *The Three Circle Model Based on Tagiuri and Davis (1996).*[4]

Introducing the Four-Circle Model to Understand the Complexity Next Gens Face

The questions that Next Gens brought to our attention illustrate the heightened complexity they observed when considering different roles. However, some of their questions did not fit the Three Circle Model—questions like how to deal with the family office, how to engage with the family's philanthropy, when to engage consultants, or how to find a new role after exiting the business. These incompatibilities led to our decision to add another circle—wealth—and a new role: nonfamily member.[5] The figure below illustrates our Four-Circle Model, which addresses how Next Gens can navigate the different norms and roles of the family, ownership, business, and wealth systems. Because Next Gens are family members, the added wealth circle resides within the family. Common norms underlying wealth are preservation, growth, and impact. The role designations W1-W4 highlight that adding the wealth circle creates four new roles, each with its own unique dynamics, namely wealthy family member, wealthy family owner, wealthy family member employed by the business, and wealthy family owner employed by the business. To provide an example, wealthy Next Gens not involved in ownership or the business (role #W1) can be envied by family members (role #1) not involved in ownership, business, or wealth—fueling conflict.

Moreover, the Four-Circle Model includes the new role #8, designating nonfamily members—whether strangers, friends, or consultants. This was important because many Next Gens wonder how to deal with individuals who are outside of the four circles of family, ownership, business, and wealth. Overall, all thirty-five questions that Next Gens raised are captured in our Four-Circle Model. The responses and commentaries to the thirty-five questions introduce approaches available to Next Gens to comply with the common norms of each circle and handle tensions where circles overlap, or the family deals with nonfamily members not involved in the ownership or business circles.

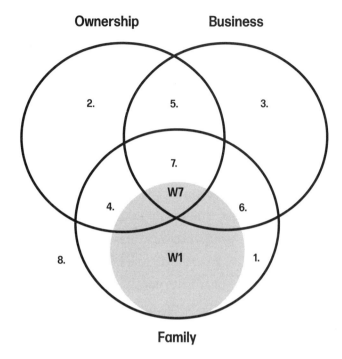

Figure 2: The Four-Circle Model.

(W1: wealthy family members; W4: wealthy family owners; W6: wealthy family members employed by the business; W7: wealthy family owners employed by the business; 8: nonfamily members)

Because Next Gens are born into a family and need to figure out how to handle their family, as well as identify how to manage their (future) connections with the other circles, the first section of the book answers questions tied to the family circle. In the following sections, we engage Next Gens' questions about and beyond the ownership (Section 2) and business (Section 3) circles. Finally, we address questions related to and beyond the wealth circle (Section 4). We introduce each of the four sections with a concise summary of common norms and challenges and conclude the book by highlighting the key takeaways that apply to each of the four circles and by offering some recommendations for the Next Gens' ride ahead.

How to Read the Book

This book is like a buffet: on four tables, thirty-five different appetizers or "amuse gueules" are neatly organized. Although all of them are nutritious, some of these dishes will taste better than others, depending on individual tastes. We recommend that you sample some appetizers at a time and come back to the buffet to taste others later on. We further recommend that you do not stop at the appetizers. This book offers over 150 additional references and over one hundred questions for further reflection that could be your main course. For dessert, you might want to visit the webpage—www.35questions.com—that accompanies this book. Additional resources, videos, and links are available for you to peruse. Finally, we would be delighted to hear from you—both in terms of your feedback and any new questions that you would like to have answered. Undoubtedly, thirty-five appetizers cannot make up an entire buffet, and the cooks are happy to prepare more dishes in the kitchen to satisfy your cravings.

Your Notes | Your Action Items ————————————

Your Notes | *Your Action Items* ————————————————

Endnotes: Motivation and Framework

1. International Family Enterprise Research Academy," Family Businesses Dominate: International Family Enterprise Research Academy (IFERA)," *Family Business Review* 16, no. 4 (December 2003): 235–240.
2. Adrian Wooldridge, "To Have and to Hold," *The Economist*, April 18, 2015. https://www.economist.com/sites/default/files/20150418_family.pdf.
3. Renato Tagiuri and John Davis, "Bivalent Attributes of the Family Firm," Working paper, Harvard Business School, Cambridge, MA. Reprinted in the *Family Business Review* 9, no. 2 (June 1996): 199–208.
4. Tagiuri and Davis, "Bivalent Attributes of the Family Firm."
5. Note: John Davis has thought about this fourth circle, but, ultimately, decided to develop an entirely new model: John A. Davis, "The Family Enterprise Model," Cambridge Institute for Family Enterprise note, 2013.

PART 1: FAMILY

by Peter Jaskiewicz and Sabine B. Rau

F amilies differ—from the single parent with a child to the clan with thousands of members spread around the globe. The size of families and the interactions among their members differ largely and are influenced by the norms and values of their society and culture. What seems normal to a family in India might be unacceptable to a family in the U.S. and vice versa.[1]

Despite some variation, common norms associated with the family are unconditional support and love. Any member of any family hopes to rely on their family's support when needed, whether or not they deserve such support. Moreover, we learn what love means in the context of our families, where we are seen how we are, as well, how we could be. The insights and observations shared in this first section of the book come from different families around the globe and thus offer context-specific examples rather than general solutions. However, they provide important starting points for reflection.

Everyone is born into a family. Most people grow up with their parents, spend their lives with siblings, and raise their children. They interact more or less frequently with many or few other family members. Family members support each other, eat and laugh together, and, yes, gossip about and fight with each other. Despite its importance from birth to death, the family remains one of the most important yet challenging aspects of our lives. For some, it is the core of their identity, the group of people that give meaning and provide love, and the tree upon which they grow their legacy. For others, it is the root of their disappointment and the group with whom they share conflict and, in some cases, seek to leave as soon as possible. Leo Tolstoy famously stated, "All happy families are alike; each unhappy family is unhappy in its own way." For Next Gens to understand their family and satisfy family norms, they need to enjoy spending time with their fellow family members, be good listeners and hosts, be empathetic, and, maybe most importantly, be able to forgive. Our interactions with hundreds of families and their Next Gens allow us to add a few more observations that help distinguish among enterprising families, both happy and not.

Taking the family for granted. The family provides insurance against failure, the place where members receive unconditional love and support. At times, it is a safe space for those stressed by the demands of the enterprise. However, we also observe that some families forget to replenish their emotional resources. They fail to celebrate the family's importance, interact with each other as a family, or socialize Next Gens into assuming roles within the family. Without the binding agents of shared memories, captivating stories, and collective achievements, the glue that unifies the family and encourages Next Gens to stick together will weaken.

Disagreeing on who is family. Many value family and see it as important, but it is common for families to disagree, without realizing it, on who is—and who is not—family. Are spouses, partners, adoptees, and best friends family? Disagreeing on who constitutes the members of a family often lays the groundwork for severe conflict around who should be informed about what, who is eligible for certain roles within the family or enterprise, or who is entitled to inherit shares.

Revitalizing family. Senior family leaders sometimes worry about their businesses and wealth but show insufficient concern for the family. When this happens, Next Gens can and should learn about their family and its patterns and leverage such knowledge to address and reverse poor family dynamics—at least in their own generation. There is no quick fix for continually failing to prioritize or consider the family. Family members, like leopards, do not change their spots and long-maintained family dynamics cannot be changed overnight. However, Next Gens have an opportunity to revitalize a family, a branch of it, or those relationships they deem important.

Based on our observations, we believe that the necessary foundation for any family enterprise is the family. If the family is nurtured and well managed, it can contribute to the enterprise or leave it gracefully. Family members can be reflective and responsible owners and stewards of the family's wealth. Whether they decide to stay or leave their enterprise, they can grow into a cohesive group that enjoys being together and leaves their mark on the world. To help Next Gens reflect upon their family foundation, we open this book by focusing on the family. We recommend that Next Gens who want to become involved in family enterprises understand the family first. What is their family about? Where does their family come from and where are they heading? For what purpose? The first part of this book sheds light on eight fundamental questions that Next Gens have asked about the family and its connection with family ownership, business, and wealth. Any enterprise requires a strong foundation, and family is often just such a foundation.

1.1
Who Is Considered Part of the Family?

Response by Gibb Dyer, U.S.

The question "who is considered part of the family" is important for both academics and consultants who study and work with family businesses as well as family business owners and managers themselves. For academics and consultants, identifying who is considered family is key to determining a family's impact on a business (and the business on the family) while those families who own and manage a business often need to decide if those who are considered family will have an opportunity to be involved in the ownership or management of the business.

Definition of "Family"

To identify who makes up a family we need to understand what people commonly consider a family to be. The definition of family is problematic today given the various types of families that exist. For our purposes, a family will be defined as "individuals who identify themselves as a family unit, are recognized by others as part of a family, and share a common biological, genealogical, and/or social history."[2]

Families come in all shapes and sizes. Common family types include the nuclear family (father, mother, and often children), extended family (one or more children living with a parent and a related nonparent adult, often a grandparent), blended family (one or more children living with a parent and a stepparent), cohabiting family (one or more children living with a parent and an unrelated adult), a single adult/parent family, and a polygamous family (typically one or more children living with a father who has multiple wives).

Family as a Social Construction and Legal Entity

These different family configurations raise interesting questions concerning who is considered family. For example, should a child consider an unrelated adult cohabiting with her mother a family member? Or should a child consider the children of a stepparent members of his family? While there are legal determinations of what constitutes a family, very often family is a social or cultural construction created by family members. For example, while a stepparent might legally adopt a child, that child may not recognize or relate to the stepparent as her father or mother. In other situations, there are parents who "disown" their biological children—the parents may be biologically related to a child, but they do not recognize that child as a member of their family, often due to what the parents consider bad behavior on the part of the child. However, when it comes to inheritance, unless a family member is explicitly denied an inheritance in a family member's will, they might still have a claim on that family member's assets—particularly if that person is a blood relative or a spouse —and those assets might include the family firm.

Family Roles in the Family Firm

We see families who own and manage family businesses having family members take on a variety of roles in the business. Ownership and management roles in the business typically consist of family members who are central to the business and have the most power. Other family members may have management roles but are not involved in ownership. Often Next Gens fill this role but hope to eventually be owners when succession occurs. Conflicts may occur when certain family members own the business but are not managers in the business. Family members who are in the business typically benefit from their salary and other perquisites that managers receive and are generally interested in putting profits back into the business to help it grow. However, family members who are owners and not managers typically want the profits from the business to end up in their pockets so they can benefit from the business' success. This creates natural conflicts between family members who are owners and family members who are managers in the business (and may be owners as well). During succession, family members who haven't been either owners or managers may want to lay claim to the firm's assets increasing the likelihood that family conflicts will occur. Even if a family member hasn't been involved in owning or managing the business, she may lay claim to the firm's assets based on inheritance or some other criteria. For that reason, it is important for a family to determine not only who is currently considered family but who in the family may have a legal claim to the family's business assets.

Family Membership and Succession Planning

Family conflicts and lawsuits are often the result of ambiguity regarding "who is the family." With that in mind, it is important for families who own businesses to identify all individuals in the family who currently or may in the future be involved in family business ownership and management, take those family members into account when making decisions regarding the firm, and make provisions for those family members who will likely not be owners or managers. The rule of thumb is for parents (or other senior family members) to leave other assets in their wills (money, property, etc.), not family business ownership, to such heirs to avoid conflicts.

These issues are also important to consultants who want to help family firms.[3] Research shows that before succession takes place the family should put together a clear succession plan, specifying which family members will be owners and managers in the business. It is important to *share* that plan with the family before succession takes place. To do this, the family needs to identify who is legally considered a member of the family and thus may have legal claims to the firm's assets as well as those who may not be considered legal claimants but are viewed to be family members with many of the privileges of legal family members. To plan for such a change, research by Ivan Lansberg and others encourages family members to have common goals or a "shared dream" along with creating ownership structures and processes to resolve these potential conflicts.[4]

W. Gibb Dyer (PhD MIT) is the O. Leslie and Dorothy Stone Professor in the Marriott School of Business at Brigham Young University. He has been a visiting faculty member at IESE in Barcelona, Spain, and a visiting scholar at the University of Bath. He has published nine books and over fifty articles and his research has been featured in *Fortune, The Wall Street Journal* and *Fast Company*. His recent book, *The Family Edge*, focuses on how "family capital" supports business growth. He has been ranked as one of the top ten scholars in the world in the field of family business.

Commentary by Marcelo De Rada Ocampo, Bolivia

My family's business is an international insurance brokerage in Bolivia. After a decade of experience working for both U.S. and Bolivian insurance companies, my father started the business in 1995 and grew it to become the largest brokerage in Bolivia in terms of revenue, clients, and number of sales agents with presence in all cities in Bolivia. In 2009, he and two partners from Ecuador and Venezuela developed a strategic alliance that made them the third-largest MGA (managing general agent) in LATAM, partnering with ten different international insurers, managing hundreds of distributors, and operating twelve offices across seven different countries.

I am the oldest of three from my father's second marriage. My half-sister is thirty-seven and lives in Florida, while my younger brother (twenty-five years old) is in San Diego, and my younger sister (twenty-two years old) lives in Miami. After studying in the U.S. and working at start-ups in San Francisco for two-and-a-half years, I returned to Bolivia to help my father in the family business. I worked as a sales operations manager, splitting my time between empowering sales agents with training and new digital tools, and the insurance partners negotiating new policy coverages, premium increases, and sales incentives. Now, while I am doing my MBA at INSEAD, I continue to support my father as an advisor, holding weekly to biweekly calls with him to discuss the strategic and operational challenges of the business.

The article is a good starting point in understanding why it is important to define who is considered part of the family in a family business. I agree with Prof. Gibb Dyer that having a clear definition is essential in helping the first generation build a fair process with regards to the ownership and ownership of the business. This can be critical when future generations start getting involved in the business and don't have the same understanding of who is considered part of the family and its impact on the business. Even just as a second generation, I frequently found myself between my two parents in discussions about the fairness of financially supporting struggling family members in each of their extended families. There were efforts of providing employment to extended family members, which ended up creating more harm than good, probably caused by the lack of clarity regarding the roles of each family member in the family firm. From my experience without clarity about the rights and responsibilities of owners and managers, succession planning has been difficult to push forward. An owner must understand and allow the manager to operate the business successfully, while the manager must also provide the owner with enough transparency on the strategic alignment and execution of the business in order to put to best use the business assets.

Questions for Further Reflection

- Who belongs to your family and why are they considered family?
- What are the views of (potential) in-laws about "who is family?"
- From your perspective, why is it important to agree on who belongs to the family?
- What does the phrase "belonging to the family" mean to you? If someone is considered family, what would you do for them and what would you not do for them?
- What problems could emerge if family members do not know that they disagree on who belongs to the family?

Your Notes | Your Action Items

1.2
How Can I Become a Respected Representative of the Family?

Response by Audrey-Anne Cyr and Isabelle Le Breton-Miller, Canada

According to a report released by PricewaterhouseCoopers in 2016,[5] as many as 88 percent of next generation members want to leave an indelible mark on their family business. However, before they can do so, they must first join the business, and earn respect and legitimacy from the family, and also from the various company stakeholders—employees, customers, suppliers, and community at large—by demonstrating their ability to be good family representatives. Representing the family does not merely imply defending its interests in the company but also exemplifying and embodying shared family values, traditions, and legacies. Thus, the legitimacy of family representatives is based upon two things. First, family representatives must embody and defend the values and interests of their family. Second, they must be able to convince the stakeholders of their business that they possess these qualities.

Becoming a Respected Family Representative: A Long-Term Process

Patience is required for a successor wishing to become a respected representative of the family as it is based on a decades-long process[6] that can be encapsulated in three stages. It begins in childhood. It is during these formative years that Next Gens develop their individual identity. This is when children are socialized to embody family and business values and begin to embrace the goals, hopes, aspirations, and ethical positions of their family. Later, during the early years of induction into the firm, Next Gens consolidate their role as family representatives in the company as a productive employee of the business. In the process they develop and reconcile their job and tasks in the firm with their personal talents and aspirations. They must also earn the respect of stakeholders in the business which includes employees, customers, suppliers, and the community at large. Finally, as they take the reins of the business, the new generation is called upon to deploy as the focal family representative. This means they embrace the more significant leadership role of becoming a worthy steward for the family and the company, building stakeholder trust and respect in the process. We shall discuss each of these phases in turn.

Stage 1: Developing an Individual Identity: Socialization and Harmony

The first step to becoming a family representative begins in childhood and adolescence for a Next Gen successor. Through their close social interactions with other family members in the family home and sometimes even with employees within the business, Next Gens are able to develop and assimilate the values and beliefs shared by their family.[7] These interactions imbue Next Gens with the values of the family. Family interactions also provide context in order for them to forge their individual identities and comportment in harmony with the family and the business. For example, the children may see their parents helping out in community charitable activities, helping out employees in need, and being available to others during times of crisis. The behavior of their parents may inspire them also to demonstrate, in their daily lives, ethics of honesty, modesty, and industriousness, not spending lavishly on luxuries or parading their wealth or status before others.

Stage 2: Consolidating Professional Identity: Reconciliation and Legitimacy

When entering the family business, next generation members must forge a professional identity that includes taking a role in the business and developing a path for growing in that role.[8] They need to acquire the experience and skills appropriate for their new functions while also representing family values and interests. By working for the firm, they must consolidate and reconcile their new professional roles with their personal interests and competencies, and their family's values. The fit between these personal talents and aspirations and their job in the firm can be facilitated by rotating through different functions in the company. Fit with the firm can also be achieved in part by being introduced by senior respected family leaders and other executives to key customers, suppliers, and prominent members of the community. It can be aided by mentorship in different positions by family leaders or significant employees working in the firm. Codifying company history through documents, artifacts, tales of past challenges and victories, and periodic gatherings celebrating key events can reinforce a family member's professional identity.[9] These activities enable Next Gens to gradually gain legitimacy and the respect of their family and other company stakeholders by serving as worthy representatives.

Stage 3: Deploying as a Respected Family Representative: Continuity and Renewal

When finally deployed as leaders and thus focal representatives of the family, members of the new generation must continually reinforce their legitimacy to maintain the respect of stakeholders. It is, therefore, important for family representatives to be able to support continuity by both acting as effective guardians of evolving family traditions and values while also ensuring the renewal of the business.[10] This can be a challenge. On the one hand, a family member must preserve what is best about a business—its values, core competencies, and its most strategic employees and their skills and relationships. On the other hand, firms confront competition from rival companies, changes in technology, and evolving economic and even political conditions. Thus, business renewal is essential. One way to convey this message to family members is to highlight the core business qualities and resources to preserve, while emphasizing constant vigilance towards emerging challenges and opportunities. By balancing continuity and renewal of family and corporate values, representatives will successfully maintain the respect and confidence of all stakeholders.

Becoming a Respected Family Representative: A Responsibility

In summary, for Next Gens, for becoming a respected family representative it is essential to build respect in the eyes of other family members and firm stakeholders. This respect can only be built over time and can be managed according to the stages we have just described. Throughout their lives, Next Gens should be aware that taking on the role of family representative is not an acquired right, but an important social responsibility.

Audrey-Anne Cyr is a PhD candidate at HEC Montréal (https://www.hec.ca/en/index.html). Her research focuses mainly on the management of social relationships in family firms and the development of social capital over generations. As part of a project led by the chair of succession and family enterprise (https://chaireentreprisefamiliale.hec.ca/en/) at HEC Montréal, she has been working on the development of a website on succession (From Success to Succession) that offers key information and tools for incumbents and successors, and promotes the development of competent and dynamic successors.

Isabelle Le Breton-Miller (https://www.hec.ca/en/profs/isabelle. lebreton.html) is a professor of management and holds the chair of succession and family enterprise (https://chaireentreprisefamiliale. hec.ca/en/) at HEC Montréal. She received her PhD from Imperial College, London, after having served in senior resource management positions in several companies. Her research, teaching interests, and publications focus on strategies, organization designs, governance structures, and succession within family businesses. She has authored over fifty publications on family firms. Since 2016, she has been a member of the College of New Scholars, Artists and Scientists of the Royal Society of Canada.

Commentary by Lindsay Jephcott, Canada

Our family is in the development, home building, golf, and investment business. We have a family office that services twenty-six family members. I'm the chief investment officer in the family office. To become a respected representative of a family, family office, or family business, there are seven main traits and skills a family member should develop. In no particular order, those traits and skills are transparency, accountability, adaptability, amiability, outstanding communication skills, respectfulness, and professional accreditation.

Transparency is essential in gaining trust from family members. While transparency may be important in every business and within one's professional designation, it is even more so when a family member is representing a family business. There is a natural tendency within families to be more suspicious of another family member who is in a position of control. When business and human resource issues arise, transparency in a timely manner leads to a higher likelihood of success.

Accountability is paramount to becoming a respected family member. This can be as simple as punctuality, showing up to events and meetings, and behaving in a professionally appropriate manner. It is also important to see tasks through to completion, and to follow up on action items that are incomplete. The ability to accept failure and constructive criticism is also a key factor. When follow through is not completed, family members may take this as a personal affront, so it is important to be thorough and to meet commitments.

As a representative of the family, one is faced with a professional divide, the need to deal with professionals in the business world, and the need to deal with family members and family politics. Adaptability is therefore an important skill to have. The skills needed to conduct oneself in a professional manner in a room full of investment bankers, for example, might not be appropriate for a more casual family board meeting. The language one uses may be adapted based on the audience. The skill is knowing when and how to adapt.

In a complex family structure, there will be many different people with varying degrees of skill and experience. To become a successful representative of the family, amiability is an important trait. One must communicate with multiple generations and personalities. A likeable personality is important so that each family member feels comfortable sharing personal information. Emotional history and complexities are ever present within a family business. One must be able to navigate these difficult situations, and to make sure one's emotions are secondary to the family members to ensure cohesiveness within the organization.

Outstanding communication skills are of great importance. With multiple personalities, skillsets, experience, and generations, it is essential to be able to communicate with each family member in a way that they can comprehend the information and feel comfortable.

Respectfulness complements the need for excellent communication skills. One must treat every family member with the same amount of dignity and respect. Reserving judgment on family members is imperative, as is avoiding negative or judgmental conversations about family members. Speaking positively and focusing on every individuals' strengths versus weaknesses, is a crucial way to gain respect.

A family representative should have the outside experience and professional accreditation required to fulfill one's job. This is more important than in other careers, as the family will want to validate that the role has been filled by a candidate who was hireable elsewhere and is a credible professional. It is advisable to bring outside experience to the family office as it can enhance best practises, strategies, and efficiencies within the organization. Ongoing education and mentorship are recommended as well.

Questions for Further Reflection

- What are the characteristics of a respected family representative in your family?
- What might be the characteristics of a respected family representative in the eyes of nonfamily members who are part of the top management team and/or board of directors?
- What are the important steps for becoming a respected family representative?
- What problems might arise if Next Gens who want to become respected representatives are not supported by Senior Gens?
- Why is good communication essential for becoming an effective family representative?

Your Notes | *Your Action Items* ————————————

1.3
We Have Always Had a Fair Deal of Conflicts in the Family. Now That I Am an Adult, Should I Do Anything About It?

Response by Kimberly Eddleston, U.S.

Conflict is a normal part of family life, but what varies is how families manage conflict and the degree to which it is destructive or productive. For business-owning families, conflict is particularly pervasive because of the intertwining of work and family roles. Family members cannot simply leave conflicts at work when they go home. It is therefore important for Next Gens to learn to effectively manage conflict—for the health of their family and business.[11]

Is the Conflict "Good" or "Bad"?

It is important to understand that not all forms of conflict are bad. Although "conflict" tends to have a negative connotation, it generally reflects disagreement or variance in opinions—something that can help families avoid groupthink and develop more creative solutions.[12] Two types of work-related conflicts that are often beneficial in moderate doses are task conflict and process conflict. Task conflict centers around disagreements related to the work at hand. For example—what strategies should we pursue? What tasks should be performed? Process conflict centers around disagreements about who is responsible for which tasks. For example—how should work be accomplished? How can we best utilize individuals' talents and skills? As one can imagine, discussions that reflect these productive types of conflict can help a family business assess its goals, adapt to changes in the environment, and ensure that the right people are assigned to specific tasks.

Relationship conflict, on the other hand, is always destructive. Relationship conflict refers to perceptions of personal animosity and includes an emotionally laden component (e.g., animosity, frustration, annoyance). It leads to low levels of decision quality, resentment, and worry, and threatens the stability of the business and family.[13] For business-owning families, relationship conflict is particularly devastating because infighting can result in a lack of attention and focus on the needs of the business. Families with greater relationship conflict are also more likely to employ family members who are impediments to the business (e.g., Fredo effect)[14] and suffer issues at succession that can lead to business failure. For families experiencing relationship conflict, it is important that family members work to improve their bonds and sense of loyalty.

Moving Past Relationship Conflict

Because relationship conflict is inherently destructive, it is important for Next Gens to put aside conflicts of the past and develop practices that support healthy relationships. As a business-owning family grows in branches, generations, and size, the family must become more proactive and deliberate in forming bonds among its members. Cousins, for instance, need to share experiences and memories that will help them cherish family relationships and prevent dysfunctional conflicts. One way to create family bonds is to plan retreats aimed at building connections. Attending workshops that focus on developing skills for effective interpersonal interactions and conflict management is also a beneficial activity.

Understanding Conflict Management Styles

When identifying productive ways that families disagree, it is important to understand the family's preferred conflict management style and learn how styles can be used to better manage conflict. Based on the degree to which the best solution is chosen and a positive relationship results, five conflict management styles exist: accommodating, avoiding, competing, compromising, and collaborating.[15]

Accommodating is a strategy of sacrifice and low assertiveness. It is when an individual is willing to give up something important to preserve the relationship. Accommodating tends to be an effective strategy when preserving the relationship is more important than winning the conflict. Although this strategy encourages family harmony, it can result in suboptimal business solutions.

Avoiding is when the source of the conflict is ignored. Avoiding a conflict often means delaying a dispute that will one day have to be dealt with, most likely making the tension harder to resolve. However, avoiding a conflict can be beneficial when disagreements are minor. In family businesses, a tendency to rely on avoidance is associated with low family satisfaction, sibling rivalry, and distrust. A major issue with this style is that it leads to long periods without expressing differences, which often results in tensions mounting and a blow up.

Competing is when individuals force their initiatives and ideas onto others without concern for others' opinions or feelings. It can involve threats or forced compliance. In family businesses it tends to escalate relationship conflict and impede performance. It also leads to anger and mistrust.

Compromising results from trying to find a resolution that partially satisfies all parties. It often creates a temporary solution, but not a long-term resolution to the conflict. Compromising can limit the discussion of ideas and decrease the likelihood of finding the best solution. In family businesses, it can help preserve family relationships, but in the long run, it can damage firm performance.

Collaborating is when individuals work together to develop mutually agreed-upon solutions that address the concerns of all parties. It can improve cooperation, commitment, and organizational learning. This conflict management style has the best outcomes for both the family and business.

Conclusion

In closing, it is important that Next Gens work together to foster productive conflict and eliminate dysfunctional conflict. Families with strong bonds and effective communication work hard to develop and maintain healthy family relationships. This should be an important goal of all business-owning families. To determine what your family's conflict management style is, Ritch Sorenson offers a free online exercise that I have used in Next Gen classes and with family business clients, "Future Family Business Owners Can Learn to Manage Conflict."[16] This is a good place to start as you aim to develop better family relationships. With better conflict management, business-owning families will enjoy a healthier family and a healthier business.

Kimberly A. Eddleston is the Schulze Distinguished Professor of Entrepreneurship, and Montoni research fellow at the D'Amore-McKim School of Business, Northeastern University. She is also an academic scholar at Cornell University's Smith Family Business Initiative. She serves as senior editor for the Entrepreneur & Innovation Exchange (eix.org), and founding editor of FamilyBusiness.org. Professor Eddleston has won multiple awards for her research and has published more than seventy articles in leading journals such as *Academy of Management Journal*, *Strategic Management Journal*, and *Journal of Applied Psychology*. In addition, she has had various levels of involvement with several of her family's businesses.

Commentary by Daniel Aponte Prypchan, Venezuela

I am a third-generation member of two families. The Aponte family, on my father's side, is in the business of farming, banking, commercial, and residential real estate and a large network of pharmacies. The Prypchan family, on my mother's side, is in the business of hospitals; we run Venezuela's largest psychiatric hospital, and development and construction of real estate both in health care and residential property. I am more involved with mother's side (Prypchan) family as I am in an inheritance lawsuit with my father's family. I am currently the manager of our not-for-profit organization in the U.S., Psychiatry, Philosophy and the Arts, and I deal with all the accounting, payroll, and other issues of all our properties in Venezuela, acting as a de facto small family office manager.

I think the question of how to deal with conflicts, especially if they are long-standing conflicts, is an important one and should be answered before a Next Gen decides to enter the family business in a more active way. Regarding the response by Prof. Eddleston, I think it is useful in guiding a younger Next Gen through the basic precepts of conflict as something all business-owing families go through. It is a great article to start to put some order to the issues you may be experiencing in your family business. However, when the issues of the family are intense and go well into the destructiveness of "relationship conflict" over generations, the level of help of this article decreases significantly.

In my experience most of the issues afflicting families in business are deeply entrenched and sometimes difficult to even verbalize. Sometimes it's not that the family doesn't know what do to, but that the family is caught in a dysfunctional dynamic that does not allow them to take action, leaving them stuck for years in pathological reactions ranging from minor arguments to outright abuse and bereavement. What do you do then?

My father's mother lied to my face about my inheritance for nine years, saying that "all will be divided fairly and by the law" whilst falsifying signatures, selling assets, and taking money to other jurisdictions. I was twenty-four when my grandfather died and I am now forty-one, and I have yet to receive my inheritance. I'm still in various lawsuits against them. My grandmother died six months ago. My father died in a plane crash when I was two and my grandmother was the person who identified his body. Most of my grandmother's actions had nothing to do with me. She barely knew me. Her actions were more about her relationship with men, her anger at my mum not speaking to them, and many more things that I will never know about. I had a feeling that this could happen, but I thought I was doing the correct thing giving them time to sort everything out and to collaborate. Not suing them earlier is the biggest regret and mistake of my life. It is important to always understand the dynamics of your family. Lack of real insight can create naivety about the ways family relationships can go wrong. I have been in therapy, I have studied family dynamics, I have done all sorts of spiritual and psychological courses and training, all to deal with my grief and my own responsibility in not knowing my family enough to preempt this sort of destructive behaviour occurring. It was there, obvious to others, but I never fully took responsibility to know and act accordingly.

Coming from two less-than-functional families owning multiple businesses, I can recommend some basic concepts that would allow a Next Gen to navigate and understand their complex family's dynamic better. Broadly speaking my key recommendations would be:

1. Understand the core values of the senior generation.
2. Connect with your family's wounds and traumas.
3. Be empathic and compassionate towards all family members.
4. Be mindful of all communications.

5. Take responsibility for your part in the dynamic.

6. Own your family's dynamics and be responsible to heal them.

7. Ethical considerations—if not you, who will do it?

This sounds simple but achieving a high level of understanding of your family dynamic is the work of a lifetime. The good news is that the more you understand the dynamic and its members, the more you will be able to stir your family into a healthier path of love and connection. Simply trying to apply any system of control over a dynamic you neither own nor fully understand will probably not work. The work of knowing one's family is beautiful and necessary.

Questions for Further Reflection ———————

- Does your family have family-specific types of conflict? If so, what are they?
- Are all conflicts in families considered "bad"?
- What is your own conflict management style when you disagree with your parents, siblings, and/or cousins?
- What could you do to help reduce the dangers of detrimental conflicts in your family?
- What are some ways to address debilitating and entrenched conflicts in families?

Your Notes | Your Action Items ———————

Your Notes | *Your Action Items* ——————————

1.4
We Are Living All Over the World. What Can We Do to Help Keep the Family Together?

Response by Christine Blondel, France

Families Living All over the World

With an increasing number of family members studying and sometimes settling abroad, keeping the family together can be a challenge. A poll conducted by the hotel chain IHG in 2019 among 2,000 people in the UK indicated that the respondents' average family spanned over 2,000 miles around the world, and that one in ten persons surveyed had a family member living 10,000 miles away. The survey also mentioned that *51% of those surveyed thought that many did not make the effort to get together.*[17] The survey was conducted in the general population, not in a pool of business-owning families, which could be expected to have a higher motivation to make the efforts to get together. However, the question remains: Do we make the effort? And if we do, which efforts can we make? What can we do to help keep the family together?

Stay in Touch

Stay in touch with the "big" family meeting or family trip: A number of families have a history of travelling and setting up businesses in different parts of the world, like Chinese, Lebanese, or Indian diasporas. Several Indian families can be an inspiration in the way they organize systematic yearly reunions to gather family members from different parts of the world. These yearly reunions generally last several days and include separate business and family moments.

Comparably, some European business families organize trips every year or so. All family members gather in their home country or abroad, for a programme that includes visits of family business facilities, sightseeing, and family activities. Travel provides casual forms of interactions, such as singing together in the bus after dinner. More simply, the general assembly of shareholders, held once a year, can be expanded beyond the formal meeting to include a lively information session about the business, exchanges, and some nice family time afterwards. Some families run two such meetings per year, and the historic family home, if still there, can be a great gathering point.

Stay in touch—there are so many other opportunities to connect: While the big family meeting is a wonderful opportunity to celebrate the family and its activities, smaller meetings can be organized by age groups, affinities, and geographies. Members of a large business family explain how they multiply occasions to meet: welcome seminar for young owners from the age of eighteen (with sessions on history, business activities, meetings with leaders, etc.), Next Gen thematic evenings followed by informal get-togethers or quarterly exchanges between young family professionals about their careers.[18]

Stay in touch without travelling: The COVID pandemic created another challenge for families spread throughout the world: family meetings or trips were no longer possible for most families. However, in parallel, the pandemic triggered a complete change in habits with the extensive use of video conferences. We have seen virtual family meetings with dozens of members who could participate using instant survey tools. Ironically, distant members who seldom attended before could be there thanks to technology—which should definitely be kept in the family tool kit. In addition to the expansion of video meetings, more traditional technical tools such as intranet platforms are still used by families to connect and share information, as well as more accessible and instantaneous messaging applications. It should be noted that intranet platforms need to be fuelled in order to stay attractive, while messaging applications require sensitivity in their use—the impact of an emotional comment can go well beyond its intention once it reaches dozens of family members. As families develop codes of conduct for their meetings, they can develop codes for the use of social media and other tools.

Interestingly in a technology era, some families still develop and distribute *paper newsletters*. These hard copies, which include information about the business, the family, and other activities (such as philanthropy, entrepreneurship, history, etc.), can easily be shared with close family members of all ages.[19]

Take an Active Role and Become Involved in a Project

Get involved: Family meetings, trips, or newsletters can be lived in a passive way (e.g., showing up at the meeting, which is already positive) or in a more active way (e.g., helping with the meeting organisation, contributing to the newsletter, etc.). A rotation can be organized in order to engage more family members in the organisation. There are many other projects in which family members can take an active role, such as contributing to the family tree and family history (e.g. filming interviews of senior members of the family), organizing owners' education, promoting the development of the family "creed" (values, vision, mission), creating a family charter, and being engaged in philanthropic activities, entrepreneurship support, etc.[20] A great way to create impetus is to ask family members—for instance, reflecting in small groups—to suggest initiatives, and ideally organize their implementation.

Think outside the box: To create a feeling of togetherness while being far away, think of objects, books, or stories that can contribute to reinforce the family identity. Some families have a family song. Some remember tales that convey their founder's philosophy. Others give personalized presents at family meetings—this could give rise to interesting anecdotes like in this family where two persons who did not know each other realised they were cousins when they saw they had the same family gift!

Conclusion

As with any challenge, those faced by families who are geographically distant have the opportunity to foster creative solutions to keep the family connected. Many family activities can be organized by a geographically diverse team. These activities contribute to the family cohesion in two ways: first, the nature of family activities reinforces shared identity and pride, and second, they offer an opportunity to engage distant members of the family. For example, a successful but geographically distant entrepreneur was happy to receive a call from a family member asking if she could mentor other potential family entrepreneurs. She was delighted to do so. In summary, the fact that business family members might be geographically dispersed does not mean they cannot stay in touch. Technology can help you as well as creativity. If staying in touch is important to you, show your interest and take an active role. Start by answering messages and finding out ways you can contribute. Your family will be thankful, and you will learn a lot and enjoy too!

Christine Blondel: Active in the field of family business since 1997, she has been exposed to hundreds of cases through her teaching, advising, and conferences. Founder of FamilyGovernance, former executive director of the Wendel International Centre for Family Enterprise at INSEAD where she still teaches. Involved in several international business schools and family business boards. Her research interests include multigenerational family businesses, fair process, and governance. She holds a master of science from École

Polytechnique France and an MBA from INSEAD, and followed several executive education programmes (governance, negotiation, mediation). She worked as a management consultant and held marketing and finance positions at Procter & Gamble. She also raised four boys, now grown-ups.

Commentary by Sophie Radermecker, Belgium

In 1885, my great-great-grandfather Oscar von Asten was a co-founder of a felt cloth factory, of which he became the sole owner in 1890. In 1922, the Peters family joined as partners. The company's first plant was located in Eupen, a small town in Prussia (now Belgium). In 1932, my great-grandfather Eduard von Asten founded a first plant in Canada, followed shortly by other plants in the U.S. and South America. After a merger of the Asten Group in 1999 with the family-owned Canadian group JWI, the Asten Group became the AstenJohnson Group. Further locations followed in the Czech Republic and China. The company AstenJohnson exists today and has done so on the Asten/Peters family side for six generations. The company is organized in the Buschberg S.A.; I am a shareholder. Today, the AstenJohnson Group is a recognized global leading manufacturer for the paper industry, supplying paper machine clothing and advanced filtration fabrics to papermakers around the world with approximately 2,000 employees. Another pillar in America is the production of non-woven needle punch textiles for the automotive, healthcare, filtration, and home furnishing industries. By emigration, a part of the family has settled in America. And through the eventful history of the "mother" location Eupen (BE), the family has expanded into Germany in addition to Belgium. Thanks to the developments in Europe and through marriage, family members from the fourth-generation onwards have also moved to Switzerland, Luxembourg, England, the U.S., and South America.

A current challenge is to keep the ever-growing "Buschberg" family together and also join the various branches that make it up. An annual general meeting traditionally followed by a dinner only partially addresses these challenges. Having this in mind, a family charter was drawn up in 2019 by a family working group. It created the function of family manager, which I currently hold. Its role is to strengthen the bonds between shareholders. A first joint family activity was a bus trip from Eupen to the AstenJohnson plant in Strakonice (CZ) with a work session and cultural program. Everything worked out fine and on the return trip a family song was composed. Already in the years before, some young members of the family were granted the opportunity as a group to undertake a sponsored round trip to the American factories. They had to support some of the travel costs to demonstrate their commitment. They presented their experiences at the subsequent annual general meeting. These activities achieved the goal to become acquainted and get to know each other.

Due to the COVID pandemic, other projects that had already been planned could not be realized. But thanks to the new media, people met and continue to meet virtually. A necessary adaptation of the articles of incorporation of business associates now allows all members to participate in meetings via the internet without having to travel far. This represents a major step forward and an opportunity for those who were previously unable to attend the annual general meeting.

Another initiative is to create an intra-family newsletter that will provide all shareholders with the same information about people, their living spaces, company locations, family history, etc.

It is also important to get the Next Gens interested in the company at an early stage—to understand it and to want them to participate as a shareholder—in order to make sustainable decisions for the future by consensus. The cohesion that develops is crucial for the continuation as a family business.

Every generation, from the company's inception to its current paradigm, has had to struggle with the challenges of its times and today must acknowledge change. Only in this way can the family and the company continue to develop. Currently, this means making central use of interactive media. Of course, interactive media can never replace physical contact and real networking among the shareholders. However, it does offer the opportunity to bring the worlds in which we evolve closer together. And the next time we meet, we will already have the impression of better knowing each other and returning to the heart of the family.

Questions for Further Reflection ——————

- How do you stay in touch with family members living nearby and at a distance?
- How do family members involved in the enterprise communicate with the larger family, including members who are not involved in the enterprise?
- What kinds of formal and informal activities does your family organize to facilitate communication among family members?
- How excited are Next Gens in your family to participate in these activities? Why or why not?

Your Notes | Your Action Items ——————

Your Notes | *Your Action Items* —————————————

1.5
How Can My Siblings/Cousins and I Assess Whether We Could Constructively Work Together in the Business One Day?

Response by Torsten Pieper, U.S.

Introduction

Henry Ford, founder of the eponymous automotive company, is quoted as having said, "Coming together is the beginning. Keeping together is progress. Working together is success." While this may sound simple, these steps are not easily accomplished. Families in business are no exception. The mere fact that an owning family has an offspring generation does not automatically guarantee it the support of a capable and committed successor group that is willing to come together, stay together, and work together to carry on the family legacy. To exemplify the challenge, a 2018 survey among 208,000 students from more than 3,000 universities across fifty-four countries showed that while over 90% of respondents intended to pursue employment immediately post-graduation, only 1.8 percent expected to join their families' businesses. This number increases to 2.1 percent five years after graduation, but still remains alarmingly low.[21] The following sections provide a series of suggestions and strategies that owning families and Next Gens can use to orient themselves and enhance the odds of coming together, staying together, and working together in the long run.

A Unifying Mission

First, it is important to understand that anybody can be in business together—regardless of their familial ties to one another. The determining factor is that one has to *want* to be in business together. This requires individuals to have a unifying mission or a compelling reason, something that gives them a shared purpose for why they want to be in business together versus starting their own independent ventures. The previously mentioned survey indicated that compared to only 1.8 percent of respondents who expected to join their families' businesses after graduation, as many as 9.0 percent planned to start their own business. This clearly indicates a preference for "going it alone" instead of joining forces in the family business.

A unifying mission should contain several characteristics to be effective. To paraphrase the military strategy genius and maverick fighter pilot, Col. John Boyd, a unifying mission should be rooted in human nature so noble that it not only attracts the uncommitted and energizes its adherents, but also undermines the dedication and resolve of any competitors.[22] By bringing its members together and aligning them behind a compelling collective purpose, such a unifying notion enables a business family to persevere through challenging conditions and to shape and cope with an ever-changing environment. Ideally, a unifying mission should be part of, and central to, an overarching family strategy that enables the owning family to define its shared goals and vision and specifies the ways in which it intends to pursue these aspirations.[23]

Communication and Relationship Quality

Staying together in the long run requires good relationships. According to our colleague and acclaimed family business expert, Joe Astrachan, the quality of a relationship depends on the frequency, length, and depth at which individuals communicate with one another.[24] In other words, the more often you talk, the longer you talk, and the more meaningful your conversations, the better a relationship you can have.

How can we improve the relationships that we have with others? A few things to consider: To enhance frequency of communication in a first step, engage the other person around things they enjoy and like to discuss, such as hobbies, interests, and the like. Later on, you can move to address more sensitive topics. Likewise, have a routine of talking at length before addressing sensitive issues. Depth of communication refers to how easily one can talk about issues that others would find too delicate or uncomfortable to discuss. The more easily you can talk about delicate issues with another person, the better your relationship.

There is a direct link between communication and relationship quality. If you talk often, for extended amounts of time, and about any and all topics, then you are more likely and more willing to identify problems and challenges early on and work on resolving your differences proactively. This is particularly relevant in business families, as it prevents people from acting in ways that may upset others, build resentment, and cause lasting damage to relationships.

Owning Family Competences

Working together requires a business family to develop and nurture certain competences among its members. Competences are a combination of tacit and explicit knowledge, behavior, and skills[25] that allow family members to adequately perform their various roles. Through our research we identified four key competences that family business members should possess: business competence, family competence, self-competence, and contextual competence.[26]

Business competence enables family members to lead or guide the organization and to oversee its management. It includes both business (e.g., financial, strategic, industry, legal, and decision-making) acumen and leadership (e.g., social and vison/value-based guidance) skills. Family competence enables individuals to contribute positively to family functionality and efficacy. It encompasses competence in family dynamics as well as communication and conflict management. Self-competence involves self-improvement (openness to feedback, and continuous learning and growth) and knowledge about boundaries and self-regulation (self-care and performing under pressure). Contextual competence (e.g., an ability to recognize trends and to think outside the box) enables family members to deal with challenges as well as leverage opportunities arising in the social, political, and economic environment. The development and nurturing of these competences should be lifelong tasks and can happen in more or less formalized ways, including institutionalized programs (such as "corporate universities" for family business members) and childhood education and mentoring along a shared set of values in each family.[27]

Takeaways

One of the facts of life is that there is no hard and fast recipe for success. However, rallying around a unifying mission, communicating often—for extended amounts of time, and about any and all topics—as well as developing and nurturing key competences among family members may enable families to come together, stay together, and work together, and thereby increase the odds of creating value for current and future generations, and for all those around them.

Torsten M. Pieper is associate professor of management in the Belk College of Business at The University of North Carolina Charlotte (U.S.), president and chairman of the International Family Enterprise Research Academy (IFERA), and editor-in-chief of the Elsevier title *Journal of Family Business Strategy*. An author of numerous articles and books on family business, he is a frequent speaker to professional and industry associations on the topics of family business cohesion, strategy, and governance. Pieper grew up in a multinational family business (manufacturer of building materials) and is fluent in German, French, and English.

Our family business was a group of companies in the industrial multi-trade sector serving clients around the globe for over forty-five years. At the time of my departure from the family business, I was vice president of the group and filling the role of the vacant president's office.

Our story with our siblings is one that unfortunately did not end in a happily-ever-after. Our father, the patriarch of our family and founder of the original business, passed away suddenly, which you would have thought would bring a seemingly close family like ours together, and that we would have supported each other and worked hard to keep our father's legacy strong. Instead, our family ended up divided and battling in court for over three years, which has resulted in the companies being impacted in profit, size, growth. In addition, our foundation was disbanded, resulting in cancelation of donation commitments. What I think is most interesting about our story is that before this crisis event happened, I thought we would have said we were a close-knit family. It is clear that was a façade that did not run deep enough to be able to climb over the Everest needed to work together and be successful in business or as a family.

Our father was the typical entrepreneur. He was a workaholic, competitive, and, though inspirational, not a "nice" guy. I honestly do not believe you can be nice and as successful as he was. Do not get me wrong, he was a great dad, but, unfortunately, kept a competitive culture within our household while we were growing up. We siblings were expected to stay at the top of our class, be the best at our respective sports, and be good upstanding citizens to the world.

He fostered a charitable culture to the outside world, teaching and instilling it in us to the point that we literally gave the shirts off our backs when people needed it. He put the employees first before our family. Unfortunately, he did not foster that same culture within our home. We were not encouraged to cooperate, support, and use our strengths to help each other but instead fought to be the best in his eyes. I believe that if we had been taught to value working together, we could have been stronger. If we were trained to see that it was us together against the world, not us as individuals alone, then we would have been more willing to look at how as a family we could be unstoppable. We each had different strengths to support and counter the other's weaknesses.

Looking back on our life together I realized we were never really "alone" as a family. We traveled a lot as a family; however, it was always with others or for a work specific conference or event, where networking and being with peers was the focus more than family bonding. We did not take the time to talk, get to know each other, and set out our family's values, culture, and charter for the future. Obviously for our foundation and charitable work, we did sit and talk about what was important to us as a family and for our legacy *outside* the house walls, but we never took the time to understand what was important to us *inside* the family. Once again it seems like a little thing, but I believe this would have helped guide us during our crisis to be all on the same road for the future instead of fighting among each other for the individual journey and path we each wanted to take.

The final thought I had with this experience in my journey is to understand why we could not find harmony and work together successfully. Though we were kept in the loop on business decisions, asked our thoughts/ideas, and always worked there for summers and after school, we were never taught proper business literacy. This came to light early in our court battle when my younger brother said he just wanted to be president of the group and I asked him what that meant to him. What he described was ownership not employment; he did not want to be president he wanted to be a shareholder, maybe chair of the board. I think this battle could have been avoided, or at least have been less tragic, if he had a better understanding of not only the business and the three circles, but also that he could have been an owner/shareholder and a member of the family, without having to be an employee.

Questions for Further Reflection ———————————————

- What brings your family members together? What pulls them apart?
- How would you describe your family's shared vision and shared mission? Would your family members agree on them?
- Do you agree with your family's values? How do these values matter?
- How would you describe the quality of relationships among members of your family?
- Are members of your family able to distinguish their role in the family from their role(s) in the enterprise?

Your Notes | Your Action Items ———————————————

Your Notes | *Your Action Items* —————————————

1.6
My Parents Do Not Talk About Their Retirement. How Can I Start the "What's Next After You Retire from the Business" Conversation with My Parents?

Response by Ivan Lansberg, U.S.

The quick answer is to approach the retirement conversation with empathy and smarts. Empathy is needed because if Next Gens can't grasp why it is so difficult to let go of a business their parents have created and/or lead successfully, Next Gens will not be able to engage with their parents constructively. Next Gens also need smarts, because to facilitate the conversation in a way that is pragmatic and focused on the needs of all stakeholders requires the kind of long-term multistep strategy needed in games like chess. Succession should never be an event; it should always be a process. So rather than one conversation, plan for a multi-year process of conversations—carefully planned so that Next Gens start with the easier, though substantive issues, and work their way up toward the most difficult ones.

The empathy element often poses the biggest challenge because there is a built-in generational asymmetry when it comes to succession. While parents were once young and can draw from that experience to understand the challenges their children face in establishing their own credibility as aspiring leaders, Next Gens have never been old, so for them to imagine the vulnerabilities their parents might feel when contemplating retirement, and shedding lifelong engagement with a business they built, will always require a more significant emotional and cognitive stretch.

So, while Next Gens ought not to be afraid of these conversations, they do need to respect the challenge the transition poses and learn to appreciate that retiring senior leaders require a system-wide approach to facilitate a process of change. This is where patience, strategy, and smarts matter.

Step 1: Establishing Credibility

The first step is to ensure that Next Gens have done all they can to establish their own credibility as viable successor candidates. As Machiavelli once remarked, "power is never given, it is always taken," an idea suggesting that the most effective successions are always driven by the aspirations and actions of succeeding generations. But *how* Next Gens acquire power in a family enterprise makes all the difference. For the burden does fall on them to provide evidence to their parents—and, indeed, to all the shareholders, employees, customers, and suppliers as well as to the communities where the business operates—that they will be in good hands under their leadership. The more that Next Gens have invested in their own personal and professional development, and the more they have demonstrated their competence to lead and add value, the easier the retirement conversations will be. This will also help to evoke in their parents both confidence and pride in Next Gens' accomplishments, and merit and pave the way to mutually respectful conversations.

Step 2: Risk Management

Succession planning is always an exercise in risk management. Ensuring that the team taking charge has the competencies that the system needs is essential. It is also critical to ensure that the outgoing seniors financial security is protected no matter what. As I often tell clients, "if you get out of the cockpit, get off the plane." The new leadership has to assume the risk for the strategic, financial, and organizational decisions they make. Otherwise, they will never earn the authority needed to lead.

Understanding the challenge that retirement poses for parents requires getting your head around the fact that succession calls for them to enable a transition to a future that doesn't have them in it. Like Moses, they must gather the foresight and generosity to lead a people to a promised land that they cannot enter. And this requires them to have the courage to face the loss of their roles, often a critical part of their stature and identities. Ultimately the transition also calls for them to come to terms with their own aging, obsolescence, and mortality. No matter how caring and empathic Next Gens are, helping their parents mourn the losses that come with succession is imperative because it's so hard for parents to do so on their own. Perhaps the most useful thing that can be done is ensuring that there are people in the system who have deep experience with these transitions and can advocate for having a succession plan in place, *and* who also have the trust and respect of the senior leaders. For example, often the most important allies that families can have for this process are the independent directors on their board. Building a strong relationship with them is a key priority for the Next Gens. If the business doesn't have a strong board, then putting one in place should be a key priority. Families should make sure that at least one of their directors is a retired business owner who has done a great job of planning their own retirement and can speak with the authority and credibility of someone with personal experience.

Step 3: Readiness

The most basic measure of succession readiness is gauging the degree to which fundamental decisions are still made by the parents. A good question for Next Gens to ask themselves is if they lost both parents today were would they be missed the most? What would happen to the ownership? What would happen to the operational side of the business? And, of course, what would happen in the family itself? Attending to the answers to these questions helps Next Gens (and hopefully the board) sketch the work still to be done.

The ebb and flow of succession in any system is driven by the biological clock. The first responsibilities that typically transfer are managerial and operational roles; the second are nonvoting shares (typically driven by estate planning prerogatives) and next comes control over the voting shares. Typically, it is the family leadership roles that are the last to be handed down. This is because the hierarchies of the family are the most enduring. As a client once told me, "the definition of a kid is someone with living parents."

You know that family leadership has been passed down when family gatherings, holidays, and rituals are no longer held in the parents' home but in the homes of Next Gens. Understanding this natural progression can provide a useful high-level GPS to navigate the transition and frame productive conversations.

Motivating parents to imagine what life would look like after the transition is also critical. Succession requires both a destination and a path. It is much easier to be pulled into roles (and into a life) that parents want than to be *pushed* out of roles they know well and are deeply attached to. Eliminating some of the ambiguity about the future and ensuring that some level of rigor has been built into the definition of the parents' roles matters. In this regard, it is critical for them to see that there are, in fact, ample opportunities available for parents to continue living engaged, purposeful, and fulfilling lives. Leaders are often ignorant about the ways in which their skills and capabilities are re-deployable in new arenas like board service, philanthropy, community engagement, politics, or even a new venture.

Also, Next Gens should bear in mind that the enemy of succession is surprise. From the moment the owners, board, and senior management start thinking about succession to the moment when the plan is fully implemented, can take as long as five-to-ten years. It is imperative to couple succession planning with a contingency plan that delineates what the family would do in the event of an unexpected occurrence. Several times in my career, I've had to help clients deal with the untimely death of the successor on whose shoulders the succession plan rested. In sum, the process calls less for Next Gens to have the retirement conversation directly and more for them to ensure that there is a the right set of conditions in place so conversations can be had between their parents and the people they are most likely to listen to on this issue.[28]

Ivan Lansberg is a senior partner at Lansberg Gersick and Associates (https://lgassoc.com). He was one of the founders of the Family Firm Institute and the first editor of its professional journal, the *Family Business Review*. After receiving his BA, MA and PhD from Columbia University, Ivan taught at the Columbia Graduate School of Business. He became a professor of organizational behavior at the Yale School of Organization and Management for seven years before going into consulting. His books *Succeeding Generations* and *Generation to Generation*, published by Harvard Business School Press, have been widely praised as landmark works. Ivan is on the faculty of Kellogg School of Management at Northwestern University.

Commentary by Paloma Rivadulla Durán, Spain

My family company Fernando Durán S.A. is the first auction house in Spain. It was created in 1969 and continues to be one of the best companies in its sector at a national and international level. We act as intermediaries; that is, we put buyers and sellers from all over the world of art and luxury objects in contact with each other using our rooms as the main venue to exhibit the objects and establish direct contact with our clients. As the objects or paintings become the property of other collectors, professionals, or private individuals on the day of the auction, it will be the experts who will stipulate a minimum estimated price, but it will be the market that will set the final price.

My role within the company is varied. Mainly, I am in charge of collecting works of art, jewelry, and watches with my mother, Paloma Durán, director of the company. We travel all over Spain valuing objects and offering our services of appraisal, transport, auction sales, and storage. Since I am the youngest person of the hired staff and since I am fluent in the world of technology, internet, and social networks, I am also in charge of updating the hardware and software of the company, installing new computer equipment, designing the website, and leading a team of programmers.

As for my mother's retirement, I have learned that it is a delicate matter for both the company and for her. A family member who has dedicated her life to running such a company should never retire.

Let me explain. My mother's bond with the company is not only a professional attachment based on legal ownership, but also an identity bond. For this reason, I would speak of a *presidency* and not of a *retirement*, because we are dealing with a special company.

It may seem paradoxical to speak of a retirement in these terms—thinking of the creation of a new position. Retirement is undoubtedly an important right, but a person like my mother will make use of this right without disappearing from the company. To make this possible, we need to create an appropriate context for her case and others like hers. It is in this sense that I speak of presidency. People like my mother deserve to always be a part of their company, because it is a question of personal identity.

The company is part of my mother's (and other family members') identity and leaving it would be like not being herself anymore. Therefore, for those who love to work within the family business, it would be necessary to create a new status within it or to create a connection that makes them part of it until they decide otherwise or until that participation becomes impossible.

For many, especially for those who find themselves in a similar situation to my mother's, a retirement that is understood as disappearance from the company creates an inner rupture—a vital tearing apart. Even more, when new generations of the family take over the company, leading the project in a different way, the change of direction and style is a threat not only to my mother, but also to the family business. This is why conflicts and delays in making decisions in favor of the company's growth arise around change. Indeed, the retirement of people like my mother must be understood in terms of a change rather than a disappearance: a change from being in management to being the chairman of the board. By changing the context in this way, the bond between my mother and the company takes on a deeper meaning; there is no rupture because there is no disengagement. I know that my mother would have wanted to devote herself to other tasks within the company instead of taking on management for so many years. I also believe that there are others who have experienced the same. Therefore, it would be interesting to consider the possibility of enjoying retirement without having to give up the family business. My mother's retirement will not mean a fall into passivity, but rather new activity: the creation of a new department within the company. It seems hard to believe or even ironic, but we will do it this way. Moreover, I am confident that this will not add to the company's burden or hinder its development. Quite the contrary, it is about creating a community that does not discard anyone before their time. We are more humane this way.

In my opinion, to be able to venture into this type of conversation, the first thing to do is to work hard and assert yourself inside and outside the company, spend time thinking about that relative who will have to retire, and listen to him or her. The three steps—work, think, and listen—help you to realize what that family member wants in relation to the company. That's how I discovered it.

Questions for Further Reflection

- How have members in the previous generation in your family, or in others you know, started to discuss their retirement from the family enterprise?
- From your perspective, is it helpful to separate discussions of retirement from discussions of succession? If so, why?
- In the family enterprise, what are the main achievements of the leaders from previous generations?
- How much do members of your parents' generation identify with the family enterprise, its products or services, buildings, and employees? Do they have a passion beyond the family enterprise?

Your Notes | *Your Action Items*

1.7
My Parents Are Well Beyond Their Seventies. How Can I Help Them Make the Transition from Work Life to Retirement?

Response by Vanessa Strike, Canada

The number of family business owners born during the baby boom (1945–1964) have either already reached, or will shortly reach, the typical retirement age of sixty-five. By 2030, all baby boomers will be older than sixty-five.[29] However, according to an article in the *Wall Street Journal*, seven out of ten baby boomers intend to work well past the age of sixty-five.[30] Baby boomers were raised in a generation characterized by a stout work ethic, and many are not ready to leave the family business. As such, there is a growing number of Next Gens who are struggling with whether they will ever be allowed to take over leadership of the family business.

Difficulty in Stepping Away
The inability of Next Gens' parents to step away from the family business is often the most significant hurdle in achieving a successful succession. Parents are often highly involved in the family business, frequently dedicating their lives to the business so that it becomes an integral part of their identity. This makes them reluctant to plan for the future. Unless they have a vision for their life after their role leading the family business, they will often resist succession planning. For Next Gens, the issue is that the decision-making power

typically lies with their parents. How then, do Next Gens help their parents' transition from work life to retirement?

The Importance of Developing a Governance Structure

The key to a successful transition can lie within (1) establishing a well-functioning governance structure and (2) being mindful and respectful of parents and other members of the senior generation, and their role in creating and developing the family business. A governance structure can formalize communication channels, solemnize the family's vision, mission, and values, adequately prepare successors, define roles, document policies surrounding succession, family employment, dividend payouts and ownership, and allow the family to come together to make decisions—all helping to unify the family. The case of Valley Carriers and the Klassen family (detailed below) provides an example of how effective and compassionate communication by Next Gens with senior leaders of the company aided in a respectful transition.

Case Example: The Klassen Family

Travis and Erin Klassen (third generation [G3] members), along with their cousins, had no ownership or leadership in the family business. They were still seen by their parents and aunts and uncles, the second generation (G2), as the younger generation who were not ready to take over the business. In response, Travis and Erin took a number of steps to begin the succession process and develop a governance structure that suited their family business. First, they developed their knowledge by attending courses on family business, and governance in particular. Second, they set up management meetings to establish lines of communication, trust, and ensure transparency. Third, they used the annual family retreat to develop the family charter, thereby engaging the entire family. The family charter identified what was important to the prior and future generations and defined and guided the family business into the future.

Fourth, Travis employed his father to help formalize a board of directors and establish an annual general meeting (AGM). Having an AGM provided for the needed transparency that had been lacking. Having a G2 member propose the initiative alongside G3 gave the proposal increased legitimacy. However, the proposal to allow G3 to become directors created tension among some of the members of G2 who felt threatened.

G3 proposed that the family business go through a freeze where G3 would join G2 as equal owners. G2 would maintain the previous equity but any growth in shares would be diluted between both generations. They proposed an executive team who consisted of G3 as the chief officers. They formalized a meeting schedule, process, and agenda and developed a communications policy. They assembled an advisory board consisting of G2 and outside professionals. The proposal had G3 taking over the management of the business while G2 remained in an advisory capacity, giving G2 a continuing role.

How the proposal was presented was key. Travis addressed the board gently and respectfully, choosing his words carefully. The language focused on their decision to *serve* the company. Travis talked about their vision and plan to *come alongside* and be *mentored* by G2. He explained how G3 wanted to *respect* what G1 and G2 had accomplished and *work alongside* G2 until they were ready to move on. It was through Travis' careful choice of language and in addressing the group respectfully that G2 realized there was agreement with each other in terms of their core values. Coming to this understanding about their alignment meant that G2 was willing to listen to G3 and was poised to make decisions about the future of the family business. During the following six months, the executive team worked with a set of trusted advisors to implement the changes from the original proposal and develop a next steps document. The document they developed included sections on "transition and succession" and "mentoring." The family found that a period of partial retirement, in an advisory/mentoring capacity, was helpful in transitioning to retirement. Having a trusted advisor with an outside perspective, who had the best interests of the business and both generations at heart and was trusted by both generations, aided in communications across generations and was crucial in implementing the succession plan.

Beyond Governance: Communication, Empathy, and Respect

Developing a governance structure that:

- Communicates the family values, mission, and long-term vision.
- Keeps family members (especially those who are retiring) informed about the business.
- Establishes ongoing communication channels to allow *all* family members to share ideas.

will help to unify the generations. Next Gens should remember to respect their parents—not to try to push them out but respect their knowledge and values. One of the greatest assets held by the senior generation is the wealth of experience and knowledge they hold from years of owning and operating the family business. Their identity is often entwined in the family business and retiring can be emotionally difficult. Communicating the desire to learn from the trove of wisdom parents can offer, with intentionality, and respecting the knowledge and values they bring, will aid Next Gens to transition into management and eventually ownership of the business.[31]

Vanessa M. Strike is a research professor at Ivey Business School, Western University. Prior, she held the CIBC Professor in Applied Business Family Studies at the Sauder School of Business, University of British Columbia, and was the academic director of the Sauder Business Families Centre. Vanessa was the founder and scientific director of the Erasmus Center for Family Business at the Rotterdam School of Management, Erasmus University. She received her PhD in strategy and entrepreneurship from the Ivey School of Business, Western University. Her research examines advisors, governance, sensemaking, cognition, and emotions in family businesses.

Commentary by Vincent Chian, Malaysia

The Chian family owns the Fairview International School network of five schools in Malaysia and one in Scotland, UK. The second son of three siblings, I am the principal of the main campus in Kuala Lumpur.

To the founders, the organization they built is the baby they created and guided from birth. When I joined the family business, I was constantly reminded that I was part of the ownership and, over time, I developed a desire to shape the business that had my name on it. Unfortunately, the more I tried to shape the business, the tighter the founder held on to the business. I couldn't understand it! If I have responsibility for the business, shouldn't I shape it to be the best it could be in my eyes? As I saw errors, I sought to correct them and faced incredible resistance from the founder. After countless arguments and verbal fights, I accidentally discovered servant leadership.

Over time, I learned to serve first and contribute; that leaders must first learn to follow well. I recognized that I did not build this company with my blood and sweat. I recognized that every time I tried to "fix" a problem, I was indirectly criticizing his leadership. I recognized that founders are living, feeling beings who want to be proud of their creation. Over time, the attitude of serving and contributing, without trying to wrestle control from him, made the founder's grip relax. The more I held back from asserting my will to change the business, the more my opinion was sought. The more I contributed, the more I was invited to contribute.

As the respect grew, I sought his wisdom and experience more. The less I sought to lead and learn, the more he felt excited to share and encourage. Previously, conversations were about demonstrating the logical "rightness" of my opinions. Even when I was completely right, these discussions almost always led to arguments. Today, I listen and learn more, and understand context—without agenda. Our conversations today are so much more enjoyable, and as I listen more, I'm amazed by the many stories of crazy challenges he had to go through. I learned that by listening, I send the message that I value him, and this has built a lot more trust between us.

As a servant leader, I recognize the burden of his leadership more than ever and it has translated to ever-increasing amounts of respect. I wait quietly for him to direct me to where he needs me to help. I don't have to find opportunities to give my opinion, it is sought. We still have a way to go but every day I see him breathe a little easier, more content that I am not here to steal the company away but to serve the vision he initially set out for the company.

Questions for Further Reflection

- What is it about your family and/or its enterprise that motivates you to get up in the morning?
- Could you organize your daily life differently if there was not a family enterprise? If so, how?
- What could the succeeding generation do to make it easier for the incumbent generation to let go?
- What roles in the family enterprise could the incumbent generation assume after "retirement"?
- What activities, outside of the family enterprise, does the incumbent generation enjoy pursuing?

Your Notes | *Your Action Items* ————————————————

1.8
How Can I Manage Family Relationships Outside of the Family Business?

Response by Arist von Schlippe, Germany

An Ordinary Question?

What does it mean for a family to jointly own a company? This is by no means a run-of-the-mill question. Vast numbers of families are engaged in entrepreneurial activities: A tentative estimate sees "115 million families around the globe . . . engaged in the process of either starting new businesses or operating young or more established firms."[32] But this number is based on data from just thirteen countries and doesn't take into account families who are active owners but not involved in business operations. Family businesses are usually multigenerational endeavors, and the number of individuals involved should not be underestimated. Scenarios range from smaller families to extended communities. While these figures indicate how many people worldwide are involved, little is known about the inner world of these families.[33] They have to address issues that other families either never will be concerned with (family ownership, succession, etc.) or will probably experience less intensely (sibling rivalry, conflicting goals, etc.). All these aspects may aggravate tensions in business families and fuel escalating conflicts, potentially tearing apart both the business and the family.

Social Systems and Their Logics

Business families face a fundamental challenge—the inevitable need to be family and business family simultaneously.[34] The term *family business* itself mirrors the dilemma when it refers to two closely interlinked systems following different logics or rationales. Family communication centers around relationships and emotional ties (whether positive or negative). Each person is seen as an individual and members share their everyday experience talking about school, parties, or work. And when it comes to decisions, families give careful consideration to the consequences of any choice for its members. The logic of communication in a business enterprise is entirely different. The focus of interest here is not the whole person but only those aspects that are necessary to perform certain tasks. All communication is scrutinized to ensure it serves the core purpose, whether directly or indirectly—mainly decision-making.

In business families, the lines between these two system-logics will frequently be blurred, and it becomes difficult to separate the contexts of business and family. For most situations context markers help distinguish which communication logic is appropriate in any given situation (e.g., office talk differs from restaurant talk). Business families lack many of these markers: the business is located in the middle of the living room, so to speak, and becomes the organizing principle of family communication. Communication about everyday issues is easily interrupted if business topics demand attention. And it's not always easy to determine which logic is active. Sunday breakfasts turn into strategy meetings, and family communication creeps into the corporate context, as in the story of the successor (CEO) whose father (board president) handed her his glasses during a meeting, saying: "Clean these for me, please!"

Duplicated Families

The tension between these logics defines the life of the business family. There is not much point in trying to be normal since such a family is *duplicated*. What does this mean? We don't emphasize so much the difference between family and business here, but rather between family and business family! It's the family that has to take on the difficult task of complexity management. On the one hand, the family is like any other, enjoying all the stages of a child's life such as first steps, school grades, lovesickness, and more. But at the same time, the family observes its members by applying the magnifying glass of the business family. Whatever happens, the consequences for the business will always be an issue. Questions will arise: Is this behavior/interest/girlfriend/boyfriend appropriate? How will it affect our future or reputation? Can we see the potential in our child to take on operational responsibility? One successor tells how at the age of six he was given a technical play kit for Christmas. Enthusiastically, he started playing before suddenly realizing that something was strange. He looked up to see five adults staring at him as if spellbound. "At the time, it was just weird," he says. "Today I know it was the business family watching me—not as a child but as a potential successor: Look, he's interested in technology!"

In Search of an Answer to Managing Family Relationships Outside the Business

So, the first steps toward an answer might not be very encouraging. It seems impossible for a family to exist outside the business family. The simultaneity of the two logics can't be dismissed. Fundamental dilemmas such as the following are inevitable:

- Who belongs? If you're born into a family, you, of course, belong to it. For business logic, in contrast, only top performers are of interest. Thus, business families often intervene significantly in their member's lives, be it the choice of profession, partner, marriage-contract, social interaction, or inheritance. Everything is scrutinized under the lens of selectivity. And since family members are often loyal, they might allow their entire life to be determined by the demands of the business (if they don't opt for rebellion).

- What's fair? Family logic assumes equality among all those involved while business logic aims to maintain its capacity for selection. This issue comes to a head in the event of inheritance. Will the one who joins the business get everything, or will family logic prevail, and all siblings receive an equal share?

- Stories! Narratives of the past play a particular role in business families. System memories stretches back far, and conflicts may drag on for generations. Children are born into this world of stories and wear them under their skin.

Final Answers and Practical Takeaways

Consciousness raising may help tackle the dilemma.[35] Being aware of not being part of an "ordinary" family may lead to the insight that complexity has to be consciously addressed (e.g., by means of regular meetings or moderated self-reflection sessions). By understanding what a business family is, it is possible to gain respect for the achievements of its members in balancing the contradicting systems of logic that are at work. This makes it easier to forgive parents and peers certain oddities and avoid falling into the trap of personal accusations when conflicts arise in potentially paradoxical contexts. Maintaining friendly relationships is the core task for every family member as the family develops over the generations.

Arist von Schlippe, professor, doctor of philosophy, clinical and family psychologist, family therapist, and coach. Chairholder at the Witten Institute for Family Business (Witten University, Germany) since 2005. His research focus and practical experiences include family strategy and governance in business families, succession, conflict resolution, and specific conditions of large business families. He has numerous publications, translated into eight languages.

Commentary by Rafael Kisslinger da Silva, Brazil and Germany

As a third-generation member of a Brazilian business family, I am responsible for our family office, especially concerning our investments outside of Brazil. I am based in Germany, near Frankfurt, while our core business, Máquinas Condor S.A., has its headquarters in Porto Alegre, Brazil. Our family has numerous members around the world and managing our family relationships outside the business has oftentimes proved to be a lot more complex than managing these relationships inside of the business. One single word explains the complexity—emotions. In the context of the family business, it is acceptable (and at times even desirable) to leave the emotions out of the picture and, instead, focus on the business tasks at hand. In the context of the family, however, this approach simply does not work. Learning to talk openly with other family members about one's feelings is not easy. And learning to listen (ideally deep listening) to how others feel is even more challenging. But both are crucial if the family unity is to prevail. In addition to sharing feelings, families must also learn to talk openly about conflicts. Avoiding difficult conversations about conflicting themes, or pretending that they don't exist, is another approach that simply doesn't work. As paradoxical as it may sound, creating a healthy conflict culture is the only way to achieve sustainable harmony in a family. Conflicts will never go away, but families can learn to be aware of them and manage them in effective ways.

When managing family relationships, it is important to notice that a fair outcome is not enough. The process that leads to any outcome must also be fair. In other words, even if the final solution is ultimately fair, if such a solution is the result of a "black box" process, it won't be accepted by the other family members. Even worse, it could actually fuel conflicts. Non-transparent processes create suspicion, and suspicion within the family is corrosive and paralyzing; it sows distrust. Fair process is about opening the black box and discussing openly how and why decisions will be made in the family. The journey matters as much as the outcome. It's not about where we go but about how we get there. When families establish fair processes, each process will help to build trust, and trust is indispensable to healthy family relationships.

I once participated in an exclusive workshop with one of the world's leading advisors for family businesses. This consultant earns a fortune by helping families to function better. And his key message was that families can actually solve every problem related to family functionality on their own once the family's communication works properly. As he explained, family functioning is based on the family's communication. And communication is the only tool that families have to improve their functioning. So, being proactive to find the time to spend together, motivated to understand the other person in their unique context, and willing to communicate regularly among each other are the core ingredients to manage relationships in a large family. If families succeed at establishing such processes, they will not only trust each other but also be happy to spend time with each other. It takes commitment and effort to manage family relationships.

As I stated initially, managing family relationships is complex because of the underlying individual emotions. Emotions flare easily when, after communication breakdowns, people do not know each other well any longer. Eventually, they will stop interacting. Unfortunately, managing emotions can be a lot more challenging than managing professional business issues, but families can learn to become "professionally emotional".

Questions for Further Reflection ———————————

- Why do you love to be around your family members outside of the enterprise?
- What stories would you like to share with your fellow family members? What stories would you only share with your fellow Next Gens? Why have you not done so yet?
- Are there resources in the family system that were never talked about? If so, why?
- Are there topics that you cannot talk about among family? If so, what are they and why can't they be discussed?

Your Notes | Your Action Items ———————————

Endnotes: Part 1

1. Peter Jaskiewicz, Michael G. Carney and Christopher Hansen, "When Trusting Your Family Hurts Your Family Business," Harvard Business Review, July 23, 2021. https://hbr.org/2021/07/when-trusting-your-family-hurts-your-family-business.

1.1 Who Is Considered Part of the Family?

2. Gibb Dyer, *The Family Edge: How Your Biggest Competitive Advantage in Business Isn't What You've Been Taught—It's Your Family* (Sanger: Familius, 2019), 15.

3. Jane Hilburt-Davis and William Gibb Dyer, *Consulting to Family Businesses: Contracting, Assessment, and Implementation* (San Francisco: Jossey-Bass/Pfeiffer, 2003).

4. Ivan Lansberg, *Succeeding Generations: Realizing the Dream of Families in Business* (Boston: Harvard Business School Press, 1999).

1.2 How Can I Become a Respected Representative of the Family?

5. "Great Expectations: The Next Generation of Family Business Leaders," *Next Generation Survey of Family Business Leaders* (London: PwC, April 2016), 1–44.

6. Kelin E. Gersick, John A. Davis, Marion McCollom Hampton and Ivan Lansberg, *Generation to Generation: Life Cycles of the Family Business* (Boston: Harvard Business School Press, 1997).
Isabelle Le Breton-Miller, Danny Miller and Lloyd P. Steier, "Toward an Integrative Model of Effective FOB Succession," *Entrepreneurship Theory and Practice* 28, no. 4 (July 2004): 305–328.
Danny Miller, Llyod Steier and Isabelle Le Breton-Miller, "Lost in Time: Intergenerational Succession, Change, and Failure in Family Business," *Journal of Business Venturing* 18, no. 4 (July 2003): 513–531.

7. Ercilia García-Álvarez, Jordi López-Sintas and Pilar Saldaña Gonzalvo, "Socialization Patterns of Successors in First- to Second-Generation Family Businesses," *Family Business Review* 15, no. 3 (September 2002): 189–203.

8. Sumaya Hashim, Lucia Naldi and Magdalena Markowska, ""The Royal Award Goes To…": Legitimacy Processes for Female-led Family Ventures," *Journal of Family Business Strategy,* (July 2020): 100358. https://doi.org/10.1016/j.jfbs.2020.100358.

9. Roy Suddaby and Peter Jaskiewicz, "Managing Traditions: A Critical Capability for Family Business Success," *Family Business Review* 33, no. 3 (September 2020): 234–243.

10. Irmak Erdogan, Emanuela Rondi and Alfredo De Massis, "Managing the Tradition and Innovation Paradox in Family Firms: A Family Imprinting Perspective," *Entrepreneurship Theory and Practice* 44, no. 1 (January 2020): 20–54.
Peter Jaskiewicz, James G. Combs, Sabine B. Rau, "Entrepreneurial Legacy: Toward a Theory of How Some Family Firms Nurture Transgenerational Entrepreneurship," *Journal of Business Venturing* 30, no. 1 (January 2015): 29–49.
Roy Suddaby and Peter Jaskiewicz, "Managing Traditions: A Critical Capability for Family Business Success," *Family Business Review* 33, no. 3 (September 2020): 234–243.

1.3 We Have Always Had A Fair Deal of Conflicts in the Family. Now That I Am an Adult, Should I Do Anything About It?

11. Andrew C. Loignon, Franz W. Kellermanns, Kimberly A. Eddleston and Roland E. Kidwell, "Bad Blood in the Boardroom: Antecedents and Outcomes of Conflict

in Family Firms," in *The Routledge Companion to Family Business*, eds. Franz W. Kellermanns and Frank Hoy (New York: Routledge, 2017), 349–366.

12. Franz W. Kellermanns and Kimberly A. Eddleston, "Feuding Families: The Management of Conflict in Family Firms," in *Family Business Research Handbook*, eds. Panikkos Poutziouris, Kosmas Smyrnios and Sabine B. Klein (Cheltenham: Elgar Publishing, 2006), 358–368.

13. Kimberly A. Eddleston and Franz W. Kellermanns, "Destructive and Productive Family Relationships: A Stewardship Theory Perspective," *Journal of Business Venturing* 22, no. 4 (July 2007): 545–565.

14. Roland E. Kidwell, Kimberly A. Eddleston, John James Carter and Franz W. Kellermanns, "How One Bad Family Member Can Undermine a Family Firm: Preventing the Fredo Effect," *Business Horizons* 56, no. 1 (January 2013): 5–12.

15. Ritch L. Sorenson, "Conflict Management Strategies Used by Successful Family Businesses," *Family Business Review* 12, no. 4 (December 1999): 325–339.

1.4 We Are Living All Over The World. What Can We Do to Help Keep the Family Together?

16. Sorenson, Rich, "Future Family Business Owners Can Learn to Manage Conflict," 2017, https://familybusiness.org/content/future-family-business-owners-can-learn-to-manag.

17. Astrid Hall, "British Families Are Now Spread All Over the World—With One in Ten Living More Than 10k Miles Away," *The Sun*, December 2019. https://www.thesun.co.uk/news/10512620/british-families-spread-over-world/.

18. Christine Blondel and Anne Dumas, "Se préparer au 'cap des 400 actionnaires familiaux,'" in *L'entreprise familiale sauvera-t-elle le capitalism?: Portraits* (Paris: Autrement, 2008), 141–142.

19. Author's Interviews Fall 2020

20. Torsten M. Pieper, "Inventory of Mechanisms to Enhance Family Business Family Cohesion," in *Mechanisms to Assure Long-Term Family Business Survival*. (Berlin: Peter Lang, 2007), 213.

1.5 How Can My Siblings/Cousins and I Assess Whether We Could Constructively Work Together in the Business One Day?

21. Phillip Sieger, Urs Fueglistaller, Thomas Zellweger and Ilija Braun, *Global Student Entrepreneurship 2018: Insights From 54 Countries* (Switzerland: GUESSS Report, 2018), 1–33.

22. John R. Boyd, "Patterns of Conflict," in *General Military Theories: A Discourse on Winning and Losing* (Unpublished Manuscript, 1987). https://danford.net/boyd/patterns.pdf.

23. Andrew D. Keyt, Joseph H. Astrachan and Torsten M. Pieper, *Family Strategy: A Framework for Families in Business* (Working paper, 2020). Available from the authors.

24. Joseph H. Astrachan and Claudia Binz Astrachan, "How Family Dynamics Shape Family Businesses," *familybusiness.org*, September 23, 2020, accessed November 8, 2020, https://familybusiness.org/content/how-family-dynamics-shape-family-businesses.

25. Fotis Draganidis and Gregoris Mentzas, "Competency Based Management: A Review of Systems and Approaches," *Information Management & Computer Security* 14, no. 1 (January 2006): 51–64.

26. Claudia Binz Astrachan, Matthias Waldkirch, Anneleen Michiels, Torsten M. Pieper and Fabian Bernhard, "Professionalizing the Business Family: The Five Pillars of Competent, Committed and Sustainable Ownership," *A Research Report sponsored by the Family Firm Institute & 2086 Society,* June 25, 2020, accessed November 10, 2020, https://digital.ffi.org/pdf/wednesdayedition/2020/january08/ ffi_professionalizing_the_business_family_v2.pdf.

27. Francesco Barbera, Fabian Bernhard, Joshua Nacht and Gregg McCann, "The Relevance of a Whole-Person Learning Approach to Family Business Education: Concepts, Evidence, and Implications," *Academy of Management Learning & Education* 14, no. 3 (September 2015): 322–346.

1.6 My Parents Do Not Talk About Their Retirement. How Can I start the "What's Next After You Retire From the Business" Conversation With My Parents?

28. Ivan Lansberg, *Succeeding Generations: Realizing the Dream of Families in Business* (Boston: Harvard Business School Press, 1999).

Ivan Lansberg, "The Tests of a Prince," *Harvard Business Review* 85, no. 9 (September 2007): 92–149.

Michael D. Watkins, *The First 90 Days: Proven Strategies for Getting Up to Speed Faster and Smarter* (Boston: Harvard Business Review Press, 2013), 1–304.

Marshall Goldsmith, *Succession Are You Ready?* (Boston: Harvard Business Press, 2009), 1–130.

Danny Miller and Isabelle Le Breton-Miller, *Managing for the Long Run* (Boston: Harvard Business School Press, 2005), 1–320.

1.7 My Parents Are Well Beyond Their Seventies. How Can I Help Them to Make the Transition from Work Life to Retirement?

29. "Older People Projected to Outnumber Children for First Time in US History," *US Census Bureau* Press Release, October 8, 2019, https://www.census.gov/newsroom/ press-releases/2018/cb18-41-population-projections.html.

30. Clare Ansberry, "When Family-Business Owners Don't Want to Retire," *The Wall Street Journal*, April 30, 2017. https://www.wsj.com/articles/ when-family-business-owners-dont-want-to-retire-1493604541.

31. Ansberry, "When Family-Business Owners Don't Want to Retire."

Vanessa M. Strike, "Valley Carriers (A): Establishing Status in a Family Business," *Ivey Publishing product* no. 9B16M095 (London ON: Ivey Publishing, May, 31 2016), 1–8.

Vanessa M. Strike, "Valley Carriers (B): Working on Versus Working in the Business," *Ivey Publishing product* no. 9B16M096 (London ON: Ivey Publishing, May, 31 2016), 1–5.

Vanessa M. Strike, "Valley Carriers (C): Reconstructing the Governance of the Family Firm," *Ivey Publishing product* no. 9B16M097 (London ON: Ivey Publishing, May, 31 2016), 1–5.

1.8 How Can I Manage Family Relationships Outside of the Family Business?

32. Jennifer E. Jennings, Rhonda S. Breitkreuz and Albert E. James, "When Family Members Are Also Business Owners: Is Entrepreneurship Good for Families?," *Family Relations* 63, no. 3 (July 2013): 475.

33. Thomas Rieg and Sabine Rau, "Uncovering the 'Missing Variable': The Family in Family Business Research," in *The Routledge Companion to Family Business*, eds. Franz W. Kellermanns and Frank Hoy (New York: Routledge, 2017), 432–458.

34. Arist von Schlippe, Tom. A Rüsen and Torsten Groth, *The Two Sides of the Business Family. Governance and Strategy Across Generations* (New York: Springer, 2021), 1–260.

35. Michael Harvey and Rodney E. Evans, "Family Business and Multiple Levels of Conflict," *Family Business Review* 7, no. 4 (December 1994): 331–348.

PART 2: OWNERSHIP

Overview by Sabine B. Rau and Peter Jaskiewicz

T he owner is the person who ultimately bears responsibility for a business. Owners have to decide who to entrust with the leadership, which strategy to pursue, which resources to allot to which projects, and more. Common norms underlying ownership are the power and responsibility derived from voting rights. Norms define the general expectations of a role. Owners are expected to use the power of their voting right to make responsible decisions that are in the interest of the owner group and other organizational stakeholders.

It is the owners who decide who should lead the business. The owners can lead the business alone, ask someone from the family to lead the business, or hire a nonfamily leader. In contexts with separate ownership and leadership systems, the owners monitor, supervise, and consult the leader or the leadership team. In other contexts, owner-managers lead themselves and do not always see the necessity for external oversight over their leadership. Whether or not owners lead the business, they are free to allocate after-tax profits (e.g., dividends) to either the business or themselves. Because most businesses need ongoing capital investment to support a certain level of stability and growth, many owners leave the majority of profits in the business. Another important ownership right is the right to sell their shares or merge with another business. Even if suggested by the leadership team, owners make the ultimate decision. Having discussed and worked with many families in business, especially with Next Gens, we can add that the following topics are often raised when Next Gens assume ownership:

Keeping the ownership group united. In most cases, ownership is shared among a few or many (i.e., more than one hundred) family owners. Because it is of utmost importance to take decisions in favor of future business development, an essential duty of the owners is to make sure that their group speaks with one voice. The groups of owners who are united and organize constant communication—business-wise and in private—are more likely to make joint and effective decisions even in challenging situations. Next Gens, therefore, often play a pivotal role. Without proper preparation and integration, however, their addition to the ownership group often tests the unity of this group.

Owners feeling entitled to lead. Owners should organize the best possible leadership team for their business. There is nothing more dangerous to a business as owners who feel entitled to leadership despite missing key competences. Although common in many contexts, becoming an owner should not entitle Next Gens to a leadership role. On the contrary, ownership obliges the Next Gens to develop their abilities and knowledge, which, when paired with a humble approach, can enable them to become responsible owners.

Feeling ashamed of inherited ownership. Some Next Gens feel ashamed because they believe that they do not deserve their heritage. While this mentality seems less obviously dangerous to the business, it is not as harmless as it appears. Owing to misunderstood humility, these Next Gens tend to stay away from both leadership and ownership roles. While the former often leads to hiring nonfamily leaders, the latter creates a power vacuum that some nonfamily leaders might use to pursue their own interests. Once Next Gens understand that inheriting ownership comes with duties as well as privileges, they can start making decisions: Either they reject the duties of ownership and sell their stake, or they accept their duties and work hard to live up to the expectations commonly

put on family owners. Once Next Gens decide, there is no need—
and no room—to feel ashamed.

Transferring ownership as the ultimate test for the family.[1]
While many family members frame the transfer of ownership as a
legal and tax-minimizing process, it is also an emotional process.
Ownership transfers from one generation to the next one, whether
as a gift during a person's lifetime, as a sale to the Next Gens, or
as an inheritance following the execution of a last will are never
easy. Transfers always touch Next Gens' deep feelings of belonging, identity, and parental love. Addressing how ownership transfers influence these feelings is crucial for developing solutions that
do not harm family relationships. Ownership transfer processes
that nurture respectful and harmonious relationships among Next
Gens are most likely to result in effective Next Gen owner groups.
Meanwhile, effective Next Gen owner groups make smooth ownership transfer processes more likely.

A family business needs strong and responsible owners who are
not afraid of taking and using this power. This section is comprised
of nine questions raised by Next Gens reflecting upon ownership
and should serve as a starting point for considering the challenges
and opportunities that come with it.

2.1
Do I Want to Assume Active Ownership Responsibilities for Our Family Business?

Response by Alfredo de Massis and Emanuela Rondi, Italy

Every family business deserves committed family owners since being forced to hold business shares can be harmful for the survival and sustainability of both the business and the family. Family owners establish the values, vision, goals, and purpose that are compatible with the family and serve as a guide for the business over the long term. Although heirs often receive ownership as a gift, they can decide how to behave as family owners and their responsibilities vary in relation to the legal structure of the business. But what does it mean to be a family owner? Ownership consists in a bundle of rights—namely the right to use, the right to appropriate rent from, and the right to transfer family business resources. Family owners are not a unitary group, and it is an individual responsibility to clearly understand the alternative roles and functions to play in the group and develop corresponding abilities.[2] Passive family owners behave as investors who own shares and collect dividends but have low commitment to the business, thereby leaving responsibilities to active family owners. Active family owners are investors who are intimately connected to the business, ensure responsible corporate behaviour (often as board members), and thus have the opportunity to contribute to the family business by behaving as stewards for the next generations. Due to the crucial influence that active family owners could exercise over the family business strategy and the bitter conflicts that may arise in the business family over ownership matters, in the next sections we examine whether and how to become an active family owner, the need for a strategy for ownership development, and the duties, competences, and related risks of being an active family owner.[3]

Fostering an Ownership Culture so That Next Gens Can Learn to Be Active Owners

Unlike managerial roles, there is usually not a clear job description for being an active family owner, so it is hard to understand what this role requires before stepping into a family business ownership group. Active family owners need to feel confident making decisions under conditions of uncertainty with a long-term orientation while balancing the needs of the family, the business, and other stakeholders. To do so, they should not only develop a good understanding of the family business but also feel psychologically tied to it, consider it part of their identity, feel proud for being involved, and get satisfaction out of its success, a concept known as *psychological ownership*.

Active ownership of a family business does not come naturally but has to be learned and cultivated. Ownership incompetence often engenders persistent foregone opportunities and harmful strategies for the family business. However, a strategy to cultivate new family owners rarely exists in the business family, and too often the need to protect the firm from its owners prevails over the aim to consider them as a precious resource. Alternatively, it might even happen that none of the owners are willing to take active responsibilities, leading the family business to be driven by managers who lack the long-term view and do not share family owners' goals. As such, the disengagement of family owners may lead to a division between ownership and management orientation, compromising family wealth and business survival. Therefore, it is important to nurture an active ownership culture in the next generation by exposing Next Gens to the responsibilities and benefits associated with family ownership. This may take the form of involving them as auditors in board meetings and setting up mentorship programs between senior active family owners and Next Gen owners.[4]

Designing an Ownership Development Strategy So That Next Gens Can Become Active Owners

Family business owners should play as a team, since the ownership group is composed of heterogeneous actors playing the owner role differently and often involving the need to wear multiple hats in the family business (e.g., managers, directors). Moreover, the ownership group might involve nonfamily owners who do not share the family culture, traditions, and values. Therefore, in relation to the different individuals involved and their relationships, the shareholder group can take different configurations and functioning.[5] All in all, family business owners need to develop a strategy for ownership development.[6] When deciding whether or not to assume active ownership responsibilities for the family business, each family owner should honestly address these questions:

- Am I ready for playing an active ownership role?
- Do I feel psychologically tied to the family business?
- How can I communicate with the senior generation and other Next Gens about my perspectives on the topic?
- If I take a passive ownership role, do I trust who will take care of the active ownership responsibilities?
- Do I have enough shares and/or influence to make my voice heard as an active owner?

As a team, current and prospective family owners should discuss these questions in family meetings as the family assembly or the family council to understand which role fits best for each owner, and to identify the ownership group configuration that is most suited to ensure the survival and prosperity of the family business in the long run. It is likely that the next generation alone may not be able to decide whether and which family members should become active owners. To avoid impasse, senior generations should stipulate shareholder agreements to shape the availability of opportunities for Next Gens to become active owners, for instance, by formalizing rules for the number of family representatives for each family branch in the board, dividing roles and responsibilities for the different duties, identifying delegates, and defining a policy for shares succession. Thus, a strategy for ownership development is at least as important as the strategies for the business and family development.

Being an Active Owner

Equipped with psychological ownership, embedded in a favourable ownership culture, and aligned with the ownership development strategy, Next Gens are not only more likely to become active owners, but also may be in a good position to pursue related financial, legal, and social responsibilities effectively. Our main takeaways are the following:

- Family business owners can be active or passive shareholders.
- A business family should nurture an ownership culture that prepares Next Gens for active ownership and avoids the risks of their incompetence, disengagement, and disagreement.
- An ownership culture also nurtures Next Gens' psychological ownership making it more likely that they will become active owners.
- Business owners need to develop an ownership development strategy that stipulates when and how which Next Gens will become active owners.[7]

Alfredo De Massis is a professor of entrepreneurship and family business who serves as coach and advisor to family enterprises and policy makers. Among various editorial roles, Alfredo is editor of the journal *Entrepreneurship Theory & Practice* and is associate editor of *Family Business Review*. He also serves on the boards of public and private organizations internationally, including in Italy, China, US, Germany, and UK. His research has been published widely in leading journals including *Academy of Management Journal* and *Strategic Management Journal*, and has been featured in various media outlets including the *Financial Times, Harvard Business Review*, CNBC, *The Sun, Daily Mirror, The Independent*.

Emanuela Rondi is assistant professor at the department of management of the Università degli Studi di Bergamo (Italy). She holds a PhD in management from Lancaster University (UK). Her research lies at the intersection of family business and social networks, with a specific interest on the role that family relationships exert on succession, innovation, and internationalization. Her studies have been published in leading academic journals such as the *Journal of Management, Entrepreneurship Theory and Practice*, the *Journal of World Business*, and the *Journal of Management Studies*. She is member of the editorial review board of *Entrepreneurship Theory and Practice* and the *Journal of Family Business Strategy*.

Commentary by Felix Zinkann, Germany

I am a fifth-generation member of one of the two families owning and managing Miele. Founded in 1899 by my great-great-grandfather Reinhard Zinkann and his partner Carl Miele, we employ around 20,000 people—roughly half of them in Germany. Our turnover in 2020 of about €4.5 billion stems from household machinery such as washing machines and dishwashers distributed in nearly one hundred countries around the world.

Our two families traditionally send only one representative each to the managing board while six of about eighty family shareholders support the company in the family council and the supervisory board. In Germany we have a so-called two-tier system with two separate boards, one managing and one supervising the company's activities. Thus, there are two potential roles to assume active ownership in our family business.

For me the phrase "do I want" needs to be split into two: "am I willing" and "am I able" to assume active ownership. Here "willing" is the dependant variable of "being able." Like every Next Gen who has the desire to one day take active ownership, I ask myself whether I have the capability to do so. Asking this question is necessary because the heart of any family business are the employees and the historical memory of the family business. Analyzing the capabilities that I have at hand and which ones I need to develop, the answer to the question becomes a due condition. If I want to assume active ownership, I have to further build my capabilities and experiences to meet the expectations coming with either of the roles.

The stakes are high at Miele, when assuming active ownership and preparing for a management position or for a seat on the family council. While my grandfather, an engineer, holds more than one hundred patents and is known for his exceptional input in innovation, my father and his partner Marcus Miele have successfully guided the business as top managers for decades. If I say yes to the question above it would mean I'd have to fill big shoes. It is crucial for any Next Gen of our two families, whether it be me or someone else wishing to take an active ownership role ensure that they are in a position to monitor or lead the company successfully without putting the company, the employees, or the family heritage at risk. Obviously, it isn't possible to ensure this 100 percent but there are a variety of steps to reduce the probability of putting the family business at risk. The first step would be to start with a suitable education and university degree. History might be more interesting to study, but less helpful for running a business. Additionally, it is crucial to gain experiences outside the family business first. These external experiences will provide different viewpoints on situations and practices which can later help an owner evaluate situations with more professional accuracy. Development and self-evaluation are also more easily obtained when gaining external experience. Feedback will likely be more honest and less biased than it might be in the family business.

Professional independence helps provide greater choice. For instance, once I've established my own career, the question of whether I want to assume active ownership in the family business is not a question of "Am I able to?" but more "Do I really want to?" From my point of view, making the choice for the family business while having a career outside of it is a precondition for success-fully joining the family business. You then do it out of passion and not out of need. This makes stepping into the big footsteps of prior generations a source of pride and honor. It's critically important to ensure that the wrong motivation doesn't get the better of you, as the price of power and responsibility can be high.

Questions for Further Reflection

- How would you describe your ownership culture?
- How does your family nurture this ownership culture? What else could be done?
- What are the characteristics of your ownership development strategy?
- At what age, do you think, Next Gens should begin their owner development and how?
- What has influenced your decision to become a passive or active owner? Are you able to switch roles over time?

Your Notes | *Your Action Items* ─────────────

2.2
If I Want to Assume the Ownership Responsibilities. With Whom Should I Discuss It, and When Is the Best Time to Start?

Response by Gaia Marchisio, U.S.

Ownership Complexity

In the late nineties, baby boomers were as old as millennials today. By then, they had accumulated about 21 percent of the wealth in the U.S. This prosperous trajectory continued, and soon we will experience the great wealth transfer, where trillions of dollars' worth of wealth will pass down.[8] In this impressive macro context, the discussion around ownership transmission seems pertinent. At the micro-level, too, it is crucial to address ownership as it is the key to understanding where true power lies in a family company.[9] The responsibilities of ownership include where to invest financial assets and whether to keep, grow, or sell the business. Like the person at the helm, owners are in charge of their ships' rudder: They provide an enterprise with the overall direction by setting its fundamental purpose, targets for profitability, risk, growth, and liquidity through ongoing adjustments to keep the ship steering straight.[10] Their success (or lack of) influences wealth preservation or destruction across generations while impacting a dynasty's continuity.[11] For all these reasons, passing ownership responsibilities on involves high stakes. Ownership-related discussions are intertwined with difficult technical aspects and complex feelings since they evoke issues related to power, money, love, mortality, and fairness.

Two additional elements contribute to generating further challenges. First, ownership includes a beneficial (dividends) and a legal component (voting rights). Depending on each family's ownership strategy, these may come together (i.e., in case of a trustee with voting shares); or separate, only the benefits, in case of nonvoting shares or a trust's beneficiary.[12] A second significant distinction is how involved Next Gens want, or are allowed, to be in management and governance; and how active or passive (glad to receive the benefits, with no participation) they choose to be.[13]

With Whom to Discuss

To address the question, it is crucial to unpack the general term "discuss" to reduce some potential ambiguity. When in a discussion, individuals engage with different intentions. There are diverse nuances. In fact, there is a difference between discussing to inform or be informed by the interlocutors. This can take place before or after a decision is made. The discussions may also include asking permission or consulting with Senior Gens. When consulting, individuals are asking for opinions or suggestions that they may or not decide to follow. That may not always be clear with everyone involved in the dialogue. As a Next Gen, being explicit about this distinction is crucial in order to set consistent expectations regarding the goals of ownership conversations.

Developing a matrix can help. One dimension would be the intentions of the conversations. Another would be determining which individuals the Next Gens would need to engage with in the various discussions, while also respecting role boundaries.[14] Several stakeholders are directly and indirectly impacted by ownership transfer and are invested in the Next Gen's life choices including family members, who may be business executives, board members, family council members (if existing), and owners. Therefore, it is important to know who needs to be informed of the intentions, consulted regarding what is possible, and able to identify those from whom Next Gens need to obtain approval. Whether with family members (of the same and previous generations), spouses, current owners, executives, mentors, and advisors, the sooner they become aware of Next Gen's interest in assuming ownership responsibilities, the better it is to initiate and engage in conversations with the appropriate intent.

It is fundamental to be prepared and know that it will take many interactions over a long time to move from expressing interests to formalizing the actual transfer of powers. The following scenarios, not necessarily related or in any particular order, could make it more concrete. First, Next Gens may want to ask their siblings or cousins their perspectives and intentions with respect to active or passive roles in ownership. Second, it is informing the mentor about an interest in taking on more responsibilities and consulting them about the next steps to make sure the Next Gen is ready. Another example would be consulting with the family council or with the board about the interest's viability. Lastly, it is crucial to sit down with the current owners, most likely parents or grandparents, to inform them about the calling, gather information regarding the existing structure and future plans, consult with them about alternative options, and ultimately get their permission, as they hold the ultimate decision-making power. In this latter example, it is critical to pay particular attention to role boundaries. The discussion would involve a Next Gen as son/daughter, young adult, possibly a parent themselves, and the future owner all at the same time. On the other end, the current owners—parents, who might be about to retire— may struggle to view their children as the adults they've become. Building the skills to keep it as a discussion between current and future owners without forgetting the family bonds and observing critical boundaries is necessary. To this end, these conversations typically happen between individuals in different life stages, with conflicting needs to be reconciled.[15] While Next Gens have a legitimate desire to express autonomy and make a mark to leave the world a better place, the incumbents may be reflecting on their life, seeking fulfillment, fearing they won't be relevant anymore, and redefining their identity. This extra layer of human complexity dramatically impacts how to approach the discussion, not just when.

Concluding Thoughts

Given this context, I recommend the following actions and steps:

- Get informed about the current ownership structure and put the strategy in place regarding both value and control distribution. While doing this, it is important not to underestimate the complexity of the inheritance law and the estate planning behind the distribution choices. These two, too often, are the main drivers.
- Ask about what types of owners and what attitude is appreciated in one's family enterprise: Are operating or governing owners welcomed? What are the conditions? What is the expected attitude for non-operating owners?
- Focus and share the passion, the why, and the meaning behind the importance of getting more responsibilities as a Next Gen.
- Get curious about how to become a more active owner. Above all, if the family culture supports a more passive attitude, it is fundamental to understand the potential impact of a change to avoid rejection.

Finally, the human complexity behind every step is a constant with a major impact. Therefore, patience, compassion, and emotional intelligence are the most indispensable skills to develop.

Gaia Marchisio. As a member of the fourth generation, understanding how to support owners has always been close to Dr. Marchisio's heart, so that she turned her passion into her profession.

With a global experience of more than twenty years, she creatively combined research, education, and advising—focused mainly but not solely—on the next generation. As the Cox Family Enterprise Center's Executive Director, she launched the MiniMBA for Next Gen owners, and founded the Family Business Clinic™, an innovative interdisciplinary advising service for family enterprises' owners seeking to create sustainable alignment. More recently, she co-authored the book *OWN IT! How to Develop a Family Enterprise Owner's Mindset at Every Age*.

Commentary by Thompson Turner, U.S.

As Gaia Marchisio articulates, ownership transitions are complicated and difficult due to both technical complexity and emotional baggage. We have experienced many iterations of this tension in our own family enterprise, which is comprised of six generations and over sixty family members and includes an operating business, a family foundation, and a family council.

A family story illustrates the emotional aspect of ownership transition. A third-generation family member who had enjoyed full control over business decisions lamented to his wife that, after significant leadership transition, the fourth-generation leaders were making too many mistakes. They were not taking his sage advice! His wife, who often provided sage advice herself, suggested to him: "Perhaps this is like riding a bike. You must allow them to fall off, get back on, then fall off again." Her husband, not convinced, responded: "But this is *my bike!*"

In terms of legal ownership, all family members in my generation (the fifth generation) already own voting shares of the company in their individual capacity. However, because of the number of family members, stock ownership does not equate to practical control by any one family member. Instead, the transition of "ownership" in our family, and the related transition of control, is more a question of leadership than legal or beneficial ownership of company stock.

Responding to the question of how to approach discussions of transitions of leadership and control, our family opted to integrate various Next Gens-specific committees and boards into the family enterprise. These Next Gens' boards are designed to familiarize the Next Gens with the concepts and responsibilities around ownership, leadership, and control, and also to identify which Next Gens have the interest, capability, and skill set to step up as future family leaders. Included in these Next Generation committees are the Next Generation Foundation (a foundation operated exclusively by fifth- and sixth-generation family members) and the Next Generation advisory board of directors (a Next Generation board that attends all company board meetings but does not have voting power). Additionally, the family council provides an avenue to family involvement for our Next Gens who wish to be involved in the family enterprise but do not possess as much business acumen or knowledge. The seats of many of these boards are filled by majority vote of family members (not by majority of shares). Accordingly, for purposes of selecting the Next Gens who will serve on these boards, each family member is on equal footing despite the number of shares he or she owns.

Through these boards, Next Gens learn about business matters or family dynamics in an environment of controlled risk and reduced tension. When Next Gens assume formal positions of control, they feel prepared and comfortable from having served on these Next Gens boards. Moreover, senior generation family members are more willing to embrace the transition to Next Gens who have proven capable of carrying the torch through consistent involvement on these boards.

Any family, especially larger families like ours, would be well-served to implement Next Gens committees and boards into the family enterprise so that Next Gens can ride the bike, fall off, and get back on before the formal transition of ownership and control occurs.

Questions for Further Reflection

- Can you list the steps it might take from a first discussion with the current owners to assuming active ownership responsibilities in the family enterprise years later?
- What drives the ownership attitude of your family? Is it something that needs to change?
- Please list common ownership responsibilities. Which of these responsibilities are exhibited by the owners in your family and why may the current owners lack others?
- What are the mechanisms for family members to become familiar with ownership responsibilities and master them?

Your Notes | Your Action Items

2.3
How Can I Prepare Myself to Be Able to Work Effectively with My Fellow Family Owners?

Response by Peter Jaskiewicz and Elizabeth Tetzlaff, Canada

A PricewaterhouseCoopers survey of 956 Next Gens in 2019 from sixty countries and territories found that Next Gens have big plans.[16] With 70 percent of these Next Gens actively engaged in the family business, by 2025; 41 percent expect to be executive directors (i.e., owner-managers); 29 percent anticipate being majority shareholders; 15 percent plan on being involved in business governance, and the other 15 percent expect to become non-executive directors. In other words, 85 percent share the ambition of becoming owners of their families' businesses.

As Marvel's Uncle Ben reminds Peter Parker, "with great power comes great responsibility."[17] Ambition, like power, has its own counterweight—obstacles. So, it could be said, "with great ambition come great obstacles." Despite their ambition, 52 percent of Next Gens have yet to be given the responsibility of a special project, and despite being "deeply engaged" in the family business, 64 percent of them admit that they are not being used as a sounding board. Worse still, 10 percent of these Next Gens feel unheard: "I make suggestions, but they are hardly ever listened to." These statistics echo the sentiment that Next Gens shared with us: We are ambitious and want to work effectively as owners, but how can we prepare for that ourselves?

Ambition, Abilities, Approach, and Acceptance

In our experience, effective Next Gens have their "A game," which includes four As—ambition, abilities, approach, and acceptance.[18]

Ambition. To have ambition is to have determination and a strong desire to achieve or see something to completion.[19] For Next Gens, this desire could speak not only to their desire to succeed as the successor, but also their determination to improve upon the advancements made in the family firm. Indeed, on one hand, we have met Next Gens who lacked ambition, stating: "I will never be as good as the incumbent." On the other hand, we have met ambitious Next Gens who were keen to learn how to accelerate their own development and were eager to leave their mark. For instance, they talked about projects to reduce carbon emissions of the family firm, unify the family before spinning off outdated business units, or implement plans in the family office to sell investments that do not comply with environmental and social standards. Without their ambition, these behaviors might not take place. Ambition is thus the first necessary quality that Next Gens need to possess. However, in order for it to be beneficial and not destructive, ambition, like energy, needs a value-oriented direction.

Abilities. Abilities help to harness ambition and give it direction. Abilities are commonly equated with accounting degrees or strategy MBAs. However, the abilities that make effective family owners are much broader and include having good people skills, being able to motivate others on the team, having healthy coping mechanisms to deal with stress, and being able to approach conflict constructively. In his biography, Charles Bronfman—the second-generation former co-leader of Seagram—describes many effective decisions that he and his brother Edgar made, but Charles also discloses that his biggest mistake was to suppress his thoughts when his brother and his brother's son brought forward proposals that were driven by their personal interests rather than business sense.[20] Charles says that he saw the problems of the family's investment ideas but admitted that he did not use his veto right because he felt pressured to comply and wanted to avoid conflicts. From Charles's story, we learn how important it is for family owners to have an encompassing range of soft skills. We can also see that ambitions that are not properly guided can ruin the family business.

Approach. Having the right abilities equips the owner with a foundation onto which they can add an effective approach to decision-making processes in family business. In our experience, as long as all parties involved feel that their voices are heard and accounted for, family owners are able to make controversial decisions (e.g., How do we deal with an underperforming family manager?)—even if they do not fully agree with each other to start with. Otherwise stated, Next Gens need to understand what constitutes a fair process, communicate, and then implement such processes.[21] We have witnessed, firsthand, good decisions failing because the family did not use an approach that allowed those involved to feel that they were all on equal footing in the decision-making process.

Acceptance. Finally, having the ambition and the ability together with the right approach leads Next Gens to the door, but in order to open it, a key is necessary: acceptance. It is not uncommon to experience the disheartening feeling of meeting everyone, having them congratulate you on the new board appointment, and then ignore you for the rest of the meeting (or the next five-to-ten years). This does not mean that the Next Gen will not be accepted, it simply means that Next Gens will need to accept that it is necessary to prove themselves in order to be recognized. Learning about ownership can look like attending family council meetings, being a board observer (visitor) in board meetings, and assuming formal roles in student groups, local not-for-profits, or regional family business associations. Rather than passively waiting for acceptance, Next Gens need to proactively work toward it. In other words, if Next Gens are able to commit to proving themselves outside and inside of the family business, then they will be more likely accepted as Next Gen leaders.

In summary, Next Gen owners' effectiveness is an outcome of their ambition, abilities, approach, and acceptance. If the senior generation does not share influence and does not treat Next Gens as owners, the latter will be less effective. Similarly, fellow Next Gen owners can be destructive. If they are poorly prepared and immature, they can torpedo processes and push away effective Next Gens. Therefore, families and Next Gens need to do their part to ensure that none of the future owners become the Achilles heel of the family and the bottleneck of their enterprise(s). Families whose Next Gens bring their "A game" are more likely to make a difference for their families, enterprises, and communities.

Peter Jaskiewicz was born into a business family in Poland and grew up in Germany. He is a full professor of family business at the Telfer School of Management in Ottawa, where he holds a university research chair in enduring entrepreneurship. His findings were considered among the most globally influential scholarship on family business in 2013, 2015, and 2017. Peter has presented his research insights to members of the European Parliament, the European Commission, and the United Nations. He is an associate editor of the leading journal in the field—the *Family Business Review*. In his advising practice, he supports the development of responsible Next Gen owners.

Elizabeth Tetzlaff is a PhD candidate at the Telfer School of Management in Ottawa, Ontario. Her research centers around exploring the impact of mental health on both the functioning of the business family as well as on the health and vitality of the family business. In addition to her research, Elizabeth is working on SSHRC-funded research study to understand how differences among families influence the longevity and success of their family businesses.

Heraeus is a technology group headquartered in Hanau, Germany. The company's roots go back to a family pharmacy started in 1660. Today, the Heraeus group includes businesses in the environmental, electronics, health, and industrial applications sectors with a focus on precious and special metals, medical technology, sensors, and specialty light sources. In 2019, Heraeus generated revenues of €22.4 billion with approximately 14,900 employees in forty countries. The company is 100 percent family-owned and has almost 250 shareholders. While my father served as the CEO of our company for seventeen years and another 20 years as chairman of the supervisory board, I was naturally aware of many developments within the company and especially concerning its family shareholders. Whether it was the draft of our first Family Governance Codex in 2005 or the subsequent development of our Next Gen and family activities, I was always interested in being involved in the family business and still participate as an active shareholder today. In my perception, the "A game," as described by Peter Jaskiewicz, holds true in reality. However, I believe their own efforts can primarily focus on the pillars of ambition and abilities whereby approach and acceptance is, depending on the family, only influenceable within limits. For me as a shareholder, our regular shareholder meetings were always a non-negotiable matter. Not that I had that conviction when I was ten years old and would have much rather gone to my friend's birthday party than to the children's program with my fellow junior shareholders. It was not until much later that I realized why my parents had instilled the importance of perfect attendance in me: It was about prioritizing the company events over my personal interests. Today some twenty years have passed since my dilemma and the commitment of being there through the years with only a handful of excuses has received acknowledgment within the family and can hardly be interpreted as anything but interest and ambition.

Regarding abilities, they are surely also driven by one's own involvement and efforts. Having studied business, I know that it allowed me to grasp concepts more quickly or simply feel more familiar with the terminologies. Nevertheless, I would strongly encourage moving away from the idea that only studied economists or IT specialists qualify for involvement in (tech) companies. I have seen too many smart and professional Next Gens, working as doctors or scientists who are able to ask clever (often out of the box) questions and participate in discussions, yet perceive themselves as unqualified or—even worse—suffer under the derogatory judgment of the older generation. This assessment not only limits the number of involved Next Gens, but also hinders the development of diverse thinking within a family business.

When it comes to approach and acceptance, I believe there is only a certain degree of influence possible. In some situations, of course, my behavior can be decisive. From my experience, the way and the timing of asking questions constitutes an example. It is not so much about *what* you say, but *how* you say it that determines whether you are perceived as a loyal co-thinker or as an insensitive troublemaker. However, I also believe that the way a family (business) deals with conflicts, is able to re-invent itself and accepts different approaches, is deeply rooted in the family's tradition. A Next Gen with great ambition and abilities and even a good feeling for the right approach, will always, to some extent, be dependent on the family to unfold and ultimately contribute to the company's future success.

Questions for Further Reflection

- How can families inspire Next Gens to develop the ambition for becoming responsible owners?
- In which areas should you, as a Next Gen, develop abilities for becoming a responsible owner?
- How can you learn to develop proper approaches to deal with issues that you will face both as a family member and owner?
- What can you do to increase your acceptance by nonfamily leaders in the family enterprise?
- What can the senior generation do to facilitate the acceptance of Next Gens in the family enterprise?

Your Notes | Your Action Items

2.4
If I Become a Non-Active Owner, What
Are My Rights and My Duties?

Response by Rania Labaki, France

Michelin, Mulliez, Wendel, and Solvay are notable examples of successful business families with several hundred family owners, most of whom do not play an active role in management or governance. Over time, family businesses tend to span an increasing number of family members and to pass down ownership to most or all descendants, whether they work in the family business or not. Only around 5 percent of the Next Gens intend to pursue their career in the family business five years after graduation.[22] Still, non-active owners can play "a responsible ownership role which proves crucial to the long-term survival of their family business."[23]

The Meaning of Ownership

The shares I inherited are a blessing and a burden at the same time. By becoming an owner, I feel proud to step in the shoes of giants and responsible to continue our family's legacy. I am, however, concerned about how to effectively contribute without an active role in the family business.
　　　　–Celia, twenty-five year old, third-generation owner

Celia's position is not uncommon among non-active owners who often struggle in finding their way in the family business. Acting as an owner means respectfully "walking the land," that is fully embracing and enjoying this status, rather than just exercising ownership faceless, on-paper-only, and controlling from afar.[24] This path is shaped by three golden rules of family ownership's benefits and responsibilities,[25] which include both financial and emotional dimensions.

Voting Right: Unleash the Ownership Power Thoughtfully

When holding voting shares, owners are granted the right to attend the meetings of the general assembly. These meetings are an opportunity to ask questions and discuss various options prior to voting important decisions that shape the strategy and its effective implementation. Some owners might find the exercise of their voting power challenging. As Celia points out:

> I attended the general assembly only once and I feel already reluctant to attend the upcoming one. I was confused because of the overwhelming display of financial information and business presentations with terminologies I am not familiar with. I did not feel comfortable asking questions or voting decisions that I could not understand. I have a small number of shares, which makes my voting power almost insignificant. I am not sure how I can really make a difference.

Just like Celia, non-active owners might find it easier to trust other active owners in the voting process. While the general assembly's resolutions are traditionally approved with the majority of votes, these resolutions are, however, binding upon all owners regardless of whether they voted or not. Non-active owners could benefit from gaining elementary knowledge about financial literacy (the financial statements and basic financial ratios), management and governance (composition, role, and functioning) by enrolling in short educational programs. They are also encouraged to consult other experienced owners or the family owners' council, composed of branch representatives, prior to the assembly meetings. This allows them to better prepare and address questions at the general assembly, express their expectations, and provide an outside view that can add value in shaping the family business future.

Dividends: Favor the Long-Term View

Non-active owners have the right to receive an annual dividend for each share they own, as declared by the board of directors. This ordinary dividend usually represents a portion of the earnings that the family business generates. In some cases, owners receive extraordinary dividends, which are larger than ordinary dividends but are not paid on a recurring basis. Should the family business incur losses, however, dividends are not distributed, unless in exceptional cases by using bank loans or retained earnings from past years.

Distributing low levels of dividends is common among family businesses in the first and second generation, preferring to use the cash to finance long-term investment projects. However, the dividends levels tend to increase with the increasing number of nonfamily owners in subsequent generations. A study shows that almost half of the non-active owners in family businesses depend on the dividends as their main income.[26] This dependency might create conflicts among non-active owners who are concerned about their finances and the active owners who are in favor of a long-term orientation of the family business.[27] By seeking financial independency, non-active owners can play a more responsible role so that the business strives and thrives, and the family harmony is maintained.

Ownership Transfer: Emotions Matter

In some family businesses, the right of transferring or selling the shares depends on conditions proclaimed in the shareholders' agreement. These include the minimal duration of holding the shares prior to their transfer, the disclosure by the owners of the intention to sell within a specific timeframe, the appropriate method to determine the value of the shares, and the eligible criteria for the new shareholders. In addition to these prerequisite conditions, the decision to sell the family business shares is both financial and emotional. When they are tempted to sell, non-active owners often do not feel emotionally attached to the business, nor are they satisfied with the financial returns in terms of their lifestyle expectations.

Selling their shares to outsiders might, however, have repercussions broader than their personal lives. Particularly when these outsiders are more short-term sighted, they might create rifts with the remaining family owners and threaten the family control of the business.[28] Pros and cons of such a decision need to be carefully considered. A family business mentor or advisor can provide guidance toward finding solutions among family owners to preserve the family business for the upcoming generations.

Conclusion

Non-active owners can engage in responsible ownership by exerting their duties and enjoying their rights while contributing to the family business continuity. These include:

- Exercising their voting power, whatever their level of ownership, based on thoughtful knowledge and communication with other owners about the family business.
- Supporting dividends choices as part of the family business continuity strategy rather than of their main financial revenues.
- Making considerate choices about the transfer or sale of their shares, by taking into account the emotional dimensions, in order to preserve the family control.

Rania Labaki, PhD is associate professor of management at EDHEC Business School, director of the EDHEC Family Business Research Centre, and Family Business Fellow at Cornell University.

She is a board member of IFERA, family business advisor at Lansberg Gersick & Associates, head of the academic committee of FBN France, and co-editor of *Entrepreneurship Research Journal.* Her current research, advising, and teaching interests revolve around the interplay between family dynamics and decision-making, governance design, and development of responsible owners. She is recipient of numerous awards recognizing her contributions to the family business field, including the Barbara Hollander Award in 2020.

Commentary by Joaquín Uriach, Spain

I am 183 years old; my inseparable bond with the family business and, above all, with the chemist's shop that my great-great-grandfather founded in Barcelona in 1838, has always led me to think that the beginnings of my life, the genesis of all that I am, should be pinpointed back to that distant date. We all carry a past that leaves its mark on us. It can be a burden, but fortunately it can also be a privilege. The history of our family businesses, our past, is both a right and a duty.

At Uriach, we have gone through several family transitions since our founding. Four generational changes in fact, and we are just embarking on a new one: from the fifth to the sixth generation. This has meant that, in each generation, several family members who were not yet proprietors, became owners in time. Most of them were active and working in the business on a daily basis when they transitioned to owners, but also increasingly larger numbers became non-active shareholders, especially in the most recent era of Uriach (fifth and sixth generation).

Each generation is different and each owner is different, whether they are active or non-active. Yet they all have a common denominator: their passion for the family business. And this is precisely the first duty of any non-active owner of a family business: to feel passionate about his or her company, to learn to love it. And you only love what you know. That's why it is crucial that they know the company inside out, from its history and values to its products. Having shares in a company must mean more than just holding a security that entitles you to some dividends. Asking questions, being curious about the company, about what it is and what it means, is the first duty. And at the same time, the first right. All non-active owners have the right to training and information from the company or the pertinent family bodies.

Passion for the family business can be acquired over time, but the best way to cultivate it is to "imbibe" it from a very young age, as a lesson imparted by your parents or relatives. Additionally, this is precisely where another duty/right emerges: that of requiring that we receive information at home and that we be involved in the business from there, so that we can become well-informed and, above all, engaged and motivated non-active owners.

However, it may well be that this passion does not materialize and that there isn't any special feeling for the family business; on the contrary, it may even be regarded as a prison and a source of family or personal conflict. In such a case, the non-active owner must enjoy a fundamental right: the right to freedom. I am referring to the freedom not to feel obliged, not to feel an obligation either to accept the role of owner or to remain in such a role. The right not to feel forced at any time to accept any responsibility that they do not wish to take on or continue to bear. One thing that is clear to me is that there is no family business anywhere in the world, no matter how big or valuable it may be, that is worth sacrificing our own ambitions or our own desires or dreams for. Don't let the dividends fool you. Freedom is a priceless commodity, or at least it is a much more precious commodity than mere dividends.

When I become a non-active owner, I must be fully aware of the fact that one of my main duties is to ensure that the company becomes more and more valuable and grows. Although this may seem obvious, it is perhaps not quite so obvious in a family business, that my duty must be to put the company and its development first, over and above my own interests or those of the branch of the family or the shareholding group I belong to. The company always comes first.

Also, the right to freedom of expression is something that is important for non-active owners. To be able to express yourself, you have to have to be in the right place, both in the family and in the business. And once you are in the family forum, you must have the freedom to make sure your opinion is heard and taken into account. It is true that family businesses, over and above the controlling-owner, are built on leadership, but above all they are built on consensus, on dialogue, and on respect for the opinions of others.

Taking on the status of non-active owner requires humility, gratitude, and empathy. Our duty is to avoid the so-called sense of entitlement or "spoilt child" syndrome of those who believe they have it all because they deserve it all, and who consider that "the world is theirs" just because they are owners. Being an owner is a privilege, but it should not give you any privileges. Being a non-active owner means that you should be thankful for being where you are and having what you have. I sometimes see non-active owners who do not appreciate what they have and act with a certain lack of enthusiasm. A non-active owner should always have a humble attitude, far removed from arrogance. Our attitude, whether it be apathetic or humble, will be key to our being good owners.

Being grateful brings us to another of the duties incumbent on anyone who becomes a non-active owner, namely the duty to contribute to society. We have been lucky enough to be born with a silver spoon in our mouths. As owners, we enjoy an ample availability of time and other resources, which allows us to contribute to the improvement of our society, our institutions, our public or private bodies. We are the privileged few and we have the duty to help others, to offer our time and knowledge to improve this world, each one of us from our own position and dimension. Our obligation is to "complicate our lives" by participating in the construction of a better world, getting involved in some way or other. Fortunately, I see many young non-active owners who do know how to be grateful for what they have by giving to others.

Our experience has also shown us that respect is a key element that every non-active owner must have among his or her duties. Respect for the past (not criticising it), for values (not playing them down), for people and, of course, for the family and its shareholders. This means that family members should respect the differences between them, especially if they are siblings. Rather than driving them apart, differences should enrich the company and the relationships between them. Family members should make the most of the fact that they are different and have different skills and knowledge. All roles are important in a family business, both those that are actively involved in the business (CEO) and those that remain within the family (social leader) or that of someone who is no more than an owner. Everyone merits respect for who they are as people and for the role that each one plays. In our family, we shareholders, whether active or non-active, have always built on differences and supported each other with mutual respect.

As I said at the beginning, to work in a family business, whether as an owner or as a manager, you have to feel passionate about it. Passion is in the blood but passion can also be taught. And passion has to be passed on. If there's no passion, it's most unlikely that there will be good ownership in a family business. This is the challenge: to keep the passion alive in the generations to come, in both those who are potential owners and those who already are owners. This is what we have always done for more than 180 years at Uriach and this is what we intend to continue to do as a key element to ensure that we have good owners and, therefore, good governance and, consequently, an excellent family business.

Questions for Further Reflection ─────────────

- Who are the owners of your family enterprise? How many shares does each owner have?
- How will the ownership structure change in the next ten years?
- What is the dividend policy in your family enterprise?
- How can shares be transferred in your family enterprise? If there is a shareholder agreement, what are its provisions?
- How passionate are you and your fellow Next Gens about the family enterprise? How can you tell if someone is passionate about the family enterprise?

Your Notes | Your Action Items ──────────────

2.5
What Mechanisms Can I Use to Monitor Whether Our Business Model Will Still Be Viable in the Future?

Response by Carlo Salvato, Italy

The Need for Continuous Renewal of a Family Firm's Business Model

Family firms that survive after the third generation—less than 20 percent do, according to most statistics—have successfully faced the challenge of relentlessly renewing their business model. A business model is the combination of factors allowing a firm to create value for its customers, its stakeholders, and, ultimately, its owners. It is a complex and often elusive blend of elements such as a firm's value proposition to its target customers and stakeholders, the resources, activities, and partnerships through which value is created, the channels and relationships through which it is delivered, and the revenue system determining how the resulting financial value flows to the firm.[29] A business model can thus be seen as the "secret recipe" for a family firm's success.

Next Gens often ask themselves whether the present business model of their family firm will still be viable in the future. The answer is simple—it will not. Recent global crises have demonstrated that once solid and profitable business models can be wiped out in a matter of a few months. Even without massive crises and pandemics, the relentless forces of competition and technological change constantly challenge the subtle balance among the components of a business model. The challenge for Next Gens is not to assess whether the current business model of the family firm will still be viable in the future. This is a passive approach towards assessing whether to join the business or not. The real challenge is to consider whether the current business model can be adapted to capture future opportunities and to avoid inevitable threats. Next Gens may assess whether their family firm is ready to address this challenge by examining two dimensions—asset recombination and people participation.

Asset Recombination in Three Steps

Next Gens may view their family firm and its current business model as a collection of assets—resources, capabilities, and technologies that can be recombined in different ways to address future opportunities and threats. Next Gens may assess whether the business model has potential for dynamic recombination in three steps.[30]

First, Next Gens should list the family firm's *core resources* (both tangible and intangible, including technologies) and *capabilities* (what people are capable of doing, individually or together, within the firm). They should try to characterize and describe them in a general manner, based on their properties and functions, not on their use in specific products and services (e.g., "digital technologies for process automation" rather than "robot technologies for the automotive industry").

Second, Next Gens should envision the new *applications* that the family firm could offer in the future with its core resources and capabilities (new products and services) and the *customers* (both new and existing) who may need these applications. New applications should be portrayed in a specific way, in terms of what they can do for potential customers and the value that they can bring to them, not simply a list of new products and services (e.g., robots with a user-friendly interface, automatically interacting with customers through artificial intelligence to ask/answer questions).

Customers should be described by zooming in to segment each customer group, or by using the concept of *marketing/customer personas*—stylized, fictional characters representing user types and all their possible needs (e.g., insurance brokers offering contracts to potential customers who dislike interacting with real employees). The combination of applications and customers will result in the identification of several new business models or extensions of the existing business model.[31] Next Gens should try to identify as many (reasonable) opportunities as possible, at least four or five, possibly ten or more.

Third, Next Gens should place the identified opportunities in a 2x2 business model innovation matrix[32] assessing them in terms of low/high-potential (both market and economic potential) and low/high-challenge in their implementation (financial, technological, competitive, and organizational, including challenges coming from other members of the family such as Senior Gen leaders). If the resulting matrix shows a few new business model opportunities in all quadrants (the only uninteresting one is low-potential/high-challenge), one can reasonably conclude that the family firm's business model has the potential to be adapted or extended in the future.

People Participation in Two Steps

Who should perform the three asset-recombination steps? Besides the thought experiment described above, Next Gens should also try to understand whether people in the family firm—including future members from the Next Gen and nonfamily managers—are willing to participate in actual business model innovation. This is probably the key issue. Identifying new and promising business models from a set of existing assets requires creativity, proactiveness, the willingness to take on risk and to collaborate to make things happen. It has to do with people's attitudes and motivations that—unlike business models—can hardly be modified and recombined. This challenge can be addressed in two steps. First, perform the three steps in asset recombination together with others, asking both Next Gen and Senior Gen members to participate. Interest and actual participation will give a sense of whether the family firm has the carrying capacity for business model innovation, or not. Second, try to discuss the business model innovation matrix with as many relevant actors as possible, to test whether possible future opportunities are actually valuable or not.

The Role of Next Gens in Renewing Business Models

Next Gens play a key role in renewing their family firms' business models by advancing proposals for innovation and change. The approach suggested in this chapter—first, assessing asset-recombination opportunities, and, second, assessing people's willingness to participate—will not give a final answer in relation to the future viability of a family firm's current business model. However, it will offer an explicit and tangible understanding of whether the family firm currently has the basic building blocks for successful business model innovation.

Carlo Salvato is a full professor of management at Bocconi University in Milan, where he teaches the family business strategies course. He is a fellow of the Family Firm Institute (FFI), where he is also the vice chair of the board of directors, a member of the executive committee, and the dean of the GEN Global Education Network. He published several papers on family firms in international academic journals and he was an associate editor of the *Family Business Review*. He is an advisor of Italian family firms on succession and Next Gen development, family and corporate governance, and corporate strategy.

Commentary by Antoine Mayaud, France

I am a third-generation member of AFM (Association Familiale Mulliez). Today, AFM's portfolio is comprised of diverse companies and brands. The group's roots date back to 1904, when Louis Mulliez Lestienne opened a spinning mill. In the 1920s, Louis helped three of his sons and one son-in-law to start their own businesses, on a joint ownership basis between them. Gérard-père, Louis' second son, joined his father in the original business and, in 1945, opened the first shop connecting the family directly with its customers. In 1961, the second generation helped the third generation to start the supermarket chain Auchan, and starting in 1978, the second generation supported numerous third-generation members to start a variety of other businesses. Presently, AFM's portfolio includes more than sixty businesses including supermarkets (Auchan; about 331,000 employees), sporting goods (Décathlon; 1,600 stores in forty countries), electronics' stores (e.g., Boulanger), hardware and do-it-yourself (DIY) stores (e.g., Adeo group overseeing, Leroy Merlin, Weldom, Bricocenter, Zodio, Aki), and restaurants (Agapes Restauration overseeing Les 3 Brasseurs, Pizza Paï, Flunch), among many others.

The Entrepreneurial Spirit

More than 800 family associates control the AFM's business portfolio today in keeping with the family's motto "All in all" (Le tous dans tout—all family in all businesses). My family has cultivated an entrepreneurial spirit across generations with some reasons for success:

- The family recognizes that business models change and, therefore, have to change (but not sell) its businesses proactively rather than reactively engaging in painful restructurings.
- The family members are encouraged to set up their own businesses, so they can align their individual passions with given

opportunities, which is better than taking over existing companies that they have little to no passion nor experience in.

- The AFM portfolio evolves and rejuvenates through various entrepreneurial transformations within the core businesses, and at its periphery through new businesses.
- Shareholders do not become passive and Next Gens gain interest in the family portfolio.
- Entrepreneurship is a great way to not only prepare Next Gen directors, but also for the family to invest in causes relevant to Next Gens.

The Family's Entrepreneurial Investment Company

The Family Council of AFM created its first investment company called Creadev in 2002—whose mission is the pursuit of majority, long-term equity investments in family and nonfamily ventures outside of retail. In 2006, the Next Gens promoted the launch of a second investment fund, Club des Entrepreneurs (CDE), this one entirely dedicated to family members. It was a response to the Next Gens desiring family investments in their ventures but in a more flexible and less dominant way than conducted by Creadev. The CDE has helped us learn from entrepreneurship for our existing businesses and start many new businesses, ensuring that the AFM portfolio evolves and adapts. As of 2019, approximately fifty family members started their own ventures in collaboration with the CDE and, therefore, with the entire family's partnership.

The Family Entrepreneurial Investment Rules

Six rules guide investments by the CDE, enabling us to update existing and add new business models to the AFM portfolio:

1. The CDE invests up to Euro 100,000 in a first round and not more than the family entrepreneurs invest themselves.

2. The CDE does not take more than 25 percent of ownership so that the family entrepreneur feels "free" relative to the family and stays in charge of his or her venture.

3. The CDE respects the idea and work provided by the family founder, and therefore, values his or her initial ownership stake higher (usually at double value compared to the CDE's value).

4. The venture has to be the main activity of the founder(s) and the main target of their investment.

5. The venture's purpose has to be the creation of jobs.

6. The founders have to adhere with the AFM's values, which are embedded in the CDE:

   o Each venture has to establish a board immediately.

   o Each founder has to participate in CDE activities that include entrepreneurial training, exchange of best practices, learning expeditions, and more.

   o Founders accept the AFM's approach to determine the value of the venture.

   o Founders have to sign an Associates Pact determining their rights and duties as well as potential sanctions in case they violate their duties.

To conclude, an entrepreneurial spirit is part of our family's DNA and has proven to be essential to update AFM portfolio's existing business models, enable the Next Gens to leverage their passion and knowledge in new ventures, keep the family united, and take advantage of emerging opportunities for the benefit of all of the family members.

Questions for Further Reflection

- What is the business model of your family enterprise?
- What are the key resources and capabilities of your family's enterprise?

- What are potential applications of these resources and capabilities?
- Who are your current customers? Who might be the future ones?

Your Notes | *Your Action Items* ——————————————

2.6
How Can I Gain Credibility with Nonfamily Executives and Board Members?

Response by Nadine Kammerlander, Germany

In the twenty-first century, many Next Gens aim to take an active rather than passive ownership role early on. For instance, they strive for board positions, where they can challenge current strategies and provide novel and fresh perspectives (e.g., on digital transformation). However, many Next Gens wonder whether the fellow Next Gen has been appointed because of their capability or because of family membership. This is a relevant concern since such appointments counter the usual age structure of many boards. A WHU study[33] found that there were hardly any members on the boards of German family firms below the age of forty and less than 20 percent were between forty and fifty.

When aiming to take over ownership responsibility, Next Gens need to be self-confident and have the family members support their decision to join the board. But it is also the firms' stakeholders, amongst others nonfamily executives and further board members, who need to be convinced about the Next Gen's qualification to advice and control the family firm. There might be some skepticism since in the past it was often a given that one or few of the children took over firm control, irrespective of qualification. Many anecdotes show that incompetent owners might hire the wrong managers and take the wrong overarching strategic decision.[34] Such competences include a general understanding of the family firm and its industry, the global and technology-related changes affecting the industry, and also the ability to engage in strategic discussions, read financial statements, and assess the performance of top managers.[35] Next Gens need to prove their knowledge, experience, and general judgment abilities. If they lack full acceptance by other stakeholders, they might have trouble being heard or listened to in board meetings. So, what can Next Gens do to gain credibility with executives and other board members?

Interaction with Family Members Before Ownership Succession

The time before succession forms the basis for all later steps. As such, it is important that Next Gens push for an objective successor selection process that scrutinizes the ability, motivation, and skills of potential Next Gen owners in a systematic way. This can provide them with convincing arguments that they were not chosen for board roles because of blood ties but because of their talent. In this regard, recent research from Switzerland has shown that it is beneficial if the successor assessment and decision is carried out by a diverse team that also includes nonfamily board members.[36]

Interaction with Nonfamily Stakeholders Before Ownership Succession

Next Gens should also think about their interactions with nonfamily stakeholders early on. Indeed, interaction with nonfamily stakeholders before taking on an active ownership role is a key success factor. Successful Next Gens report that they have been present in the firm and know key stakeholders from an early age. While this might go along with the drawback of being seen as "the CEO's kid," it also builds up trust in the Next Gen's intentions. A successor reported that after her decision to become an active owner, the external stakeholders felt relieved as they knew the firm would be continued as a family firm and be in good hands. In addition to trust, the Next Gens also need to think about what relevant knowledge they should build up before succession in order to gain credibility. This could be achieved by founding their own firm or getting a proper business-related education at a top university.[37]

Interaction with Family Members after Ownership Succession

Once ownership succession has officially taken place, the roles of the various family members change. Often, the senior generation is still—formally or informally—present in the overall firm decision-making, even if the Next Gens have already taken over an active ownership role. Now it is important to set rules for interaction to maintain a professional relationship amongst generations and to manifest the solidity of the Next Gen's power. For instance, it is important to keep family conflicts out of any board meetings and to send clear signals that the senior generation backs the decisions of the Next Gen.[38]

Interaction with Nonfamily Stakeholders after Ownership Succession

Young and female Next Gens especially complain about a lack of respect from long-tenured (nonfamily) managers. So, what can they do to quickly gain credibility? Many successful Next Gens highlight the necessity to immediately show high levels of competence. This can be achieved, for instance, by shaping the firm's strategy (e.g., regarding digitalization) and asking the right questions. Other measures include building up the right team of top managers. A Next Gen from an HR company reported that making sure to work with the right people—and replacing some of her father's intimates—was a key success factor for role in the family business.

Practical Implications

The need to convince family-internal as well as family-external stakeholders about one's own competences bears important implications for Next Gens. First, they need to show "presence" in the firm (e.g., at firm events) from early on in order to prove their commitment to the firm. Second, Next Gens should dedicate time and effort to gain business-related knowledge and experience, for instance, through business school education and gaining their own managerial or entrepreneurial experience. Third, Next Gens should make sure that there's a systematic and neutral process in place that assesses their suitability as active board members. Lastly, they need to make sure to contribute sufficiently and constructively once they have assumed their active ownership position—for instance, by stimulating change regarding digital business models.

Conclusion

In sum, the examples show that gaining credibility is not a one-time effort but a continuous process. Indeed, some Next Gens reported that it took from a few months up to five years until they had gained full credibility. The right strategies in place, as well as support by family members and nonfamily mentors, might speed up the process.

Nadine Kammerlander is a professor of family business at WHU—Otto Beisheim School of Management in Germany, where she also leads the Institute of Family Business and Mittelstand. She earned her PhD at the University of Bamberg (Germany) and worked several years as strategy consultant. Her research, teaching, and consulting centers around topics of family firm and family office entrepreneurship, leadership, and governance. Her research has been published in leading international journals and was honored with multiple national and international awards. Prof. Kammerlander is also a board member in the Association of German Supervisory Board Members (VARD e.V.)

Commentary by Anonymous, Europe

Our Family Business

I would define our purpose as facilitating entrepreneurship. Our objective is to identify an entrepreneur who deeply shares our values, character, sensibilities, and frame of mind (i.e., someone you can work with for decades), who has an idea that has dynamic growth potential, and where we as a family can add value in some form. Once we find such an entrepreneur, we try to create the best environment for them to succeed by doing four things:

1. We become the sole capital provider for the entrepreneur and in doing so allow the entrepreneur to start thinking and executing for the long term, and not the next milestone or the next round of funding.
2. We give the entrepreneur and his or her team total autonomy in making decisions. We do not interfere or overrule their decisions even though we have the power to do so. However, we also hold them totally responsible for the performance of the business.
3. We help and support them actively where we can really add value—this varies with each business and can range from heavy operation assistance to strategy and M&A activity.
4. We treat them like true partners and not subsidiary agents, and we build a rapport with them where they know that we will always support them.

My Role in the Family Business

My role is to support entrepreneurs we have already decided to back and to identify future entrepreneurs who we can back. I do the former in two ways:

1. We establish formal detailed budgets, which are reviewed and discussed in detail at formal monthly or quarterly reviews.

2. I regularly speak to the entrepreneurs and the senior management to help them in areas where they need support. I do the latter by constantly meeting people who are referred to us or that I have met somewhere.

We do not take a top-down approach where we analyse industries/sectors/geographies and then from there narrow down where we think there will be opportunities. We create opportunities around the people we meet with whom we feel a strong chemistry. Our referrals or introductions usually come from people who know us, and understand our approach and our philosophy. The most critical variable for us is the person.

My Lessons Learnt

Gaining credibility with nonfamily board members and managers is simple: Never demand respect because of who you are but rather earn respect because of the quality of your contributions. In family businesses, most nonfamily executives and board members will assume that you will have some level of arrogance because you are part of the family. You must never act in a way that confirms this assumption. In whatever role you play, be the first one at the office and the last one to leave, be the person with the most knowledge of material to be discussed, and go the extra mile to deliver a little more that you were expected to do. Never act in a way where you assume people will respect you because you are a family member. Always act in a way where it is your duty to earn the respect of others. The impact of these types of actions will be magnified because most will assume that you will use the opposite approach. In my case, I define success as reaching a point where the entrepreneur will come to me to discuss something—not because I am the family member mandated to oversee his or her business, but because engaging with me will help him or her make a better decision.

Questions for Further Reflection ───────────

- Do you, as a Next Gen, aim to take over ownership responsibilities? If so, why?
- What is your family's process to familiarize Next Gens with the roles of nonfamily executives and board members along with the expectations for Next Gen owners?
- Do you know all nonfamily executives and nonfamily board members of your family enterprise? What are their strengths and weaknesses?
- What capabilities have you developed as a Next Gen that are, or will be, valuable to the family enterprise?

Your Notes | Your Action Items ──────────

2.7
We Sibling/Cousin Owners Are Living All Over the World. How Can We Keep Effective Control of the Nonfamily Managers Running the Family Business?

Response by Cristina Cruz, Spain

Business-owning families are facing increased challenges associated with cultural and demographic changes. The younger generation appears to be highly mobile and internationally oriented. The good news is that these global citizens are more open to change and more receptive to collaboration across borders than their predecessors. However, the high mobility and geographical dispersion of Next Gens pose additional challenges for family owners. When family members start to spread out geographically, communication can start to break down, even in today's wireless world. The problem with family business is that most conversations are informal, happening around the lunch and dinner table. If members are far from this table, they miss many conversations creating problems of miscommunication. Geographical dispersion also complicates infusing a sense of legacy among Next Gens. Family members develop commitment through frequent family interactions, with storytelling, symbols, and rituals becoming the foundation of the family legacy. When family members no longer live close to each other, these interactions are minimized, making Next Gens less connected to the family and its business. This raises the question of how globally dispersed family owners can effectively monitor their nonfamily executives from afar and make effective decisions. Through interactions with successful business families from all over the world I uncovered three best practices that geographically dispersed business families develop to address these concerns.

1. Stay in Touch: Foster Family Communication and Cohesion

Remaining as a cohesive functional group is an imperative requirement to address miscommunication issues (e.g., Next Gens find out about a business issue from a nonfamily member) and to foster a family legacy for geographically dispersed families. However, as families grow and ownership fragments, maintaining family cohesion proves to be a difficult task. Indeed, if one thinks of cohesion as family unity, the task becomes almost impossible. It is highly unlikely that a group of fifty cousins would want to vacation together, hang out all the time, and sit together around the lunch table. While being best friends is not needed to ensure business family cohesion, having the cousins spend time together means building trust that is needed to become successful business partners. It also means keeping them informed about major company and family events.

The best way to keep Next Gens engaged and informed is through the extensive use of technology. Long-lived business families have created their own intranet, co-organize important family events, and facilitate communication among family members. Others have gone further, using formal social platforms to exchange ownership and governance information and updates. For instance, two next generation entrepreneurs from European business families founded Trusted Family, an online platform with the mission to "connect and manage board, shareholders and family members, from anywhere, at any time, on any device."[39]

2. Show Commitment: Develop Responsible Owners

In addition, to ensure family cohesion, geographically dispersed business-owning families also need to become an effective and competent decision-making group. To get there, they need to instill a sense of commitment and responsible ownership in Next Gens. This may sound easy when family members grow up close to the factory, but can business families raise responsible owners when they are spread around the world?

The first thing business families should do on their way toward developing responsible Next Gen owners is to be clear about purpose. To be effective, the purpose should be backed up by shared values. Just as important, the purpose should be actioned based on certain principles that would guide family members behaviour and the family firm's strategic decision-making. Having a well-articulated purpose would facilitate decision-making by creating a framework that will help to align key goals by setting expectations about what any family owner can expect from the firm and what the firm can expect from them.

Next, families should ensure they develop competent Next Gen owners. Ownership competence is not an easy task for geographically dispersed families, as most of their members have never been exposed to learning experiences within the firm and family. This is why it is so important that such families create an education committee. The committee should survey the family to define the key topics (e.g., governance, digitalization, wealth management) that create ways of carrying out activities that engage and educate members on these topics. For instance, the committee could organize plant visits, inspirational talks during annual meetings, or even an entire program for developing responsible owners with an educational institution.

We recently developed a program for the fourth generation of a family with more than thirty cousins spread all over the world. The plan included sessions on mainstream business disciplines such as finance and marketing. It also included a "responsible ownership module" with workshops and sessions on how to successfully enact their ownership role, and to contribute the success of the firm and the functionality of the family. We also developed a "corporate intrapreneurship" module for Next Gens.[40] As part of it, cousins worked (virtually) on teams to develop a business opportunity that could potentially add value to the family business. The overall program was a success. At the end of it, the Next Gens were a more cohesive group, they gained deep knowledge of different businesses, and they understood the importance of having an entrepreneurial mindset to control the family business in the future.

3. Structure the Family and the Business: Implement Sound Governance Structures

Geographically dispersed business families face traditional issues of separating ownership and control. While ensuring family cohesion and developing responsible owners would alleviate these concerns, family owners need to develop proper family and business governance structures to effectively oversee the business as owners. Business governance implies setting up the right incentive system for nonfamily managers and ensuring that the board provides family owners with effective mechanisms to monitor nonfamily managers, without the need of direct oversight by family owners. Family governance requires the development of formal communication channels (such as setting up a family council and/or a family assembly) to discuss what help different family owners need to define their roles as owners, as well as to make large business-owning families speak with one voice.

Effective governance enables family owners to focus on fulfilling their responsibilities toward the family legacy, while empowering nonfamily managers to work toward the sustainability of the family firm.[41] In the end, geographically dispersed families face the challenge of developing a group of cohesive and responsible family owners among Next Gens that are neither (physically) close to the family nor to the firm. To overcome the physical distance barrier, families should invest heavily on mechanisms that strengthen family bonds, develop a sense of belonging, and clarify the role and expectations for each member of the family, while ensuring that proper family and business governance are in place for the family to be united and control the business effectively.[42]

Cristina Cruz (PhD, Carlos III) is professor of entrepreneurship and family business studies at IE Business School in Spain. She is the academic director of the IE Center for families in Business. Her research focuses on corporate governance issues in family firms and on the entrepreneurial behavior of family owners. She is an associate editor of the *Family Business Review* and recently became a fellow of the Family Firm Institute.

Commentary by Michel von Boch, Germany

Villeroy & Boch's strong roots in European culture have shaped the development of a worldwide premium brand around ceramics, from the company's foundation in 1748 to the present day. The group operates two businesses: bathroom and wellness offering ceramic sanitary ware, bathroom furniture, wellness products and fittings, and dining and lifestyle manufacturing and distributing dinnerware, crystal ware, cutlery, indoor furniture and accessories. Present in over 125 countries, the company has thirteen production sites, employs 7,100 people and generated revenues of €801 million in 2020. In 1990, Villeroy & Boch went public, issuing nonvoting preferred shares on the Frankfurt stock exchange and voting ordinary shares, which are since kept among the descendants of the founders, now in the tenth generation, pooled and managed by a family council.

Management Board, Supervisory Board, and Family Council

Villeroy & Boch operates within German law, the German Corporate Governance Codex and international regulations of Good Governance, and has implemented a dual-board system. The supervisory board controls management and provides guidance on the strategic, long-term perspectives and nominates the management board in charge of day-to-day operations and running the business. The family council, whose chairman I am, aggregates the common interests of the family shareholders vis-à-vis third parties and functions as a primary point of contact for the company. It further supports the transmission of ownership of the company across the generations.

Keeping Control

Ever since going public with the company, the family has been integrating nonfamily members at executive and non-executive positions and has carefully managed the balance of professional skillsets in the sole interest of a successful business. With over 300 family members spread across several countries, the family council plays a central role in bringing the shared interests together bottom-up and disseminating relevant information top-down via various formal and informal channels. The information flow plays a critical role in keeping a diverse set of profiles united around the pursuit of a 273-year-old legacy. Our operating model is defined by only a handful of written rules and upholds a long-standing oral tradition of dialogue, diplomacy, and negotiation with a critical, single focus on the pax familia. While sometimes complex and time consuming, this approach has proven its power.

At the same time, the dual shareholding structure and ownership of the voting rights provides the family with an efficient control mechanism via the general assembly, allowing for its voice to be heard on the appraisal of the yearly dividend, designation and discharge of the supervisory board, including three family members and three independent directors, discharge of the management board and participation in major decisions requiring a formal approval.

Practically Spoken

Keeping effective control based on the rules and processes outlined before for us works through communication, communication, communication. Prior to the COVID-19 crisis, we met regularly for our official family-council meetings. This was accompanied by frequent phone calls to plan the meetings. Additionally, we often meet informally at our home base in the Saarland where the company was founded and where the headquarters is located. Thus, for we siblings and cousins, coming together for dinner, enjoying each other's company and chatting is the basis of our trust, supports our values, and makes it easier to work together effectively. Now, in times of the coronavirus, we meet frequently in video conferences and additional phone calls, but we all hope to come back to face-to-face meetings soon. This rather unique combination of a robust governance, external talent, strategic family experience, and formal and informal communication has demonstrated its resilience throughout the challenges of time in the greatest interest of all shareholders and leaves us as a family confident about our future.

Questions for Further Reflection ———————————

- How do you define being an effective owner?
- How can you and your fellow Next Gens as (future) owners prepare to become effective at overseeing the managers of the family enterprise?
- What tools can you and your fellow Next Gens use to become a cohesive and effective group of owners?
- What tools can you as Next Gens use to monitor the managers of the family enterprise?

Your Notes | Your Action Items ———————————

2.8
It Is Difficult to Imagine That We Can Become Responsible Business Owners One Day. What Type of Development Path Can We Pursue to Learn More about Becoming Responsible Owners?

Response by Rosa Nelly Trevinyo-Rodríguez, México, and Miguel Ángel Gallo, Spain

Developing the talents of Next Gens as potential, responsible owners is a high priority for 67 percent of global families in business and their family offices. But the success of such ownership education programs and internships is mixed.[43] Why is it that some Next Gens manage to become responsible owners and others do not?

Becoming a responsible owner takes time, effort, and commitment. It's a continuous, never-ending process influenced by our knowledge and business competence, as well as by our motivations, emotions, and experiences. Viewed in this way, what type of actions shall Next Gens embrace in order to build up and nurture a solid, responsible business owner track?

1. Committing to the Owners' Role: Exploring Ownership Matters

Becoming a (future) good family business owner implies voluntarily embracing the (future) ownership role and committing to it. Yet, in order to do so, Next Gens are expected to have enough information, education, and professional skills. Understanding owners' rights and responsibilities as well as learning about corporate law, governance structures, estate planning, fiduciary arrangements, talent management, employee relations, business financial statements, and tax matters are all fundamentals in order to join the starting line of the family business "responsible business owner track."

Next Gens must also pursue a specific training related to their *own* family company. Attending company visits, taking part in meetings with top management teams, and having briefings with high-profile managers, executives, and board members will help in this process. Gaining knowledge of their family business history, values, and vision will help Next Gens realize their heritage. In addition, grasping the family firm's strategy, market potential, business units and operational processes, products and services, and budgetary elements will allow Next Gens to better understand the here and now of their business.

2. Communicating Well: Active Listening and Empathy

Making conscious, individual efforts to get to know, care about and enjoy all family members is essential if a long-term personal and professional relationship is to be sought. Trust-building for Next Gens begins with developing the habit of calling or texting each family member every month—just to stay tuned. Yet, communicating well takes practice, effort, active listening, and empathy.

Case in point: Mathias wants to talk to his older brother—the CEO of the family business—about starting his own new enterprise. He needs a sounding board rather than more time to think alone. Both agree to meet for coffee that evening. After greeting each other, Mathias starts sharing his ideas for about two minutes. His older brother interrupts him and brings up certain business problems he is facing. Then, his phone rings. After the fifteen-minute call, the CEO brother says, "Bro, just look at the size of our family firm. We are a global business. Considering setting up such a tiny enterprise is nonsense, and anyway, we are not investing in it, so don't even bother. Let's focus on the actual business problems we have to solve, okay?" He stands up, gives his brother a pat on the shoulder and leaves.

Communicating well requires stopping whatever we are doing to pay attention, listen, and value what the other person has to say—while not assuming what the other wants—and interpreting the emotions behind the words. Feeling heard and understood builds up trust and caring among family members. Patronizing and ignoring a family member's ideas and feelings shuts down the communication process and drives division and indifference.

3. Nurturing Legitimacy: Learning to Carry Out an Insightful Use of (Future) Power

Legal ownership and its voting rights are the most straightforward types of authority owners can exert. Legitimacy is, on the other hand, an intangible asset tied to knowledge, prestige, and good reputation deriving from moral authority that provides the basis for cementing alliances, inspiring people, and influencing decision-making. While legal power is granted, legitimacy—both in the family and in the business—is gained, nurtured, and constantly upgraded. Next Gens must strive to attain legitimacy early in their life (even before having or exercising legal ownership), and committing themselves to advance it by practicing compassionate attitudes, such as:

- **Humbleness.** Avoiding the "I know it all/I deserve it all" attitude. Valuing others and being open to learn and seek feedback from predecessors, employees, advisors, and other family members.[44]

As an illustration: When Susan was appointed to the board of directors of her family company, she recognized that even when she had an MBA and seven years of working experience, she was not fully prepared to serve as a board member. Thus, she asked for help. The board assigned her an external mentor who accompanied her as full-fledged member of the board of directors for one-and-a-half years. "It was the most valuable experience I could have had. It allowed me to practice and learn—that is, to make errors without messing up with the firm—and to become a valuable board member."

- **Coherence.** By respectfully noticing inappropriate or disrespectful behaviors among family or nonfamily members, and taking action on them, Next Gens live and reinforce their values, gaining credibility and good reputation.
- **Family Diplomacy.** Next Gens must consider the welfare of all stakeholders and become skilled at the practice of consensus building, committing themselves to cultivate, build and rebuild the family business owners' relationships. Fostering family-wide activities (i.e., family assemblies) to promote inclusion and transparency helps to integrate family members (owners) and to align their collective interests.
- **Gratitude.** Being conscious and thankful of all the positive things one has received from the family and business, valuing the efforts (sacrifices) made by predecessors and realizing that ownership rights are not granted, is fundamental for Next Gens to build up their moral authority. Moreover, since stewardship and gratitude go hand in hand, this practice also entails nurturing the family's legacy and preparing, in due course, a potential successor.

To Wrap Things Up

Committing to forge a responsible owner career is a never-ending process that involves family and business acumen, personal interest, passion for doing well by doing good, communication and consensus building skills, the practice of humbleness, coherence, family diplomacy, and gratitude as well as tons of prudence and moderation. A responsible Next Gen owner turns out to be an engine and a vehicle of family cohesion. Their commitment to behave in a professional and judicious way—family- and business-wise—compels other family members (owners) to stick together, and in this way, secures the future of the family's shared business dream.

Rosa Nelly Trevinyo-Rodríguez, PhD, has been contributing to the family business practice, knowledge creation and dissemination over the last twenty years. She is CEO of Trevinyo-Rodríguez & Associates—an organization that advises business families—founder of the Tec de Monterrey Family Business Center and Author of the bestseller *Family Business: A Latin-American Perspective*. Dr. Trevinyo-Rodríguez serves as a board member in leading family-owned companies, advises single-family offices, has delivered more than 150 executive courses and C-Suite international conferences, and became the first Latino president of the Academy of Management International Theme Committee and chair of the Management Consulting Division.

Miguel Ángel Gallo, PhD, is emeritus professor of general management at IESE Business School (Spain), where he served as full professor (1975–2003) and IESE PhD Program Director (1980–1990). He was founding director of the first Family Business Chair in Europe—acting as its chairman from its inception in 1987 until September 2003. His areas of specialization include strategic management, boards of directors and family business. Prof. Gallo is fellow of the Royal European Academy of Doctors, Strategic Management Society and serves as honorary president of the International Family Enterprise Research Academy (IFERA). He has participated on the boards of prominent firms Grupo VELATIA, Fuertegroup, and Grupo Senda.

Commentary by Mauritz, Michael, Johanna, Sebastian, and Wilhelm Aminoff, and Robert Schulman, Finland

The so-called "Cousin Companies" are a group of enterprises currently in transition to the fifth generation of family ownership. They are involved in four types of businesses: technical trade, technology, real estate, and asset management. Among other things, they provide machine tools and factory automation, human-centric lighting solutions, and quality vehicles for personal and professional use. As the Next Gen owners, our main role is to prepare ourselves as much as possible to take part in ensuring the continued success of both the family and the businesses. This entails a balance of business and accounting education, developing good practices and fair processes, building family and management connections, as well as creating working structures for collaboration within and between generations. Furthermore, as Next Gens, it is also important that we discuss our values, and while we should remain humble, we must also, at times, dare to assert ourselves.

The question of this chapter really lies at the heart of what we are doing as Next Gens. We are pursuing a structured development plan with the explicit goal of becoming "responsible owners." At the onset of this project, our generation sat down with a facilitator and thought about what we value in a board member, a leader, a family member, and an individual. Five core categories resulted from these discussions: personal independence, competent and reflective board member, trusted representative of the family, effective Next Gen group, and experienced professional. Together these categories form our so-called Next Gen Scorecard—a compass for the personal and professional development of Next Gens. The idea is that by co-creating a multi-year plan and pursuing items in each category of the Next Gen Scorecard, Next Gens are able to track and structure their personal and professional development.

Trevinyo-Rodríguez and Gallo's answer mentions all of the Next Gen Scorecard's elements, but also highlights the issue of personal commitment. Ultimately, to become responsible owners, an enormous amount of work is required in the long term. Before embarking on this journey, it is important to really commit to it—to choose to be a responsible family business owner. The answer also brings up an important distinction between authority and voting rights. Authority comes from a place of knowledge and trustworthiness and is given implicitly through interpersonal relations, whereas voting rights is a matter of circumstance. Decisions made through discussion, convincing arguments, and trust receive far more buy-in than those that must come down to a vote. Nurturing familial ties and interpersonal relationships and continuously honing the skills required to responsibly own the businesses is a sure way to become involved and trusted—but stay humble and modest!

Questions for Further Reflection

- What is the typical path to Next Gen ownership in your family?
- What is your family's accepted process for ownership transition?
- How can you, as Next Gens, develop humbleness, passion, prudence, and commitment among other traits?
- When do you, as Next Gens, start to develop such values? How can the family support Next Gens in this context?
- When does the family undermine the development of Next Gens in this context?

Your Notes | *Your Action Items* ———————————————

2.9
Which Networks Are There to Exchange with and Learn from Other Business Families?

Response by Marta Widz, Switzerland

Peer-to-Peer Exchange and Learning

Next Gens have long recognized the benefits of interacting and exchanging with peers, and the desire to learn and grow together. The coronavirus crisis only reconfirmed the importance of peer-to-peer networks as a safe harbor for family business owners to connect and to go through a phase of extreme uncertainties with the feeling of solidarity. Jacek Ptaszek, the Next Gen and executive team member of JMP Flowers, the largest producer of flowers in Poland, and board member of the Family Business Network (FBN) in Poland,[45] reflects on how the FBN Poland supported its family business members in 2020:

> We extended our virtual platform that we previously used for board meetings only, and offered virtual support groups to everyone in the network. We met up to six times a week to discuss how to combat the day-to-day challenges of the crisis. The attendance rate was at 80 percent! Then, we introduced 'sharing your history' evenings, during which family business owners presented their entrepreneurial journey. How emotional and educational these evenings were! Next Gens learned about the legacy of other family businesses and took a deep dive into the stories of their own families,

reconnected with their own heritage, built their collective family identity, and developed the family purpose.

Leading economists, politicians, psychologists, film directors, and actors were invited to the virtual cafés, to the joy of Next Gens. Needless to say, FBN Poland expanded the network. Many new family businesses heard about their activities, joined a virtual session on a test-and-trial basis and stayed.

Family Business Peer-to-Peer Platforms

Peer-to-peer networks are one of the most fulfilling and fun ways for the Next Gens' lifelong learning journey. Next to the multiple national and local family business associations,[46] there are a few global networks that include:

Family Business Network (FBN):[47] Driven by the motto "by families, for families, together across generations," FBN unites over 4,000 family businesses, and is the largest global peer network for family businesses. Its flagship conference, FBN Global Summit, attracts a few hundred participants year by year. FBN is a matrix organization in which members can connect within local chapters, and within interest groups, called communities. The latter include the Next Gen[48] community of 6,400 Next Gens; Polaris,[49] which drives responsible capitalism, and entered the partnership with the United Nations to launch the Family Business for Sustainable Development (FBSD) initiative,[50] Entrepreneurs community,[51] Now Generations,[52] Large Families,[53] and Family Office[54] communities. Examples of FBN community-specific gatherings include the NxG Entrepreneurship Day, NxG Summit, and Polaris Circle, as well as a range of gatherings organized by the thirty-two national FBN member associations. Two other peer-to-peer networks are the World Economic Forum (WEF) Family Business Community[55] and the Hénokiens.[56]

World Economic Forum (WEF): It unites family businesses and offers educational modules as well as has a Next Generation community, Family Business community retreats, Next Generation meetings, Impact Summits, and regional meetings.

The Hénokiens: It is the international association of forty-nine bicentenary family companies and offers The Next Gen Association.

Blended networks unify family business owners with other family business experts, such as advisors and academics. Family Firm Institute (FFI)[57] is an exemplary global network of "thought leaders in the family enterprise field" to "educate, connect, inspire." FFI offers cross-field networking at the FFI Global Annual Conference, within local and thematical FFI chapters. FFI publishes the *Family Business Review* (FBR)[58] and the *FFI Practitioner*,[59] recognizes academics and practitioners that drive the field of family business forward with a series of awards,[60] and provides education via the FFI Global Education Network (GEN).

Examples of national blended networks include the Family Business Australia (FBA),[61] or the valuable partnership in Canada between the Family Enterprise Foundation (FEF),[62] the Canadian business families and the Family Enterprise Advisors (FEA)[63] underneath the umbrella of Family Enterprise Canada.[64]

Exclusive for the Next Gens or Theme-Specific Platforms

In a quest for responsible wealth management, social purpose, sustainability, and entrepreneurialism, Next Gens could embark on other peer networks:[65]

- The ImPact: https://www.theimpact.org/
- Toniic: https://toniic.com/
- Nexus: https://nexusglobal.org/
- CREO Syndicate (CREO): https://creosyndicate.org/
- Ashoka: https://www.ashoka.org/en-ch

- YPO (Young Presidents' Organization): https://www.ypo.org/

In Search of Peers

Identifying a suitable network may, however, not be a straightforward journey. Benjamin Firmenich, fourth-generation owner of Firmenich, the world's largest privately held producer of fragrances and flavorings, founded in 1895, looks back:

> I was born into a business family. Our DNA is to think in an entrepreneurial and creative way, act in an ethical and sustainable way, and to transmit the wealth to the next generation. I was looking for other Next Gens like me, and I came across Nexus, a network uniting Next Gen philanthropists, impact investors, and social entrepreneurs, headquartered in the U.S. Inspired by Next Gens opening up on the topics of wealth and family business, experiencing how they let themselves be vulnerable, I brought Nexus to Switzerland and co-initiated the Geneva Nexus Salon, a local meetup of the Nexus Global Youth Initiative.

For Benjamin it was clear: Unlike his brother, who worked in the family business in a series of roles, Benjamin wanted to "give a human face to investments and contribute to the well-being of our planet and global society" outside of the family business. Benjamin teamed up with Cedric Lombard, Next Gen of Lombard Odier, a Swiss private bank founded in 1796. Reaching out to their own personal wealth and the families' seed funds, Benjamin and Cedric founded Impact Finance.[66] Benjamin explains:

> Nexus Switzerland opened the door to the World Economic Forum Family Business Community, where I met the executive director of The ImPact, an organization my family joined. This is also where I first heard about the Harvard program on impact investing for Next Gens, which I later

supported to transmit to Switzerland at the Center for Sustainable Finance and Private Wealth at the University of Zurich. Thanks to Nexus, I met exceptional people and some of them have or still play an essential role supporting me with my mission.

Benjamin's story is a journey of self-discovery; a journey of developing a purpose and externalizing the Firmenich family values in an alternative way to traditional succession.

The Future Is Bright

There are multiple platforms for Next Gens to indulge in, to bond over shared experiences, to learn, and to support one another to endure the coronavirus crisis and beyond.[67] Wishing you a great exchange and learning journey, together with your peers!

Dr. Marta Widz embraces the worlds of research, education, and advisory in the family business field. She obtained her PhD from the Center for Family Business at the University of St. Gallen, Switzerland, and is a research fellow at IMD Business School, Lausanne, responsible for the family business awards. She is the member of IFERA, AOM, and FFI, and served as a co-chair of the 2020 FFI conference program committee. Marta presents frequently for family business audiences (FBN, the Hénokiens). She is an alumna of the London School of Economics (LSE), Global Alliance for Management Education (CEMS), and the Warsaw School of Economics (SGH).

Commentary by Izabella Wałkowska, Poland

Plastwil, our family company, is in the global business of rail sleeper and rail fastening system manufacturing. We also produce other components for the railway infrastructure, and metal and plastic components for the automotive industry. I took over the company after my mum. I am the second-generation owner. Based on my values, I develop the company with a focus on our employees, the environment, and our local community. As the CEO, I expand the business, together with my team, into new markets.

Lesson Learned

Marta Widz covers various peer-to-peer networks in her chapter. I highly recommend you read about these networks and find out which ones might be most interesting to you. If you find a good fit, join the network(s)! I did it and it was one of the best decisions I have ever made. I chose to join FBN ten years ago and have been a member since, earlier on as a Next Gen and right now as a Now Generation member. I hope to encourage you to find the right organisation(s) for you by telling you about my experiences with FBN.

FBN is an organization where membership is only granted to owners and family members from the biggest family businesses around the world. I have had the chance to directly learn and draw inspirations from them over the past few years. I could visit many family-owned businesses and learn from stories told by founders themselves or the Next Gens who came after them. These stories helped me to understand both the parents' path and the path ahead of me.

FBN and other organisations are places where you can meet new people, join unforgettable parties and trips, but, above all, take part in professional workshops and lectures about various topics, such as family relations, succession, environmental protection, asset management, charity, and corporate social responsibility among others. This is an enormous opportunity to combine fun and learning, where everyone can find something for themselves. Workshops continue in smaller subject groups online throughout the year, exchanging experiences of people from different companies, industries, and countries.

We discover synergies underlying the family and the company at various levels, as well as opportunities and challenges coming out of this synergy. Next Gen meetings are organized all around the world at local offices and international meetups. A Next Gen can only be a person under forty years of age. Subjects of meetings are always adjusted to younger people, who might still be searching for their path or already know what role they would like to play in their family business, but at the same time may still have certain various reservations they find difficult to talk about. One thing that I discovered only after a while was that those meetings are not only going to be an opportunity for you to make new friends from all around the world and exchange knowledge, but to find something deeper. It is important to have some familiarity with the exchange of experiences involved in being part of a company or building the company for years to come, and how such involvement is intertwined with family.

Both family and business are tied together in ways that are difficult to separate. If a family is most important, but the company is most important, too, we touch upon some very delicate issues that make it hard to be open. It is not easy to discuss challenges, problems, and issues related to people close to us, as much as it is not easy to talk about emotions. Sometimes we are left alone to deal with things like that.

We managed to build something unique at FBN, which is a platform of trust. This is the key to having an open discussion about family and business. Next Gens can talk only within their own group if they like, or ask seniors from other companies and countries, as well as advisors about their recommendations. We managed to build strong relationships and friendships, which have lasted for years. Thanks to that, we support one another and develop not only during our meetings, but outside of them, too. I think our experience is similar to the one of other families.

I have discovered that no matter where you are in the world, we all face challenges, opportunities, and chances ahead. Let us meet in peer-to-peer networks to mutually give and receive something unique. See you there!

Questions for Further Reflection

- What network activities have members of your family been previously involved in?
- How many family enterprise role models do you have outside of your own family?
- Where do you learn about best practices and improve your knowledge?
- Where do you engage in dialogue with peers and topic experts?
- Please develop an annual calendar of network activities that you and fellow Next Gens could pursue to broaden your knowledge, experience, and personal networks.

Your Notes | Your Action Items

Your Notes | *Your Action Items* ————————————

Endnotes: Part 2

1. Peter Jaskiewicz, Alfredo de Massis and Marleen Dieleman, "The Future of the Family Business: 4 Strategies for a Successful Transition," *The Conversation,* April 15, 2021. https://theconversation.com/the-future-of-the-family-business-4-strategies-for-a-successful-transition-156191.

2.1 Do I Want to Assume Active Ownership Responsibilities for Our Family Business?

2. Craig E. Aronoff and John L. Ward, *Family Business Ownership: How to Be an Effective Shareholder* (New York: Palgrave Macmillan, 2011).

3. *Succession*, directed by Jesse Armstrong (2018; New York, NY: Home Box Office (HBO)), TV-MA.

4. Torsten Pieper and Joseph Astrachan, "Developing Responsible Owners in Family Business," *familybusiness.org*, December 3, 2020. https://familybusiness.org/content/developing-responsible-owners-in-family-businesses.

5. John Baron and Rob Lachenauer, "The 5 Models of Family Business Ownership," *Harvard Business Review*, September 20, 2016. https://hbr.org/2016/09/the-5-models-of-family-business-ownership.

6. "How to Build your Ownership Strategy?" *Family Enterprises Foundation,* accessed February, 2021. https://familyenterprisefoundation.org/videohome/professionalizing-ownership/how-to-build-your-ownership-strategy/.

7. Note: The authors are grateful to Helmut Senfter, Deputy Chairman of Senfter Holding AG, and Dario Voltattorni, the Director of the Italian Association of Family Businesses (AIDAF), for providing feedback that was useful to fine-tune and support the knowledge conveyed in this chapter.

2.2 If I Want to Assume the Ownership Responsibilities. With Whom Should I Discuss It, and When Is the Best Time to Start?

8. Alex Pigliucci, Kendra Thompson, Mark Halverson, *The "Greater" Wealth Transfer: Capitalizing on the Intergenerational Shift in Wealth* (Accenture, 2015), 1–8.

9. Ivan Lansberg, *Succeeding Generations: Realizing the Dream of Families in Business* (Boston: Harvard Business School Press, 1999).

10. Wendy Sage-Hayward, Gaia Marchisio and Barbara Dartt, *Own It!: How to Develop a Family Enterprise Owner's Mindset at Every Age* (New York: Palgrave Macmillan, in press).

11. Amelia Renkert-Thomas, *Engaged Ownership: A Guide for Owners of Family Businesses* (Hoboken: Wiley, 2015).

12. Patricia M. Angus, *The Trustee Primer: A Guide for Personal Trustees* (New York: Advisory Group LLC, 2015), 1–72.

13. Craig E. Aronoff and John L. Ward, *Family Business Ownership: How to Be an Effective Shareholder* (New York: Palgrave Macmillan, 2011).

14. Kelin E. Davis, John A. Davis, Marion McCollom Hampton and Ivan Lansberg, *Generation to Generation: Life Cycles of the Family Business* (Boston: Harvard Business School Press, 1997), 1–320.

15. Erik H. Erikson and Joan M. Erikson, *The Life Cycle Completed (Extended Version)* (New York: W.W. Norton & Company, 1998), 1–140.

2.3 How Can I Prepare Myself to Be Able to Work Effectively with My Fellow Family Owners?

16. "Agents of Change: Earning Your Licence to Operate," *PwC's Global NextGen Survey* (Germany: PwC, 2019), 1–26.

17. *Spider-Man*, directed by Sam Raimi (2002; Culver City, CA: Columbia TriStar Home Entertainment), DVD.

18. Mira Bloemen-Bekx, "Enriching the Early Phases of the Succession Process: An Explanation of the Role of Social Mechanisms in Business Families" (PhD diss., Hasselt University, 2019). Authors' note: Mira Bloemen-Bekx speaks of ambition, abilities, and acceptance.

19. *Oxford English Dictionary*, 3rd ed. (2001), s.v. "ambition."

20. Charles Bronfam and Howard Green, *Distilled: A Memoir of Family, Seagram, Baseball, and Philanthropy (New York: HarperCollins, 2017).*

21. Ludo Van der Heyden, Christine Blondel and Randel S. Carlock, "Fair Process: Striving for Justice in Family Business," *Family Business Review* 18, no. 1 (March 2005):1–21.

2.4 If I Become a Non-Active Owner, What Are My Rights and My Duties?

22. Thomas Zellweger, Phillip Sieger and Peter Englisch, "Coming Home or Breaking Free? Career Choice Intentions of the Next Generation in Family Businesses," *Family Business Center of Excellence* (St Gallen: Ernst & Young, 2012).

23. Torsten M. Pieper and Joseph H. Astrachan, *Mechanisms to Assure Family Business Cohesion: Guidelines for Family Business Leaders and Their Families* (Kennesaw: Cox Family Enterprise Center, 2008), 1–42.

24. Sharon A. Alvarez, Udo Zander, Jay B. Barney and Allan Afuah, "Developing a Theory of the Firm for the 21st Century," *The Academy of Management Review* 45, no. 4 (October 2020): 711–716.

25. Author's note: Some legal rights and obligations of ownership might vary according to the legal jurisdiction, the articles and by-laws, the type of shares, and the shareholders' agreement.

26. Peter May and Matthias Redlefsen, "Ten Rules for Non-Active Shareholders," *Campden FB*, July 1, 2005. https://www.campdenfb.com/article/ten-rules-non-active-shareholders.

27. Rania Labaki, "Financial Behaviour of Families in Businesses," in *Managing Ownership and Succession in Family Firms*, eds. Aleksander Surdej and Krzysztof Wach (Warsaw: Scholar Publishing House, 2010), 40–55.

28. Rania Labaki and Gerard Hirigoyen, "The Strategic Divestment Decision in the Family Business Through the Real Options and Emotional Lenses," in *Challenges and Opportunities for the Strategic Management of Family Businesses*, eds. Jesus Manuel Palma-Ruiz, Ismael Barros-Contreras and Luca Gnan (Hershey: IGI Global, 2020), 244–279.

2.5 What Mechanisms Can I Use to Monitor Whether Our Business Model Will Still Be Viable in the Future?

29. Alexander Osterwalder and Yves Pigneur, *Business Model Generation: A Handbook for Visionaries, Game Changers, and Challengers* (New York: John Wiley & Sons, 2010).

30. Marc Gruber and Sharon Tal, *Where to Play. Three Steps for Discovering Your Most Valuable Market Opportunities* (London: Pearson Education Limited, 2017).

31. Larry Keeley, Helen Walters, Ryan Pikkel and Brian Quinn, *Ten Types of Innovation: The Discipline of Building Breakthroughs* (New York: John Wiley & Sons, 2013).
32. Marc Gruber and Sharon Tal, "Attractiveness Map," in *Where to Play. Three Steps for Discovering Your Most Valuable Market Opportunities* (London: Pearson Education Limited, 2017).

2.6 How Can I Gain Credibility with Nonfamily Executives and Board Members?

33. Christoph Achenbach, Jan Eiben, Peter May and Gerold Rieder, *Beiräte in Familienunternehmen* (Vallendar: WHU – Otto Beisheim School of Management, 2009).
34. Jonas Soluk and Nadine Kammerlander, "Digital Transformation in Family-Owned Mittelstand Firms: A Dynamic Capabilities Perspective," *European Journal of Information Systems* (in press, 2021): 1–36.
35. Claudia Binz Astrachan, Mattias Waldkrich, Anneleen Michiels, Torsten Pieper, Fabian Bernhard, "Professionalizing the Business Family: The Five Pillars of Competent, Committed, and Sustainable Ownership," *FFI- Family Firm Institute,* January 2020. https://www.researchgate.net/publication/341219385_Professionalizing_the_Business_Family_The_Five_Pillars_of_Competent_Committed_and_Sustainable_Ownership.
    Ethel Brundin, Emilia Florin Samuelsson and Leif Melin, "Family Ownership Logic: Framing the Core Characteristics of Family Businesses," *Journal of Management & Organization* 20, no. 1 (January 2014): 6–37.
36. Stephanie Querbach, Miriam Bird, Priscilla S. Kraft and Nadine Kammerlander, "When the Former CEO Stays on Board: The Role of the Predecessor's Board Retention for Product Innovation in Family Firms," *The Journal of Product Innovation Management* 37, no. 2 (March 2020): 184–207.
37. Nadine Kammerlander and Larissa Leitner," When Entrepreneurs Raise Entrepreneurs," *familybusiness.org,* September 17, 2018. https://familybusiness.org/content/When-entrepreneurs-raise-entrepreneurs.
38. Colette Dumas, "Understanding of Father-Daughter and Father-Son Dyads in Family-Owned Businesses," *Family Business Review* 2, no. 1 (1989): 31–46.

2.7 We Sibling/Cousin Owners Are Living All Over the World. How Can We Keep Effective Control of the Nonfamily Managers Running the Family Business?

39. "The Leading Platform for Family & Shareholder Governance," *Trusted Family*, 2020, https://trustedfamily.com/company/.
40. Cristina Cruz and Laura Jimenez, "Solutions for Entrepreneur Families: How to Transfer Wealth While Keeping Ambition Alive," *White Paper* (Zurich: Credit Suisse AG – IE, 2016), 1–72.
41. Sam Bruehl and Rob Lachenauer, "How Family Business Owners Should Bring the Next Generation into the Company," *Harvard Business Review*, July 24, 2018. https://hbr.org/2018/07/how-family-business-owners-should-bring-the-next-generation-into-the-company.
42. Claudia Binz Astrachan, Matthias Waldkirch, Anneleen Michiels, Torsten M. Pieper and Fabian Bernhard, "Professionalizing the Business Family: The Five Pillars of Competent, Committed and Sustainable Ownership," *A Research Report sponsored by the Family Firm Institute & 2086 Society,*

January 8, 2020, https://digital.ffi.org/pdf/wednesdayedition/2020/january08/ ffi_professionalizing_the_business_family_v2.pdf.

2.8 It Is Difficult to Imagine That We Can Become Responsible Business Owners One Day. What Type of Development Path Can We Pursue to Learn More about Becoming Responsible Owners?

43. Richard Hockley, Isadora Pereira and Gabriele Schmidt, *UBS Global Family Office Report* (London: UBS AG, 2020). https://www.ubs.com/global/en/wealth-management/uhnw/global-family-office-report/global-family-office-report-2020.html

44. Rosa Nelly Trevinyo-Rodríguez and Josep Tàpies, "Effective Knowledge Transfer in Family Firms," in *Handbook of Research on Family Business,* eds. Panikkos Poutziouris, Kosmas Smyrnios and Sabine B. Klein (Cheltenham: Elgar Publishing, 2006), 343–357.

2.9 Which Networks Are There to Exchange with and Learn from Other Business Families?

45. "The Family Business Network Poland: Association of Family Businesses," *The Family Business Network Poland* (website), 2020, https://fbnpoland.org/.

46. "FBA-Family Business Association Home Page," *Family Business Association* (website), 2020, https://familybusinessassociation.ch/index.php.

47. "Family Business Network Homepage," *Family Business Network International* (website), 2019, https://www.fbn-i.org/.

48. "Next Generation," *Family Business Network International* (website), 2019, https://www.fbn-i.org/communities/next-generation.

49. "Polaris," *Family Business Network International* (website), 2019, https://www.fbn-i.org/sustainability/polaris-our-raison-detre.

50. "Family Business for Sustainable Development Homepage," *Family Business for Sustainable Development* (website), 2019, https://fbsd.unctad.org/.

51. "Entrepreneurs," *Family Business Network International* (website), 2019, https://www.fbn-i.org/communities/entrepreneurs.

52. "Now Generation," *Family Business Network International* (website), 2019, https://www.fbn-i.org/communities/now-generation.

53. "Large Families," *Family Business Network International* (website), 2019, https://www.fbn-i.org/communities/large-families-0.

54. "Family Office," *Family Business Network International* (website), 2019, https://www.fbn-i.org/communities/family-office-0.

55. "Family Business Community," *The World Economic Forum* (website), 2021, https://www.weforum.org/communities/family-business-community.

56. "The Henokiens Homepage," *the Henokiens International Association of Bicentenary Family Companies* (website), 2017, www.henokiens.com.

57. "Family Firm Institute Homepage," *Family Firm Institute* (website), 2021, https://www.ffi.org/.

58. "Family Business Review (FBR)," *SAGE Journals* (website), 2021, https://journals.sagepub.com/home/fbr.

59. "Family Firm Institute Practitioner Homepage," *Family Firm Institute Practitioner* (website), 2021, https://ffipractitioner.org/

60. "Awards," *Family Firm Institute* (website), 2021, https://www.ffi.org/awards/.

61. "Family Business Australia Homepage," *Family Business Australia* (website), 2021, https://www.familybusiness.org.au/.

62. "Family Enterprise Foundation (FEF)," *Family Enterprise Foundation* (website), 2021, https://familyenterprisefoundation.org/about/foundation/about-us/.

63. "Family Enterprise Advisors (FEA)," *Family Enterprise Canada* (website), 2021, https://familyenterprise.ca/fea-designation/.

64. "Family Enterprise Canada," *Family Enterprise Canada* (website), 2021, https://familyenterprise.ca.

65. "The Impact Homepage," *The Impact* (website), 2015, https://www.theimpact.org/. "Toniic Homepage," *Toniic Institute* (website), 2019, https://toniic.com/. "Nexus Homepage," *Nexus Global* (website), 2018, https://nexusglobal.org/.

"CREO Syndicate Homepage," *Clean, Renewable and Environmental Opportunities (CREO) Syndicate* (website), 2020, https://creosyndicate.org/.

"Ashoka Homepage," *Ashoka Switzerland* (website), 2021, https://www.ashoka.org/en-ch.

"YPO Homepage," *Young Presidents' Organization* (website), 2021, https://www.ypo.org/.

66. "Impact Finance Homepage," *Impact Finance* (Website), 2020, https://www.impact-finance.com/.

67. Kurstyn Loeffler and Jennell L.S. Wittmer, "The Value of Family Business Peer Groups during a Global Crisis," *FFI Practitioner,* November 4, 2020. https://digital.ffi.org/editions/the-value-of-family-business-peer-groups-during-a-global-crisis/.

PART 3: BUSINESS

Overview by Sabine B. Rau and Peter Jaskiewicz

Joining the family business is a major challenge for any Next Gen. Whether they contribute at a lower level of the hierarchy throughout their working lives, work their way up into middle management, or even make it into the highest leadership position—that of the CEO—working in the family business is not easy. The norms underlying the business circle are merit and performance. If a Next Gen assumes a role in the business, the evaluation of their behavior in this role will be based on their merit and performance. The more Next Gens advance, the more they are scrutinized.

Assuming leadership responsibilities in the family business is a particular challenge for Next Gens if they are the second generation. Founders not only lack the experience of being a successor, but the business is also their "baby," leading them to interfere with Next Gens' leadership even after retirement. Defining clear boundaries of their respective roles is a precondition for successful Next Gens—whether they are regular employees or future business leaders. Therefore, to be successful, Next Gens must be as qualified as any suitable nonfamily candidate for the same position. Education, experience, and prior promotions to a similar position outside of the family business are strong indicators of Next Gens' potential.[1] Although usually part of a team, the Next Gen is relatively more powerful than others because of their link to the owning family. This power comes with the expectation that the Next Gen will be the first at work, work the hardest, and be the one to turn off the lights at night. Such behavior helps legitimize Next Gens and, over time, enables them to guide and motivate team members and subordinates to work together toward a joint goal. Communication skills are therefore also essential. Finding the right balance between distance and closeness is especially important when the incoming employee is a family member who is often younger than their non-family peers and subordinates, though the "right" balance between closeness and distance with employees differs across cultural contexts. In summary, being meritorious and performing above expectations paired with strong communication skills and empathy are a good starting point to succeed in the business circle.

Having discussed and worked with many families in business, especially with Next Gens, we frequently observed the following topics as Next Gens join and work in the family business:

Taking mistakes as learning opportunities. Being a hard-working Next Gen does not mean being perfect. Whatever we do, we make mistakes. By assuming responsibility for their own mistakes, a Next Gen becomes a role model. Other members of the team as well as employees will, to a certain extent, copy their behavior. Instead of denying or covering up mistakes, these mistakes can serve as learning opportunities for the entire team. Putting mistakes on the table, analyzing them thoroughly, and taking steps to avoid them in the future helps build a learning culture that allows room for trial and error and thus sets the stage for innovation. However, we also understand that this is easier said than done in cultures in which family members have to save face at all cost.

Feeling obliged to join and eventually assume leadership. In many families, although not openly discussed, there is an underlying hope among parents that at least one of their children will join the family business and move up the ranks to business leadership. Depending on the societal and cultural context, this wish is often stronger for sons than for daughters who have greater freedom to decide whether to join (and advance in) the family business. As a Next Gen, one should only join and work toward a leadership position if the motivation stems from passion for the business, not from felt obligation toward parents. The latter often leads to mediocre results and ultimately harms the business and the family.

Being afraid of the reactions from the family. The decision to appoint a Next Gen as a leader of the family business comes with a certain level of loneliness for this leader. They have more responsibilities than other family members, are under more scrutiny, and are more prominent and visible. To ensure that fellow family members accept the new family business leader, communication is essential. Proactively addressing questions and fears among family members is one important step. Staying humble and not assuming a prominent role when the family meets privately is another.

Securing the support of relevant stakeholders. A Next Gen working up her or his way into a leadership position is not only under scrutiny from fellow family members; nonfamily managers, employees, customers, suppliers, bankers, and the larger community are also watching. To lead the family business successfully one day, these stakeholders must support the future family leader. Why? Because even if the Next Gen has an excellent education and credentials from their previous career, they need resources to succeed at each rank, whether financial resources, information, or access to networks. Resources, in turn, are only offered to those who are viewed as legitimate by stakeholders. Therefore, communication is essential (again). The ascending Next Gen leader must secure the support of relevant stakeholders by addressing them early on in a way that is both modest and self-confident.

A family business needs strong Next Gens. Communication in all its different facets is essential for any aspiring Next Gen employee and leader. Clear rules in the family and the business are the foundation for good cooperation within the business and between leaders, owners, and other family members. Rules could address, among other topics, whether or not business matters are discussed over dinner at home, or who is entitled to decide when a family member can work in the business or against which criteria such decisions will be made. A qualified and experienced, yet passionate and humble Next Gen is a strong signal for a promising future of the family and its enterprise. The following chapter addresses nine questions from Next Gens concerning entering, climbing the ranks, and leaving the family business.

3.1
Why Do Many Next Generation Members Fail to Succeed with the Family Business?

Response by Sabine B. Rau, Germany

Next Gens' difficulties with the family stem from four major areas:[2] the individual, the business, the family, and unclear or inadequate roles for the Next Gens. Although 41 percent[3] of Next Gens want to play an active role as executive director in the business in the future, there are many who try but fail.

Qualification, Experience, and Motivation

> "Father, this is my resignation letter. I will study medicine and become a doctor."
>
> "Thomas, for heaven's sake, you are my successor, you do a great job, you are respected by everyone, you have an MBA from Harvard and year-long experience as a strategy consultant with BCG before you joined. It's crazy to quit now."

While it sounds awkward, Thomas is making the right decision to avoid failure in his family's business. Looking at the three elements required to avoid failure on the individual level, Thomas satisfies two of them. He is highly educated, and he did work outside the family business with obvious success shown by being promoted by his employer. But even if he could compete against nonfamily talent because of his excellent education and his experience, his motivation does not suffice. Realizing that becoming the next CEO of his family's business would satisfy his parents' dreams but not his own, he resigned. Other Next Gens who have not been as courageous as Thomas often either fail or become unhappy, in the worst cases leading to conditions like depression and addiction, among others.

No Success without Being Accepted

Isabel, a second-generation member of an international family business producing additives for pet food, is angry and depressed at the same time. A few months ago, she had to leave her job at a multinational conglomerate to take over as CEO as both of her parents were infected with COVID-19. John, the long-standing marketing director, refused to accept her order to engage a social media expert and to use LinkedIn and Instagram to communicate with their customers.

A major reason for failure is not being accepted by long-standing managers and employees or by suppliers, banks, or customers. Isabel is well-educated, experienced, and motivated, but without acceptance by important stakeholders, relevant resources will not be at hand, whether financial resources, information, knowledge, or other. Earning acceptance is crucial. Isabel has one hundred days to establish herself in the first sight. Accepting the culture, norms, and rules is the starting point; being able to change them bit by bit, however, is more challenging. Isabel's success depends on taking her time to talk to as many employees, managers, customers, and suppliers as possible, listening carefully, not promising too much, and finally building alliances. A mentor outside the family business to reflect upon the information gathered and to develop a plan for communication and for decisions to take is very helpful.

Old Roots of Actual Conflicts

"No, no, no!"

"But, Jean, we need to increase our capital to further develop this project."

"I know, Justin, and again: No! You might be the elected manager from our family, but I am still an important shareholder. My father warned me about you before he died, and he was right."

Without support of his family, Justin's failure is likely. On one hand, support is needed from the non-active family owners as well as from family members. Families are long-standing, interdependent systems in which every decision, every event rocks the family. In this case, the father of Jean was dismissed by Justin's father because of diverting business funds for private use. Events like this one leave traces which decades after the family members involved have passed away still influence their offspring's communication and their way of working together. Before joining his family's firm, Justin needs to become aware of those old family topics and talk to family members to secure support. Here, especially talking to Jean and clarifying that the conflict of their fathers is not any longer their own conflict is crucial. A family constitution (e.g., defined rules and processes how to govern the business and the family) would be helpful.

Clear and Adequate Roles

"Darling, could you get me a cup of coffee?"

"Dad, I am not your 'darling,' I am a key account manager for our automotive customers."

"Gosh, Andrea, don't be so sensitive."

Family businesses consist of four interdependent systems. Here, Andrea's father addresses his daughter within the family language although the topic and the team require business language. To avoid the confusion coming with inadequate communication, roles of all individuals involved should be clear and they need to be adequate in terms of qualification and experience. Working in the family business, Andrea and her father should stay within their role as employee and boss. Andrea is not an owner, neither is she family, nor is she wealthy when she communicates as a key account manager. It is tempting to use the power coming from being a shareholder, a daughter or a son, or from being financially independent and not needing the job when talking with colleagues but doing so is one of the reasons for the failure of Next Gens.

Summing up

When a Next Gen decides to join the business, failure is a risk that comes with this decision.

- Being at least as educated and experienced as nonfamily candidates are required to be, is a prerequisite to avoid failure.
- Next Gens must be highly motivated to take on the responsibility to shape the future of the family business.
- Being aware of how important acceptance—by the management, employees, suppliers, banks, and customers—is, helps to avoid failure.
- Old roots of conflicts need to be addressed before joining to secure support of all family members for the Next Gen member.
- Finally, clear and adequate role definitions help to avoid failure.

Sabine B. Rau is one of the most renowned experts on moderating succession processes and co-creating family protocols (also called family constitutions). She holds visiting professorships at the Telfer School of Management (University of Ottawa) and at Berlin's European School of Management and Technology (ESMT). She also teaches at the Université de Luxembourg. Before she started her academic career in 2001 as a research fellow at INSEAD, Sabine founded her own business and worked for her family's business. In 2003, Sabine took over the presidency of the International Family Enterprise Research Academy (IFERA), which she led until 2007. She now serves on several boards of family businesses as an independent director.

Commentary by Anonymous, Asia

Our family business manufactures materials for packaging commodities and industrial components of automobile companies in Asia. I am a Next Gen, whose current role is that of an external advisor. I am not fully immersed in the business's operations but hope to enter it one day. In my experience, many Next Gens fail to succeed with the family business for one or several of the following three reasons.

Senior Generation's Unwillingness to Let Go

The human psyche is designed in a way wherein spending enough time doing something not only becomes a part of you, it becomes you. Ergo, letting go of it becomes a challenge. For an owner who has spent many years at the family business's helm, it becomes a challenge to let go, which in turn makes a handover all the more challenging. An owner keeping a firm grip makes a leadership transition more difficult. It delays the next generation from having access to business information and curbs their creative freedom and motivation to enter the family business. This delay, in turn, hinders them from exercising their ideas which could help address the business's current challenges and reap opportunities. Two solutions are (1) more open communication between the two generations to discuss whether there is a shared way forward and (2) the younger generation leaving the family business behind to prove their capability and realize their ideas. While the second solution helps the Next Gens, it does not directly address the senior generation's will not to let go. I could see myself as a part of the latter. In my experience, while justified to some extent, the senior generation's will to hold on must be dealt with in due time because a transition is inevitable.

Senior Generation's Lack of Communication

The lack of intergenerational communication bears the risk of reduced interest on the Next Gens' part while redirecting the Next Gens' interest elsewhere. If the plans to pass on the business were developed, and family communication was strong—ideally before the Next Gens left home for college and work—the family would have a stronger foundation for later leadership succession. In this case, both generations could agree early on the same mission or, at least, they would have sufficient time to engage in regular dialogue. In my view, inadequate communication is a significant impediment for families to move forward. It is only as an adult that I realize how important it would have been to engage early on in regular intergenerational communication about the family business and its transition.

Senior Generation's Lack of Trust in Next Gens

The senior generation leaders' lack of trust in Next Gens is a familiar scenario that often appears independent of the actual merit and experience of many Next Gens. Their ideas are not trusted, and their approaches are scrutinized. Such skepticism might be a natural reaction and a valid justification for the senior generation, given that the different generations arguably do not share the same values. However, the trust gap has to be bridged if Next Gens want to join and stay in the family business. Next Gens have grown up differently, which should be an opportunity and not a threat to the senior generation and the family business. Suppose both generations can develop mutual trust. In that case, they can mold their thinking, and the lessons they have learned over time can provide opportunities to rejuvenate and strengthen the business. However, without some trust and some mutual learning, the ideas of Next Gens to change the business model are often rejected upfront. Open communication and continuous interaction throughout adolescence can help prevent this issue. Conversely, global education and work experiences might or might not help solve this issue because they usually physically distance the senior from the next generation.

In conclusion, I have experienced that each Next Gen has to learn their lessons, accumulate relevant experiences, and earn trust. However, all of the above is more challenging and less impactful for the family business if the senior generation leader is delaying the transition of letting go and does not realize that a dialogue is the need of the hour.

Questions for Further Reflection

- What is your motivation to succeed in the family's enterprise? Do you feel obliged or passionate about it?
- What are the qualifications and experiences that nonfamily members would need to be accepted for the same position? Are these qualifications and experiences that you already have or still lack?
- What are the old conflicts, in the family or in the enterprise, that you might inherit when you join (or do not join the enterprise)?
- When, and how, should entrenched intergenerational differences be addressed?

Your Notes | *Your Action Items* ——————————————

3.2
How Can Next Generation Members Prepare Themselves in the Long Run Before Joining the Family Business?

Response by Andrea Calabrò, France

Ready for Boarding?

Belonging to a business family is surely a privilege that often carries numerous challenges that family members must face at certain points of their life. Entering the family firm as a manager (in whatever functional area) is a key milestone to getting ready to occupy positions that are more strategic such as becoming the next family CEO.[4]

Unfortunately, the process of entering the family business is not often formalized, making it more challenging to identify overlap between what the Next Gens want to achieve (and can offer) and what the family business needs (and can offer). If the process was formalized and known to all family members, it would allow more clarity and fairness. Moreover, the degree of uncertainty around entering the family business would be lower. However, because those processes are often not formalized, and mostly managed through a case-by-case approach, becoming a manager in the family business remains more uncertain and less straightforward for Next Gens. It is important for Next Gens to develop and pursue their own action plan to prepare for the possibility of a managerial position in the family business.

How to Get Ready[5]

Next Gens' action plan should include the following parts:

1. **Strategic education**

   Education and training are the foundation for the managerial roles Next Gens' might attain in the family business one day. It is therefore important for them to avoid education and training that is too far away from their potential managerial role. Being assigned to jobs that they do not feel qualified for or that do not match their personal expectations can be a source of personal frustration and conflicts with the previous generation that if unsolved can jeopardize the well-being of the Next Gen, the family, and the family business. Next Gens interested in working as managers of the business need to make sure they satisfy general skills usually required for managerial positions before joining the family business. The use of body programs, tailor-made programs for Next Gens led by a senior professional advisor, including training on the acquisition of specific competence and personal coaching, can help guide and support Next Gens' preparation.

2. **Relevant work experiences**

   Preparing properly is surely a must to feel confident in the managerial roles Next Gens assume. However, becoming qualified to work for the family business is as important as pursuing a career that provides the Next Gens with financial independence and legitimacy. Next Gens should work in other business environments before entering the family business. These experiences could be made in other family businesses that the owning family knows in order for Next Gens to learn some of the dos and don'ts of working in one's own family business. Another recommendation for Next Gens is to work in sales as related experiences provide the Next Gens with direct feedback independent of who they are. They succeed at selling or they don't. But they gain the opportunity to interact with different people over time.

3. **External validation**

Once Next Gens have their strategic education and relevant experiences, it is important to make an external assessment that will help them to determine a) if they have acquired the skills and have the capabilities to fill a managerial position, b) if there is a good fit between who they are or want to be and what they are required to do in the new position, and c) to identify potential next steps and actions that need to be taken before they can join the business in that position.

4. **Connected integration**

Once they enter the business, Next Gens need to understand, analyze, and visualize what is needed to make a successful contribution to their managerial position. To this aim, they need to understand the position better: Who held the position in the past? Were they a family or a nonfamily member? What was their leadership style? Why did they leave the position? What does it entail to make a good job in this position? How has this position been seen previously? Knowing the history, purpose, and value system of the family business will further support Next Gens' understanding of what is expected of them while enabling them to do a good job that adds value to the overall well-being of the firm and the family.

5. **Exploring paths**

Once well acquainted in the managerial role, Next Gens should explore new approaches to doing their job better. They need to remember that it is not about getting the job, but getting the job done. Moreover, they should use the position to explore novel opportunities with other parts of the family business. Next Gens should remember that managerial positions and businesses evolve.

6. Constant communication

Next Gens entering the family business need to exchange and network with other family members—within and across generations to avoid being disconnected. Furthermore, Next Gens need to talk through job expectations and ask their nonfamily managers for regular feedback in their role as an employee. This includes never complaining about work-related treatment at family meetings or with board members. Finally, peer-to-peer networking with Next Gens from other family businesses will provide them with important lessons and experiences from peers who face similar challenges or have already navigated them.

Nurture Your Readiness

The previously mentioned actions all enable Next Gens to get ready. The awareness of being ready is a status that Next Gens will get over time; it will make their entrance in the family business smooth. Next Gens not being or feeling ready, however, is still a common situation. Often Next Gens are forced to assume managerial roles when a parent falls ill, or a designated replacement of a senior family members leaves. This scenario often comes with Next Gens feeling trapped in the family business as they lack the choice to exit (at least in the medium term) and lack the ability to make a difference. A family business CEO from the United States,[6] operating in a scrap metal processing business, described his own lack of readiness as follows:

> I didn't have a choice. I had to run the business. I mean Sunday was the funeral and literally Monday morning I was at work. . . We could have been out of business in a month if I wouldn't have taken on the business. There was really nobody else to run it.

Summing up

- Before entering the family business, Next Gens need to be qualified and pursue their own career path to become financially independent and gain legitimacy.
- Next Gens should seek external validation of their skills and competencies before assuming a managerial position in the family business.
- Once in the family business, Next Gens need to assume their new role, connect with other parts of the business, explore new paths, and communicate.
- Being ready and feeling ready supports a smoother and more promising entry into the family business.

Andrea Calabrò is co-director of the IPAG Entrepreneurship & Family Business Center and professor of family business & entrepreneurship at IPAG Business School, France. He is global academic director of the STEP (Successful Transgenerational Entrepreneurship Practices) Project Global Consortium. He has published journal articles on family firms, internationalization, and corporate governance in leading international journals such as: *Strategic Management Journal, Entrepreneurship Theory & Practice, Family Business Review, Harvard Business Review,* and *Journal of Business Ethics.*

Commentary by Roland Szymański, Poland

I am a third-generation board member at LARS Group, which is a holding of brands manufacturing electronics for HVAC and smart building industries (Auraton), LED lighting (LARS), helicopter services, and technical maintenance of the aircrafts (Helicenter).

There are many ways that Next Gens can prepare themselves in the long run before joining the family business. Planning, good communication within the family, and trust seem mandatory in order to provide good succession. But these strategies need to be combined with the qualifications and the individual character of the particular successor. One of the most common ways to objectively evaluate individual skills is to find a job outside of a family business, preferably in a big corporate structure that provides unbiased assessment and many ready-to-use schemes that can be easily replicated into the family business later on. I had a short episode in a corporate bank, just to have a glimpse of how such a big structure works. A corporate career is not for everyone and it is equally important to know what one wants to do and not do in life. I decided to take a different approach. I created a start-up that was connected with my biggest passion—flying. Having the financial backing of my family, I started running a helicopter service center, something that I believed the emerging Polish market needed. It seemed like madness to the financial advisors of the family, but, frankly, back then Poland was lacking experts in the field of general aviation. LARS Group was a trading and manufacturing company with no experience in aviation services. However, the mixture of true devotion coming from passion and strong financial backing resulted in creating the biggest helicopter maintenance center in Western Poland. Today, Helicenter is a part of the family group but starting a small business from scratch with no experience was one hell of a business training. There is no one golden rule on how to prepare to join the family business. Yet there are methods that are more suitable than others. What the next generation is lacking in the beginning of the business journey is experience. Accomplishments in business are important, but even more vital are failures and personal mistakes that we can learn from. Making these mistakes in a controlled environment that cannot seriously harm or destroy the family business seems critical in the personal development of a young manager.

Financial bonuses for accomplishments should be balanced with the formal responsibilities for failures, no matter if it is a corporate structure or a small start-up. The family business can provide that extra bonus, which is financial security. If you screw up, you still have the roof over your head! Many start-up owners do not have this luxury, so use it wisely.

Questions for Further Reflection

- Do you need to join your family business, or can you choose between several options of which joining the family business is only one? How have other family members approached this decision in the past?
- What other work experiences outside of the family business have you accumulated? What are benefits of such experiences before joining the family business?
- Are you clear about your potential role in the business and the dos and don'ts that come with it?
- Have you developed a personal development (or action) plan to get ready for entering the family business? If so, what are some of the key topics that you address?

Your Notes | Your Action Items

Your Notes | *Your Action Items* ————————————————

3.3
How Can Next Generation Members Make an Informed Decision on Whether to Join the Family Business?

Response by Fabian Bernhard, France and Germany

Current surveys indicate a decline of Next Gens' intention to follow in their parents' footsteps and join the family business. For example, a study conducted by the consulting company EY in 2017 found that only 3.5 percent of all Next Gen members wanted to take over their parents' firm directly after college graduation and 4.9 percent planned to do so five years later.[7] More than ever, young Next Gens have opportunities and career options outside the family business which previous generations may not have had. With that kind of freedom of choice, how can Next Gen members make an informed decision on whether they should join the family business?

Joining the Family Business

In most cases, the question of a career choice comes up when the potential successor enters late adolescence or young adulthood. During this phase of life, which is often characterized by uncertainty, career preparation for the family business begins with the fundamentals: a thorough self-assessment, inquiry into one's skills and goals, and an evaluation of possible career options. This process should be approached openly, allowing for several possible directions. The family business is one choice but, particularly early in life, should not be the only choice.

For the next generation, engaging in self-reflection is an important process. Not spending time on the fundamentals and not gaining a deeper understanding of the dynamics of the family business may result in feeling trapped in a career that Next Gens do not like or a lifestyle they cannot afford.[8] As a young college graduate, it may be tempting to accept a job offer from a family business that is far beyond anything else being offered to their peers. However, accepting such an offer, before getting any outside experience, can put the Next Gen in a gilded cage, potentially making them adopt an attitude of entitlement, and permanently undermining their credibility among co-workers, family members, and potential outside employers.

The following three steps may help Next Gens develop deeper insights into the potential roles they can take on in the family business setting.

Step 1: Self-reflection

Next Gens regularly benefit from advantages others do not have. For example, many Next Gens grow up with an inherent understanding that they will eventually take over the family business. While this can represent a great opportunity, such expectations can also reduce young Next Gens' motivation to explore and establish who they are as individuals, encouraging complacency, and stunting their personal growth. Thus, it can be useful to gain experience outside the family business. Furthermore, engaging in tools related to genealogy,[9] identification of one's values and beliefs,[10] or personal career and goal-setting exercises (e.g., developing a life plan[11]), can be a first step to help young Next Gens develop a greater awareness of Self. Such self-reflection is essential in making sense of one's roles in a family business environment.[12] Outsiders from the family business system, such as mentors, coaches, and trusted advisors, can support reflection exercises that lead Next Gens to explore life goals in more depth.

Step 2: Recognizing Options, Normalization with Others, and Receiving Objective Feedback

While every family business is unique, next generation family members and their families often face common challenges. Young members of family businesses often feel isolated. They believe that their problems are unique to their situation. Communicating with other business families in one's social circle can help develop a deeper understanding of how others have managed their transition into the family business. Also, joining formal and informal networks, including industry associations, university centers, or societies dedicated to family businesses, can help encourage Next Gens to observe, understand, and learn from others in similar situations within their peer groups. Finally, mentors can provide Next Gens with insights into typical challenges related to joining the family business. Struggling family members will realize that this difficult decision is not unique to their case but is "normal" among others in their situation. Building on this realization, Next Gens can further develop self-awareness and identify their strengths, weaknesses, possible roles, and current expectations in the family and business environment.

Step 3: Open and Effective Communication about Plans for the Future

It is common for family businesses to falter when it comes to openly discussing controversial topics, such as succession and associated expectations. An absence of open dialogue between the current generation and Next Gens can lead to incorrect assumptions, which often result in disappointment, disillusionment, and eventually conflict. If establishing effective communication is difficult, coaches and advisors can provide opportunities for young Next Gens to practice forthright and meaningful conversation and facilitate dialogue to help overcome communication barriers between family member like the resistance of addressing sensitive and emotional topics or disagreeing with more senior family members.

Conclusion

It is difficult for young people to figure out who they are, who they want to be, and how they can get there.[13] The process can tap into fears, insecurities, and a great deal of emotional resistance. It is tempting to let someone else decide what direction their life ought to take and what career they should follow. The most influential people for most young people, especially for Next Gens, are their parents. For those who are unaware of their own goals, following a parent's script can be one of the more subtle challenges to recognize. Taking ownership of one's own life, however, is key to personal fulfillment, happiness, and a successful career. It is therefore important that Next Gens invest significant time reflecting on their career options and seek advice from outsiders such as peers, family business networks, advisors, and career service coaches. Finding one's own path, be it within the family business or outside of it, takes time and should include self-reflection, exploration of all options, honest feedback from others, and open communication with the family.[14]

Fabian Bernhard is an associate professor of management and part of the Family Business Center at EDHEC Business School in Paris, Lille, Nice, and London. He is a research fellow for family business at the University of Mannheim and for psychology at the University of Frankfurt in Germany. Equipped with the insights from his own family's business, Fabian Bernhard worked several years for a renowned financial consulting company in New York. Since 2017 he has been on the board of directors of the Family Firm Institute (FFI). In his academic work he specializes in the emotional dynamics in family businesses and the preparation of Next Gen leaders.

Our family enterprise is active in several fields, including manufacturing, services, real estate, and trading. Its origin dates back to 1908, when my great-grandfather started the trading business, which has grown to a portfolio of separate companies since then. I am the managing director of the pharmaceutical business and a board member of the holding.

To answer the question: "How can next generation members make an informed decision on whether to join the family business?" I travelled through memory lane and remembered different occasions that have shaped my thoughts on the subject. While I started my career outside of the family firm, I knew that I would eventually join the business because I have always imagined myself here. Because I didn't know how it would be to enter the family business, I am happy to share my lessons learned in the hope they prove useful to Next Gens, pondering whether or not to join the family business.

I joined the family business initially without an exact role, task, or mentor. I was hired because of who I am—a family member. While I was able to organize myself, find my way through trial and error, it is worth mentioning that other family members facing similar challenges were less fortunate. In the following, I will elaborate on the lessons I learned since I joined the family business, and then I will provide some final thoughts:

1. In the first few months, I learned that being a family member isn't a license but a vast responsibility due to the sensitivity and the scrutiny that my behavior would evoke among family and nonfamily members. In the first years, I made costly mistakes while I figured out my path and learned to satisfy the family's expectations. While I lacked a mentor, employees lacked guidance on dealing with a family member. Therefore, my first lesson is the importance of having a mentor and a clear role and

responsibility, as well as finding your place—how to work together with employees, run projects, and add value.

2. Once I found my place, my career was fast-tracked with quick promotions and early exposure to critical decision-makers and essential stakeholders. I embraced the networking opportunities given to me and learned tremendously from the people I met. Many of them are now part of my network, and I am glad I can consult and work with them. Therefore, my second lesson is the importance of building relationships early—within and outside of the family business.

3. As my career progressed, I was promoted to different positions in several family enterprises. I was fortunate enough to enjoy new assignments, which I saw as opportunities to get to know other companies and people. My third lesson is that it takes time and effort to understand a new role, satisfy associated expectations, and hopefully make a difference in it.

4. As my responsibilities grew in each new position over time, I realized that I enjoyed the freedom and ability to lead and make strategic decisions. I developed a particular interest in creating something new: starting new companies, developing new products, and entering new markets, which have added immensely to my self-satisfaction. Therefore, my fourth lesson is the importance of making a meaningful contribution to the family's legacy and creating opportunities for my extended family and the next generation.

Now that I have worked in the family businesses for more than thirteen years, I also want to share some thoughts about the unique consequences of joining the family business in the long term.

1. As a family member in my culture, you are fortunate to have a high level of decision-making autonomy coupled with a high level of job security.

2. Feeling loyalty to the family enterprise has given me purpose and meaning. It has also given me the ability to inspire others and shape our organizational culture.

3. Your co-workers' and family members' expectations mean that leaving the family business isn't an option. I will most probably stay here until retirement, even though the workload is intense and can be overwhelming.

4. Whether you outperform or underperform as a family member, the consequences are minor. If you care about a commensurate salary, you might be disappointed that family members usually earn less than market salary. Conversely, if you underperform, you still enjoy the safe space that the family enterprise offers.

5. There is more *inter*-generational than *intra*-generational learning, which puts more responsibility on the eldest children in each generation to mentor and guide younger siblings and cousins. The younger ones also have the luxury of learning from the costly mistakes of their elder peers.

6. When you perform well in your managerial role, you are expected to assume more leadership in the family business. The high expectations can make you lonely. You cannot complain or vent, and it is hard to make friends at work. As a family member, you have to act extra cautious, be extra polite, and work extra hard. Just because family and nonfamily members do not know how to deal with you does not mean that they do not put the highest expectations on you.

Whether to join the family enterprise is an important decision that ultimately depends on whether you can derive satisfaction and pride from the unique trajectory ahead of you. In my case, it worked out. I have always understood that every family member's work and efforts shall create value and wealth for the entire family—including future generations. As long as I can contribute to the family's legacy, help develop my fellow Next Gens, and increase our businesses' market value, I am at peace.

Questions for Further Reflection ————————————

- As a Next Gen, do you have a family or nonfamily mentor with whom you can reflect upon whether and how to join the family business?
- How much have you familiarized yourself with both family business management in general and, more specifically, the management of your family's business?
- What work experiences have you had in your family business to familiarize yourself with it?
- What have you learned from the experiences of Next Gens from other families in business who decided to join their family's businesses?

Your Notes | Your Action Items ————————————

3.4
What Are the Ground Rules Between Nonfamily Executives and Family Members Joining the Family Business?

Response by Pramodita Sharma, U.S.

Mr. Smith, as Carolyn had always known him, had worked at her family's business since she was a child. A regular visitor to their home, her parents respected him for his competence, wit, and integrity. He seemed to take special interest in her perhaps because she was the oldest of three siblings. He expressed pride when she enrolled in the nation's top business school. But since she joined the company full time, something seemed different as an awkward unease grew between them. Why?

From infancy, the descendants of an incumbent leader or next generation members develop a sixth sense of being sized up by nonfamily executives working in their family's business. With time, these inquisitive glances become more piercing as speculations of the descendants' role and influence on the business grow. Like a frog in tepid water slowly brought to boil, some juniors find it difficult to express their unease or call it out. Others use their position deftly to build collaborations and partnerships of mutual interest with nonfamily executives by embracing three principles or ground rules.

1. Run Slow to Run Faster

When asked how forty-one-year-old William Etti, a lifelong distance runner, improved his marathon time from 5:51 to 3:57 in two years, he explained, "by doing most of my runs at a slow pace my marathon finish time was much faster."[15] He said that running at a conversational pace with a buddy, with an occasional pause to catch breath, helps to build energy aerobic systems essential for runners' speed and longevity. Carolyn is well aware that she is bursting with new ideas and eager to make changes that she feels are imperative to the survival and renewal of her family's well-established business. The running analogy suggests that the *important question is not whether or not her ideas should be put into action, but rather the timing and pace of those actions—* implementation of change accelerates when the team, particularly established and competent nonfamily professionals like Mr. Smith, bring their best selves to the game. Thus, to accelerate her progress and impact and sustain it for the long-term, she must start slowly and "understand before seeking to be understood."[16]

2. Reimagine Together

Concerned about the predictions of population growth and food shortages by 2050, Dr. Chris Nelson, a molecular scientist and second-generation member of Kemin Industries in the U.S., personally interviewed 10 percent of Kemin's entire work force, 200 people, to understand how each sees their company in twenty years. From this exercise, emerged Kemin's purpose: "to sustainably transform the quality of life of 80% of the world's population by 2030." For an individual to be considered *sustainably transformed* by Kemin, they must consume its products at least five times a day.[17] Such collaborative reimagination helped to direct the collective energies of family and nonfamily members alike, to develop sustainable plant-based materials to accomplish this clearly articulated and measurable goal. Across the Atlantic, in the Netherlands, Marlies van Wijhe, a fourth-generation member of the Royal van Wijhe, a manufacturer of Dutch Paints and Coatings worked closely with family and nonfamily peers and seniors to articulate their aspired goal to ensure that all 10 million buildings in their country would be covered with durable paints made from bio-based renewables using the circular-economy process. Lofty goals like these become achievable because the desire to leave a better world for the next generation is equally shared by family and nonfamily members.

3. Scenic Route to the "Chief" Suite[18]

The Automatic Manufacturing Ltd. (AML) of Hong Kong, designer and manufacturer of industrial automation controls, follows a transparent career development scheme to enhance the entrepreneurial grit and self-efficacy of its Next Gen leaders. In consultation with incumbent family leaders, Next Gens develop an educational and venture creation plan with clearly established and measurable milestones to accomplish over two decades in order to qualify for consideration of any chief-level positions at AML. Close working relationships and mentorships by carefully selected nonfamily executives is an integral part of this training and development plan. For example, supported by the family's angel investment scheme, juniors work closely with nonfamily executives to establish a new venture independent of AML that is subsequently merged with the parent company after a few years of a successful run. Similar thoughtfully created meandering career development patterns that adroitly weave in close interactions with and mentorship by nonfamily executives is followed by the British luxury leader goods manufacturing Ettinger family, as well as the American Kanfer family that manufactures Purell Hand Sanitizers.

Conclusion

These principles of (1) carefully managed pace and timing of the next generations' integration in family business, (2) reimagination of the enterprise with nonfamily executives, and (3) a career development plan focused on building necessary capabilities and relationships are yet to be codified into formal training and educational programs. Therefore, they tend to be overlooked in family firms. This amplifies the assumed importance of factors like luck, personality, or wisdom as the drivers of productive and collaborative, performance-enhancing relationships between descendant family members and nonfamily executives. While the transgenerational leadership change is inevitable, the longer career and life spans extend the potential of developing nonreplicable family firm competitive advantages by carefully planning and exploiting the under-appreciated and utilized potential of the "working together" period between next generation family members and senior nonfamily executives.

Pramodita Sharma is the Schlesinger-Grossman Chair of Family Business at the Grossman School of Business, University of Vermont. She served as the editor of *Family Business Review* from 2008–2017. Her research on succession, governance, innovation, next-generation commitment, entrepreneurial leadership, and sustainability in/by family enterprises is published in over fifty articles and ten books. Since 2015, she has published *Entrepreneurs in Every Generation* (https://www.bkconnection.com/books/title/entrepreneurs-in-every-generation) and *Patient Capital: The Role of Family Firms in Sustainable Business* (https://doi.org/10.1017/9781316402528), and ten articles in journals like *Entrepreneurship Theory & Practice*, *Family Business Review*, and *Journal of Business Ethics*. *Pioneering Business Families of Sustainable Development* (https://www.e-elgar.com/shop/usd/pioneering-family-firms-sustainable-development-strategies-9781789904413.html) is her most recent book.

Commentary by Kanishka Arumugam, India

Our family business EKKI is one of India's advanced pump and water technologies manufacturers under the EKKI and Deccan brands. Established in 1981, our family business has recently been pivoting from a pump company into a deep tech water technology firm. With four state-of-the-art production centers, the group is considered a world leader in the niche field of open-well sump submersibles and is also a growing leader in the pump and water tech business in India. The group has forged a joint venture with HOMA, a globally established German waste-water pump technology provider that operates in more than one hundred countries.

I am the co-chief executive and a second-generation member, son of the founder, and joined the company in 2015. On our board, we are working with eight managers of which two are from our family, namely my father and myself. I was thus forced to find a good way to work with nonfamily executives from my start in the company and, like many Indian Next Gens, I did not have any specific training nor was there a structure to help me to find my way. Today, I am a co-CEO of the EKKI Group. I work in the areas of strategy, business development, and technology management.

One element of working together is the specific culture of our family and our family business. My father and my uncle are from an agricultural background; thus, we value hard work, humbleness, and a frugal and simple way of living. These values helped me a lot when starting. Being the son of the owner gave me a great amount of liberty, but this liberty led at the same time to deprivation. I did not have a clear path or a structure; the dos and don'ts I had to find out myself. So, as Pramodita Sharma wrote in her commentary, carefully integrating the Next Gen was not what took place in my case. What helped me a lot was my high-level education. I graduated from Oxford. I was also helped by my experience as a manager at well-renowned international companies in the water and technology market, Xylem Water Technology, Italy, and Forbes Marshall, India. This generated at least a certain level of acceptance, although I joined when I was rather young. In India, seniority is important. I remember when I suggested hiring a CFO and the long-standing executives voted for an older person while I argued that meritocracy is more important than seniority.

The third point that helped me to get along with the nonfamily managers was that I brought an important project along when I joined. Thus, re-imagining the business together with the nonfamily executives as Pramodita Sharma suggested in her article, was exactly what happened in our case. Bringing HOMA, a renowned German pump specialist, to India as a partner for EKKI opened the path to think ahead for the whole management team. In our family, we think of our employees, as well of our nonfamily executives, as members of our family. So, as a business family, we started to dream and plan for a future for EKKI together with HOMA. We will hire more people in the future, and with each new nonfamily executive who joins after I have joined, I hope that it will be a bit easier than with those who have been here before I was. Building the future of EKKI together is a strong bond for us as a management team and I am proud to be part of it.

In summary, I believe that it is easier for Next Gens to work with the nonfamily managers effectively if they (1) are humble and come from a humble family, (2) accumulated relevant work experience at well-known firms internationally, and (3) bring home a project or opportunity that can help advance the family business.

Questions for Further Reflection

- What do you value about the personalities, capabilities, and experiences of the nonfamily executives of your family's business?

- How do the nonfamily executives in your family's business fare when compared to their peers at competing firms?
- What are your comparable and your complementary capabilities and experiences?
- What are the ground rules for establishing regular and respectable exchanges with your fellow executives once you assume an active role within your family business?

Your Notes | *Your Action Items* ——————————————

3.5
When and How Should Family Members and Their Partners Be Hired in the Family Business?

Response by Lloyd Steier, Canada

Although the statistics vary, studies have long attested to the low survival rate of family businesses beyond a few generations. Some of the most commonly cited reasons for their mortality are the lack of preparation of the next generation and inadequate family hiring.[19] Indeed, managing the successful hiring—and onboarding—of employees is a critical function for all organizations. This challenge is usefully captured in the book *Good to Great*[20] and the famous metaphor that compares leaders of great companies to bus drivers who focus on: "getting the right people on the bus, the wrong people off the bus, and the right people in the right seats." This process is particularly challenging for family firms because they must also balance the advantages and disadvantages of nepotism (the practice of those in power to favour relatives usually by giving them jobs). Nepotism,[21] when managed correctly, can generate unusually motivated, competent employees who work harmoniously across generations. On the other hand, managed incorrectly, it can create dysfunction, poor performance and firm failure. Although some family members may assume that they have a seat on the proverbial bus by virtue of their position in the family, the rigours of the marketplace are not kind to incompetent heirs or dysfunctional organizations. In other words, the stakes are high!

Some family members begin working in their firm at an early age whereas others do not join until later in life. Some firms embrace the hiring of partners whereas others prohibit the practice. When firms have reached a sufficient size or age to contemplate hiring outside the family, many find it useful to have a policy of hiring family members only when they meet the requirements of a vacant position. Even trickier than hiring is developing an onboarding process. There is no single one-size-fits-all recipe as to the "when and how" of onboarding family members or their partners. The family business landscape exhibits considerable variation as to the practice. Using illustrative examples of the challenges facing family firms, this article offers common guidelines for hiring and onboarding family members as well as their partners.

Before offering the guidelines, it is useful to illustrate the problems that can occur when they do not exist. Consider the following example:

> My mother and father are family-first people and I also believe in that principle however it has its limits. When I took over the firm, we needed to do a valuation and one of the related actions I elected to do was hire a group of consultants and family business advisors. Their report was unsettling. A number of family members as well as their spouses worked in the firm. Some were compensated three times more than nonfamily members even though they were doing similar work. A few had company vehicles even though there was no discernible business purpose for their use. Family first was evident in hiring and promotion decisions. Some of the negative consequences included a lower-than-expected valuation of the company and poor morale among nonfamily members that included an exodus of talented people.

The example illustrates that unwritten rules develop over time; here, they are destructive. To co-construct helpful rules with all family members, the family, together with an experienced moderator, can develop a family protocol. In the family protocol, guidelines are agreed upon.

Five Guidelines for Hiring and Onboarding Family Members

1. **Appropriate apprenticeships.** Working within their own firm often exposes family members to important roles, routines, and relationships necessary for running the firm. In certain industries, this experience is a key ingredient for success and can be acquired at a young age. However, for other firms and industries, experience outside of the firm (or higher education) may be invaluable. Apprenticeships should be aligned with industry practice and strategic needs of the firm.

2. **Strive to ensure "fair process for all" in the workplace.** Fairness is important for morale as well as productivity. Examples of polices that achieve a greater perception of fairness include: Hiring and promotion decisions aimed at ensuring the person has the right skills for the job. Hiring and promotion based on merit with the path to promotion clear to all. Hiring family members ahead of more qualified employees can lead to serious dissatisfaction. Compensation should be commensurate with work as well as comparable for all who do similar work.

3. **When onboarding family members, organizational receptivity to the practice needs to exist or be developed.** Although many family members report positive experiences with non-family mentors in the workplace, others report experiences to the contrary. The following example provides an illustration of

what can go wrong when people are "parachuted in" with little planning:

> My father was determined that I have the same work experience he had as a youth. When I was 16, he got me a job as a labourer at one of our remote sites. Times had changed, the firm had grown substantially and, although I did not recognize it at the time, there was significant labour unrest. No matter how hard I worked or tried to get along, I was shunned and bullied. Things got so bad there was a serious concern that I would be physically harmed. Management eventually had to charter a helicopter to get me out. Years later, the experience still haunts me.

4. **Establish mechanisms to facilitate communication and manage family conflict.** As the Three Circle Model[22] of family businesses richly illustrates, unless managed, the three competing rationalities of family, business, and ownership invariably lead to conflict. Family conflicts, albeit inevitable, should not spill over into the business. Useful mechanisms that define ground rules and facilitate communication among family members include family protocol, family meetings, family councils, and advisory boards.

5. **Ensure compliance with legal and tax regulations regarding the hiring of family members.** These regulations vary by country.

Every Family Crafts Its Own Strategy

Although the above guidelines provide a useful frame of reference, ultimately every firm should craft a strategy that works for them. Factors such as size, age, generational involvement, and strategic intent will invariably come into play. Overall, simple straightforward guidelines often work best. For example, Jack Mitchell,[23] chairman of Mitchell Stores, reports that they successfully integrated Next Gens by subscribing to just two basic rules:

- "After graduating from college or the equivalent, you must work elsewhere for at least five years before you can join the family business."
- "You must be a good fit for an actual job at our company."

Conclusion

In conclusion, an ongoing challenge for family businesses is balancing the natural tendency toward excessive nepotism with the long-term needs of the business. Establishing policies regarding onboarding family members is a work in progress that must take into account family dynamics. These dynamics often change over time as family complexity evolves from a nuclear family to configurations such as multigenerational families or networks of families. Useful guidelines for meeting the onboarding challenge include appropriate apprenticeships, fair process, organizational receptivity to the practice, mechanisms to manage conflict, and compliance with regulations. More broadly, two overarching themes regarding the onboarding process of family members are effective communication mechanisms and hiring and promotion based on merit.

Lloyd Steier is a professor of strategy, entrepreneurship, and management at the University of Alberta School of Business. He also holds a distinguished chair in entrepreneurship and family enterprise and is the founding academic director of both the Centre for Entrepreneurship and Family Enterprise and the Alberta Business Family Institute. He has worked extensively with family firms as well as their advisors. His research and service have been recognized through awards such as the Family Firm Institute's "Barbara

Hollander Award" and the Family Enterprise Research Conference's "Lifetime Influence and Impact Award."

Commentary by Matthias Beggerow, Germany

The Bitburger group in Germany, with 4,000 employees and €1.3 billion in sales, has been wholly owned by the Simon shareholder family (40 partners) for over 200 years—the core business of the company being the brewery group. After entrepreneurial diversification, the portfolio today includes participations in companies of various industries, such as mineral water, screw tools, start-up companies, etc. Two seventh-generation shareholders work in the six-person management team, which used to be owner-managed. Today, the family is represented by six family members in the ten-person shareholders' committee (GA). I have been a member of the GA for 20 years and a spokesperson for the family board. The selection of family members for the supervisory board, and the advanced training of Next Gens are also among my responsibilities.

I would like to comment as follows: Whoever is interested in working for a family business should already have shown enthusiasm for the company and for the shareholder family. Not only is a high degree of acceptance in the family important, but also qualified vocational education, together with professional experience gained outside the family business, foreign languages, and time spent abroad is necessary. The appointment process must be transparent in every respect like the candidate's profile and the process's timeline. An external and independent assessment of the candidate is necessary. Moreover, there must be realistic chances for external applicants. Assessment centers and previous professional experience play an important role, too. A family shareholder is never treated in the same way in the company as a nonfamily employee.

This shareholder always has better access to confidential information and the company's management. Therefore, skills such as social competence, empathy, and self-reflection are also of great importance. Moreover, it is important to find the right nonfamily superior who can manage the employed family shareholder fairly (e.g. regarding job appraisals, salary adjustments, etc.).

For the best possible decisions, a company culture is needed in which a family member can lose a selection process or even be removed as a manager or employee ("company first"). Like many of the larger German family-owned companies, we limit the possible employment of shareholders to the top management level. For the shareholders, however, an important task is to assume a position in a supervisory body. The best candidates are determined in free and secret elections. The candidate's profile, CV, and letter of motivation are required and made available to all shareholders. In preparation of such tasks, our Next Gen education teaches values such as reliability, punctuality, diligence, ability to listen, prudent use of social media, humble respect, and no claim to leadership due to family affiliation. The Next Gen should develop a keen interest and understanding of business and strategic issues for the family business early on. Their possible development path should be known to Next Gens. Let me finally mention two experiences illustrating the wide range of topics that could come up on such a development path. A shareholder asked me whether her son could start an apprenticeship in the company because he had only received rejections elsewhere. I denied the request because it would convey the wrong values. On the other hand, allowing Next Gens and family stakeholders to listen to the speech of a managing partner who addresses employees, customers, and guests found my full support. The speech offered great added value for stakeholders of our family business in addition to the Next Gens who attended.

Questions for Further Reflection ―――――――――

- Do you have an established and accepted process for deciding whether or not to hire family shareholders in your family business?
- Do you agree with the criteria, process, and people making the decision?
- How would you proceed if you had to fire a family member's spouse?
- What are the rules for communication and mediation in case the hiring of a spouse leads to a conflict?

Your Notes | Your Action Items ―――――――――

3.6
Who Should Decide Whether a Family Member and/or Their Partner Is Qualified to Work in the Family Business?

Response by Jennifer M. Pendergast, U.S.

It is a recognized best practice for family enterprises to set guidelines for the employment of family members to ensure they are qualified for their roles. A study of top family enterprises found that only 38 percent are led by family CEOs, demonstrating a willingness to seek out the best leadership talent.[24]

Who Decides on Family Employment?

To ensure that family members are qualified for employment, typical requirements include earning a college (and perhaps graduate) degree, working outside the business, following the same terms of employment as nonfamily members (e.g., compensation, benefits), participating in the same performance review process as nonfamily employees, and meeting or exceeding the benchmark of nonfamily candidates applying for the same position.[25] While the rules are fairly typical, what is less common is specifying who is responsible for defining and enforcing them.

Family employment is one of several issues where the interests and concerns of the three circle stakeholders in family enterprise governance (family, owners, and management) overlap, with motivations that are not necessarily aligned. Clarity around how each of the three circles plays in decisions around family employment is crucial. Who decides must be defined at three levels:

1. Who decides the rules of employment?
2. Who evaluates the individual family candidate against the criteria specified in the policy?
3. Who holds the organization accountable to following the policy?

Family systems need to determine what role each of the three circles will play at each level as well as how they will interface with each other to ensure effective decision-making. The answers will differ depending on the family's and the enterprise's life cycle stage, and the owners' philosophy regarding the purpose and value of family employment.

Purpose and Philosophy of Family Employment

Family enterprises often start with the purpose of creating employment for founders and even their next generation. Over time, the purpose evolves to a broader set of goals related to financial returns and service to various stakeholder groups (employees, customers, community). As purpose evolves, so does the family's philosophy regarding the role and value of family employment. For example, a couple emigrated to the U.S. and founded a food products company that distributed products grown in their native country to the restaurant industry. The founders' goal was to create economic security for their family, including their children, all of whom worked in the business. When it came time to re-evaluate how employment requirements would be defined for the third generation, their second-generation parents acknowledged that they wanted the business to provide the opportunity of employment but not necessarily a guaranteed job. And, further, they wanted to make funds available to family members to pursue entrepreneurial opportunities, creating job opportunities outside of their family business.

Families vary greatly in their philosophy regarding family employment. At one end of the spectrum is believing that a family enterprise is not a family enterprise unless it is led by a family member. At the other end is when family employment is viewed as a contributor to family conflict and a barrier to top-quality leadership. While a handful of families espouse a philosophy that prohibits family employment, later-stage companies (e.g., third-generation ownership or beyond) typically create strict qualifications for employment but welcome family members who are qualified and interested.

Because legal documents (e.g., bylaws, shareholder agreement) do not typically address who has authority to define employment rules, then it's up to the owners, board, and management who must decide. While these stakeholders should have a vested interest in top-quality leadership, the potential desire to support family employees can create conflict. Ideally, owners should define the employment philosophy (e.g., desire and rationale for family employment). Management should create and implement employment policy guidelines, with input from owners and approval of the board. And, most important and often overlooked, whomever holds the system accountable to the rules must be specified.

Who Is Responsible for Tough Decisions?

To be effective, family employment policies must address who has responsibility to implement and oversee them. Typically, implementation would fall in the hands of the management. The HR function has responsibility for evaluating candidates for hire as well as managing for the performance evaluation process. However, the challenge a manager faces in turning down a family candidate should be acknowledged. Similarly, the decision to let an underperforming family employee go is extremely difficult. So, a system to monitor compliance to the policy needs to be created.

In later-stage companies, a family employment/development committee of the board may oversee entry, development, and evaluation of family employees. If the philosophy is that family employment is desirable, then proactive tracking, encouragement, and development of qualified candidates is important (e.g., internships, coaching). To avoid conflict, independent directors are good candidates for the committee, supported by HR professionals in the business. Family employees are constantly tested by stakeholders to determine whether they are fit to serve, so independent oversight of their progression through the business provides credibility.[26]

A real-life example: In a large, multi-generation family enterprise, the CEO's daughter worked in the business with two of her cousins. The CEO's brothers were concerned that his daughter would be prioritized for key assignments to increase the likelihood she would be selected as CEO one day. In this case, the employment policy specified clear guidelines for tracking performance of family employees and responsibility for managing career paths and development plans. The independent board directors were responsible for the review of individual development plans, careers paths, and performance evaluations. This process gave family members comfort that the CEO's daughter would not be unfairly advantaged.

Takeaways

While policies have become standard, clarity on responsibility for enforcement and compliance is typically not a standardized policy. While owners should have responsibility for setting family employment philosophy, they need to step back to allow implementation and enforcement of the rules to rest with business leadership and the board. Creating a central role for an independent board, which has fiduciary responsibility for ensuring that the business is well-run, creates necessary accountability and objectivity around the evaluation of family employees.

Jennifer Pendergast, PhD is the John L. Ward Clinical Professor of family enterprise at Kellogg School of Management, Northwestern University. Pendergast received her PhD from The Wharton School in strategy. She consulted for twenty years with large multigenerational family enterprises on family and business governance and succession before returning to academia to become executive director of the John L. Ward Center for Family Enterprises.

Commentary by William L. Darley, U.S.

W.S. Darley & Co. (Darley) is a family-owned and operated business whose mission since 1908 has been to passionately serve the world's first responder and tactical communities by providing high quality, safe, and innovative products with unmatched commitment and service. I, William L. Darley, am a fourth-generation descendant of our company's founder, William S. Darley.

Family members are encouraged to consider making Darley a home for their career aspirations, but only if it is a fit for both them and the company. Darley has employment policies for hiring family members that are written in our Darley Family Constitution. Some of these policies include, but are not limited to, education requirements, outside work experience, market pay for their position, and clear and explicit job expectations and responsibilities. One of the most impactful employment policies for family members is to work outside of the business for three years to gain perspective and insights from working for nonfamily managers.

I was working in commercial banking for a mid-sized bank out of their Chicago office when an opening in international sales at our family business became available. After going through the interview process and meeting with several different stakeholders (both family and nonfamily managers, and the BOD) I was offered the job. My first role was to manage and grow our international customer base around the world. Our family business has had a global footprint since World War II, and today we provide life-saving equipment into approximately one hundred countries every year. After five years as an international sales manager, I moved to our government contracting division as a supply partner manager. Our company works with hundreds of suppliers each year to efficiently equip our war fighters through our government contracts. I work to manage, develop, and find new supply partners with the latest and greatest equipment, technology, and solutions. As a Next Gen working in our family business, I know how important it is to hire the right person for the job. Our family's business has been blessed with 113 years of operations, largely due to our continued effort of hiring the best people and then supporting those people. I have seen our management team adapt from mostly family members to now majority nonfamily members. We believe hiring future Darleys who are qualified is a crucial part of "The Darley Way" culture, but never at the expense of a better candidate with a different last name. Today Darley has twelve family members who work in the business, seven from G3 and five from G4. Working family members are spread among different divisions at Darley, with roles ranging from the executive team to middle management to entry-level positions. Working family members are subject to the same rules as all employees but are expected to be held to a higher standard of conduct and contribution. As our family tree continues to grow, we will certainly continue to monitor and adapt our family employment policies, as necessary.

Commentary by Anne Eiting Klamar and Christian Klamar, U.S.

I, Anne Eiting Klamar, am a fourth-generation former CEO of the company, now chairing our mostly independent board of directors. I also am chair of the Eiting Family Council and the largest shareholder in the company. We are a fourth-generation family business transitioning to the fifth generation with one out of six G5s working in the business. We manufacture for exam rooms and clinical spaces in the medical, dental, and animal health markets, including furniture but also digital diagnostics and imaging.

Jennifer Pendergast's chapter was insightful for me because she looked at governance best practices for employing family members in a family company. I think it is a shared responsibility between ownership philosophy toward family employment, management, and the independent directors on the board. My father, as G3, never worked anywhere else—same with my two siblings. There was no formal policy, but the expectation was clear. I went to medical school and was later brought in as CEO. I often wonder if my siblings think about how much they may have missed having a career only in the family company. The four G5s of college age and older have all sought external employment, and one very qualified G5 now works in the company by merit. It may well fall to the fifth generation to develop more detailed guidelines regarding necessary qualifications of family members to work in the family business.

I, Christian Klamar, am a fifth-generation son of a former CEO and current board chairwoman. While I follow the company's major initiatives, my main role is to learn what family governance practices the preceding generations have established, and to educate myself on how these need to be adapted as the family and company grow.

Ms. Pendergast's response rang true on more than a few points. While the continuity of family management is helpful (and maybe even crucial) in the formative years of a family enterprise, the scale of the business can quickly outgrow the competence of the family. In our case, previous generations have a long tradition of working in the company. However, as my generation comes of age, we have all sought outside employment. One of us now works in the company but had consistently proven her qualifications to the family and management before her hiring and continues to do so. I believe that family members should be allowed to work in the company to provide stability and demonstrate shareholder support and commitment. But moving forward, I think that our family's espoused values should include a commitment to education and demonstrated self-achievement before a role in the enterprise is earned.

Questions for Further Reflection

- Do you know the rules that are used in the family business for evaluating the quality of family members applying to work in the family business? What do you agree and disagree with regarding these rules, and why?
- Who is responsible for deciding whether a family member is qualified to work in the family business?
- If these rules are not followed, who is responsible for enforcing them?
- Does your family have a history of hiring qualified or unqualified family members? Is it a success story or one laden with conflicts? Why?

Your Notes | *Your Action Items* ─────────────

3.7
When and How Should Family Members Be Promoted in the Family Business?

Response by Reinhard Prügl and Peter May, Germany

Promotion (or non-promotion) of family members is one of the most critical decisions because it needs to find a balance between family and commercial logics.[27] For that reason, this question is an extremely challenging one. It is important for the future of the company, the future of the family, and for the personal future of the individual family member. We look at the interplay of three crucial considerations regarding the question of when family members should be promoted: role clarity, role competence, and role acceptance.

When Should Family Members Be Promoted (or Not)?

Role clarity (Willingness): First, why do I want to be promoted? Do I desire to be promoted? Do I feel obliged, or do I expect financial or other advantages, or do I need for financial reasons to be promoted?[28] Based on the level of commitment, Next Gens should ask themselves why they want to be promoted and if the answer to that question is not yet clear, they should not seek promotion. Next Gens should also ask whether they are driven by their own motivations or the family's needs.

Role competence (Ability): Second, a member of the next generation who is motivated and sure that being promoted in the family business is their preferred career path, the crucial question is: Does the Next Gen fulfil the requirements in terms of skills, knowledge, and ability needed for the job? Those competencies serve as important signals. Interestingly, recent research finds that signaling occurs over a much longer time frame compared to nonfamily businesses. Signals are sent and perceived in the enterprising family as well as in the family business context, and negative signals are used by family members to exclude themselves from the pool of family members potentially being promoted within the firm.[29]

Role acceptance (Stakeholder support): Third, the question remains whether other family members as well as other crucial stakeholders like key nonfamily employees, key customers, and suppliers as well as banks and regional communities are likely to accept the Next Gen in the new role. In other words: When being promoted, family members need to ensure the support of major stakeholder groups in order to be effective. Here, narratives play an especially crucial role during leadership transfer.[30] Useful narrative strategies include the linking of Next Gens' actions to former family members having been promoted within the firm, displaying emotional ties, emphasizing external endorsement of qualities, or promoting the personal qualities of Next Gens by associating themselves with key people in the industry.[31]

How Should Family Members Be Promoted?

Family businesses can be particularly successful when their owners are guided by two basic principles: (1) professional ownership and (2) fair process. These two principles also provide a helpful guideline for answering difficult questions regarding the cooperation of family members.

Professional ownership puts the company at the center and asks: What answer would the company want from a professional owner? One who does not ask: "What is best for me," but rather: "What is best for the company?"

Fair process turns to the family. It aims to avoid unnecessary disputes and offer the malignant family virus of envy, jealousy, and mistrust as little as possible to attack. To this end, it ensures that all personnel decisions about family members in the company are made fairly. That means that there are clear rules, every decision is compliant (i.e., the agreed-upon rules are strictly followed, and that everything is fully transparent and verifiable). Procedural fairness perceptions can, for example, be increased by involving family-external parties into the promotion process of family members (e.g., an advisory board).

Contextual Considerations

The answers to those questions not only depend on the members of the next generation, their parents, or corporate governance rules in the family firm, but crucially on the cultural background in which they operate. Business families from the West tend to prefer a business-first ideology. They put the interests of the company above those of the family and therefore place high demands on family members in the company. In other cultural environments, a family-first approach is more likely to be followed. Here the company is the natural place to serve the family members. Differences between the two cultures in terms of answering our question can be quite large. Accordingly, members of the next generation should be aware of their culture. As both authors predominantly gain their insights in the cultural context of the "German Mittelstand," that is small- and medium-sized businesses that form the backbone of the Germany economy and usually withstand economic turbulence, the authors are fully aware that their insights might be culturally biased and not applicable in other cultures.

Summary and Practical Implications

- Next Gens should only be promoted in the company if they are motivated intrinsically. Wanting to please the parents due to a sense of obligation or wanting to prove it to the siblings are not good motives. We have only one life and we should not waste it.

- Next Gens should only be promoted in the company if they are able to fill the job they are sitting on. Professional skills and personal qualities are essential. A company, especially its asset value for the family and its social significance for the people working in it, is too important to make it a place of self-awareness and self-realization for individual family members.

- Selection decisions need to be taken in a professional manner and as independent of personal judgments as possible. Parents find it difficult to judge their own children. Uncles and aunts might be even less able to do so. Support from outside (e.g., advisory board members) and recognized procedures (e.g., assessments) are helpful in granting a high level of perceived fairness in the promotion process.

- A clear development and promotion plan must be agreed upon and should include clear development goals and promotion steps, as well as how results are measured and what the consequences of reaching and missing goals are. Especially helpful are mentoring and coaching offers as well as support in the selection of individual offers for personality development. This also includes programs to improve management skills (e.g., programs dedicated to the particularities of successfully running a family business) and access to business (e.g., FBN) or scientific (e.g., university-based family business centers) networks and education programs.

- Finally, Next Gens should not underestimate the benefits of starting the career outside the family firm by gaining leadership and management experience in a well-established company or by starting their own venture. Outside experience can enable unbiased feedback of how good one really is, experience of what it's like to be managed, and, importantly, outside experience offers a plan B as an external career has a market value even if things go wrong in the family business.

Reinhard Prügl is full professor and academic director of the Friedrichshafen Institute for Family Entrepreneurship (FIF), Zeppelin University, Lake Constance, Germany. His overall research interest is focused on the intersection of marketing, innovation, and family business, particularly from the perspective of the next generation of enterprising families. His work has been published in renowned journals such as *Journal of Management Studies, Family Business Review, Journal of Family Business Strategy, Research Policy, Journal of Product Innovation Management,* and *Marketing Letters.*

Peter May, founder of PETER MAY Family Business Consulting, is a leading family business expert. According to a survey conducted by internet portal Family Capital, he is one of the one hundred most influential people in the world of family business and "Germany's number one family business consultant." Peter May is an honorary professor at WHU—Otto Beisheim School of Management in Vallendar and held the Wild Group Chair of Family Business at IMD from 2008 to 2009. Peter May has developed numerous concepts for advising family businesses and business families and founded some important initiatives such as the world's first family business codex in Germany (2004).

Commentary by Yoon Li Yong, Malaysia

Our family business, Royal Selangor International, is located in Kuala Lumpur, Malaysia. My great-grandfather started it in 1885. He was a tinsmith in the growing tin industry and began making products for households. We have never mined or smelted tin. Instead, we focus on adding value to tin. Our business has a strong brand and makes beautiful home products, many of which were designed in our workshop. The third generation was my father and three siblings. This generation internationalized the business to Europe, Australia, and the U.S. in the 1970s and built a network of offices, distributors, and wholesalers.

Today, we have a total of about 600 employees with most of us based in Kuala Lumpur. The family business is still privately held, and we have completed succession to the fourth generation. In our industry, product life cycles are long. Some of our evergreen products are twenty years old. However, the industry has shifted over the last thirty years; living has become less formal. The household items and gifts industry has, therefore, gone through some consolidation with brands either being bought out or shuttered. One has to be very passionate to work in this business but, then again, being constantly surrounded with beautiful things is a pretty good motivation.

In the fourth (my) generation, most of my relatives have been in some way or form involved in the business. Today, only two of us— my cousin and I—work full time in the business. I am the managing director; he is the executive director. I was an engineer by training before I did my MBA in 2004. In 2005 I joined the business as a retail manager for a few years before taking over product, manufacturing, and marketing as a general manager. From there, I worked my way up to where I am now. So, how are family members hired and promoted? Let me highlight our rules and our values.

Our Rules

- Every family member has to work elsewhere for at least two years after leaving school.
- If a family member is good at what they are doing and fits the company's needs, they might be invited to work here.
- We engage our nonfamily directors and managers for hiring family members.
- Once a family member is invited, they apply for a vacant position and undergo the standard recruitment process.

- Every family hire reports to their head of department, who may not be a family member.
- Every family hire starts as a regular team member.
- If the head of the department is a nonfamily manager, they make promotion decisions, and twice a year, they review possible promotions and provide employees with feedback. On average, we promote good employees every two to two-and-a-half years. The family council, however, can fast-track family members who excel in their jobs.

Our Values

Our family council includes six members elected every three years from eligible voting members of the family forum. We organize a large family retreat every eighteen months. At every second retreat, we elect a new family council. A critical outcome of past retreats was the creation of our family charter. Our philosophy is to work together to generate solutions that meet the needs of both the business and the family. We communicate, work together, and practice integrity and love. We see our most important priority as remaining united as a family through spending time together and providing understanding and support to each other. We should maintain a balance of work, family, and play. We encourage family members to contribute views and ideas, to ensure participation regardless of age or experience. We recognise our responsibilities to resolve conflict through a process, to listen and communicate, and to unite in the face of external threats. We value our success, history, and legacy; and through our family council and family forum we work to pass on to the next generations what has been so ably passed on to us.

Our Family Vision

Our Family Vision is to propagate the Royal Selangor name globally to be synonymous with pewter and good design leading to a vital and dynamic brand. We recognise that employees are a valuable asset. We will recruit, develop, and retain outstanding talent, both family and nonfamily, based on merit. The business will continue to be majority-owned by the family, in order to maintain the legacy of Royal Selangor. The board of directors will have family and non-family members. Family members not directly involved will have their views and interests represented through an active family council, and an evolving charter of good family governance. The business will be a good corporate citizen through its interaction with the community.

Questions for Further Reflection ───────────────

- Are you familiar with the history of your family business promoting family members?
- Do you agree with the practice of promoting family members in your family business?
- Do you think this practice should be updated? If so, how?
- Do you have a family constitution/charter detailing how family members are hired and promoted?
- If you want to be promoted, as a Next Gen, within your family business, what do you do?
- How do nonfamily managers and board members see the practice of promoting family members?

Your Notes | *Your Action Items* ─────────────

Your Notes | *Your Action Items* ────────────────

3.8
When and How Should Family Members Be Let Go from the Family Business?

Response by Andrew Keyt, U.S.

The Dilemma

Sarah Jones, the CEO of her family's $200 million manufacturing company, was sitting in her office, wondering what to do about the declining professional performance of her brother, John. Her father had recruited her back to the business five years ago, after a ten-year career with General Electric. Her brother, in contrast, came straight into the business following college at the urging of his father. John had wanted to pursue acting, but his father said, "That's ridiculous, you are going to come work for me. This is the place for you." John started in the parts department and started to enjoy the process of managing the parts and inventory side of the business, but he still longed to pursue his dream.

When Sarah came back to work for the family business, her father felt that John would resent his older sister having more authority, and to try to prevent that tension promoted John to be an executive vice president, a title that would match his sister's. Because John wasn't quite prepared for this position, even the minimal responsibilities given to him by his father began to become difficult for John. It has now been four years, and John's poor performance has become apparent to not just Sarah but to many of the nonfamily executives. Sarah is now wrestling with how to fulfill her responsibility as CEO to hold John accountable, and her role as an older sister to support her brother and help him succeed.

Meeting the Challenge

Working for your family business can be one of the most rewarding experiences when the business is going well, and one of the most difficult experiences when family members aren't performing well. Because both an individual's personal and professional lives are enmeshed with each other, dealing with performance issues with family employees can tear at the fabric of our family relationships. It also can impact the credibility of the family within the organization. Research has shown that 53 percent of family business employees see the Next Gens as less impressive than their predecessor and 63 percent expect the Next Gens to mismanage the company (Edelman Trust Barometer, 2017). So it is important that family members understand how to manage family employment with great care.

Sustaining the health of our family relationships through the process of firing a family member starts long before the family is faced with the decision to fire a family member. It starts with having an effective family employment policy that makes the processes from hiring to firing clear and transparent for all family members. Employment policies help to avoid some of the following common mistakes that the Jones family made:

- Putting family members in positions that they aren't qualified for.
- Not defining job responsibilities.
- Not having clear measures of accountability.
- Not providing regular feedback.

Most family employment policies focus only on the requirements that family must meet in order to work in the business and whether a job must be open in order for them to be hired. A comprehensive employment policy should be much broader. It should also address how family members will be evaluated, how they will be given feedback, the process for promotion decisions, and the process for firing a family member.

Having robust hiring, evaluation, and advancement processes and procedures that are clear and transparent from the beginning reduces the likelihood that performance problems escalate.

Identifying Performance Problems

Having a policy is just the start. A family must also identify performance problems and talk through them as soon as they become apparent. An effective performance management system will include:

- Clear job descriptions and performance goals.
- Regular conversations about performance and feedback.
- Performance improvement plans and support to help improvement.
- A process that is clearly objective and fact based.

Executing this process objectively can be challenging, so many families are establishing family employment committees that include independent directors, and/or outside experts to work with those inside the organization to give real and effective support in guiding the careers of family members.

Having the Conversation

Even when given feedback and support and the opportunity to address the feedback, family members sometimes need to be fired. The challenge then is how to have this conversation in a way that fulfills both our responsibility as a business leader to hold an employee accountable, and our role as a family member to show love, care, and support. Treating the firing of a family member just like any other employee will sow the seeds of family break-ups and buyouts, so a family must approach these conversations with care.

Hopefully, if the family has been working through a performance improvement process and giving regular feedback, supported by clear examples and data, the conversation about letting a family member go should not come as a surprise. From the beginning, this conversation should be delivered with love and caring, and take a compassionate tone, saying things like, "We love and care for you and want to help find a place where you can be successful, and that does not appear to be here."

As an expression of that care and love, a family should give the family member some space and support to help them find a soft landing. Providing career counseling, networking assistance, and financial support over a defined period of time can soften the blow of being asked to leave the family business. Once the decision has been made, we must be clear that this is not a negotiation, but you are giving them support.

Accept the Reality

Even if the family does this well, they must know that emotions will run high and that it's important to understand the difficulty and pain that this conversation will present for the family members, and oftentimes their spouses, and extended relatives. Showing empathy, support, and care is important, but it still may not be enough. A family needs to be prepared that it may take some time for the family member and others to deal with the sense of loss, and it may take months or even years for the pain of this loss to dissipate. Showing love, support, and care in the process will limit the potentially explosive impact of making such a difficult decision.

The process of working together as a family with a shared sense of purpose can bring great joy, but it comes fraught with peril. To manage the potential downside of working together, a family should do three things:

1. Create a clear employment policy.
2. Give objective and transparent feedback.
3. Always lead with a sense of loving and caring for them as a member of the family.[32]

Andrew Keyt is an internationally known business strategist and succession planning expert for family-owned businesses and the author of *Myths and Mortals: Family Business Leadership & Succession Planning*. He has established a reputation globally for his exceptional ability to advise large family-owned businesses, resolve family conflict, and restore communication. As a former clinical professor in family business at Loyola University Chicago, Andrew has created educational programs for Next Gen leaders, family business owners, and directors in both academic and non-academic settings. The founder of Keyt Consulting, Keyt advises families on how to meet the challenges of family business succession. For more about Andrew Keyt, please visit www.andrewkeyt.com.

Commentary by Philippe E. Brenninkmeijer, Germany and Switzerland

A sixth-generation member of an old business family, I resigned from our family business C&A/Cofra in 2015. The process was challenging. Here is what I learned.

When deciding that you will look for your path outside of the family business, whether this decision is voluntarily or involuntarily, it is always important to consider the fairness of the process through which the decision is made and implemented. Working for the family business can be fulfilling. However, it can also be or become a burden and unnecessarily increase one's life-stress level. As such, deciding to leave the family business can be a valid one.

Of course, leaving a family business is not like leaving any other company, as the linkage is not comparable. At any other company, after the contract's termination, there is no further need to stay in contact. When one leaves a family business, however, one always remains connected by something much thicker. Blood! Also, how you initially join a family business is fundamentally different. Most likely, from childhood on, you have accompanied your parent to the place of business and have learned that it is not only a job but part of your history, DNA, and destiny. This is so important to understand when to either decide to start the termination process or likewise decide to resign. As in the end, you are giving up a part of your identity.

Therefore, it is imperative to strive for the highest possible level of fairness. I would even go so far as to recommend an independent expert to moderate the final decision, as this will add another level and should help ensure that the decision is made as fact based as possible. Facts are essential in order to come to a sound decision, especially since feelings do play a pivotal role in family businesses. However, when explaining the decision to the family member it is essential to understand their subjective thought process and under-stand what the business means to their history, DNA, and destiny.

In all likelihood, the family member will not be happy with the decision so you must give them time to mourn and digest the change. Offering the availability to talk can ensure that the family member does not drift too far off in his ideas and reasoning. Though the business relationship might have ended, you are still—and will always remain—part of the family. If you succeed in making clear to the family member that they still are and will always be a loved and respected and valuable family member, whether inside or outside the business, you have solved a challenging situation.

Questions for Further Reflection ───────────────

- Do you have policies in your family business for the whole process of hiring, onboarding, evaluating, and firing family members?
- Do you agree with how your family business has let family members go or do you think the practice should be updated? If so, how?
- Does your family have a history of conflict around family members leaving the family business?
- Do you believe it is a good practice not to allow family members to work in the business? Or should they only be allowed to work in the top management team?

Your Notes | *Your Action Items* ───────────────

3.9
When Does It Make Sense to Engage Family Business Consultants?

Response by Evelyn Micelotta, Canada

No matter how large or small, family businesses often look for advice from consultants. Management consultancy is a global business worth US$160 billion in 2019,[33] providing solutions in various areas of management. In the world of family businesses, the involvement of a family in the ownership and management introduces unique features and may generate additional challenges.[34] Should a family business select a consultant with established experience in working with family businesses? In my experience, yes. A generalist consultant may focus on the business system without sufficiently considering the complexity generated by the family system. Family business consultants, instead, focus on how the business system, the family system, and the relationship between them should be managed. It can be unproductive—and even dangerous—to hire business consultants unfamiliar with the family system. Understanding that the value of family business consultants is their ability to operate at the intersection of family and business, we need to address two related questions.

Question 1: Will the Issue at Hand Benefit from the Advice of a Family Business Consultant? How?

There are three managerial areas where the advice of a family business consultant is likely to be beneficial. First, when the engagement of a consultant is aimed at filling a gap, either in resources (e.g., time and knowledge to establish a social media presence), in specific expertise (e.g., the implementation of a new tool in the family business, e.g., ERP), or in consensus (e.g., transfer of ownership or management). A family business may be occupied with day-to-day operations and not be able to devote time to collect and process strategic information; seeking the support of a consultant and his/her team allows the family coalition to speed up this process and obtain the desired outcome much faster and cheaper. Second, when the issue at hand is one that requires expertise and knowledge outside of the core business of the family firm, for instance an IPO or a sale. In these circumstances, a key function of a family business consultant is to reduce power and knowledge asymmetry, while protecting the integrity and the interests of the family and the company. Third, family businesses typically benefit substantially from external advisors where there is the need to reassess basic organizational processes that connect the family and the business system. For instance, if a business needs an upgrade in its family governance structures, a family business expert is needed to ensure that changes in the family are understood. Some of the issues that affect governance issues might include the rising numbers of family members in later generations that should support, rather than undermine, family harmony and effective organizational decisions like the introduction of a family council. This final form of engagement of a consultant is particularly critical and delicate in family businesses. The role of the consultant is not to bring outside expertise and apply it to the family firm, but to manage a process of co-creation with the family coalition. The underlying principle of this engagement is to understand the rules and structure of the specific family firm and to offer an array of potential solutions that support the family goals and may help prevent future conflicts. Importantly, this is where the consultant cannot (and should not) provide a one-size-fits-all solution but a tailor-made solution for the specific family and its business.

Question 2: Is the Family Ready to Hire a Family Business Consultant?

Consultants are top experts who engage in both delivering value and learning at the same time. To effectively advise a family business, it is essential for a consultant to develop an in-depth understanding of the business and the family behind it (i.e., situational knowledge).[35] In family businesses, grasping the real source of a persistent problem is particularly critical, however, it may take a long time, especially if there is not much willingness in the family to discuss old grievances or reveal complex, and potentially dysfunctional, dynamics. Equally challenging is to capture key information from nonfamily managers who may be reluctant to share knowledge about the family with outsiders. Hence, when thinking about hiring a consultant, families need to honestly assess whether they are able and willing to provide the expert with the needed situation knowledge about the family and its dynamics. It is possible that family members will not agree on the status quo. That is okay; an experienced family business consultant should be able to ask the right questions to make sense of the situation. However, the consultant will be powerless if most of seemingly private details are not revealed. Such consulting projects not only waste time and resources but can even make families worse off.

Example: A Bridge to Cross a Generational Divide

A situation in which hiring an external consultant turned out to be critical was the one facing Mushroom Inc., an international European family business in the mushroom business. The founder and CEO of Mushroom Inc. had been procrastinating succession for a long time, even though the successors had been ready and pushing for years. The situation stalled to a critical point, with distrust and conflict surfacing. Further conflict was only avoided when both generations agreed to engage a third party—a trusted consultant. As the successor explained:

You need an external expert for that, who is also a trusted figure. The first generation and the second generation were constantly having fruitless arguments. There should be someone who can take into consideration both interests and can be neutral. Fortunately, we did have that. My father had a consultant who was respected by both parties. He moderated us and helped us to develop and apply rules for the transition.

Trust in the family consultant, combined with deep situational knowledge about the family firm, enabled this advisor to be successful in helping this family company navigate the treacherous waters of succession.

Conclusions

The decision to open the doors of your business (and your family home oftentimes) to a consultant is an important one, that should be considered carefully. Hiring a specialized family business consultant is the best option, given the peculiarities of family businesses. Hiring a consultant makes a lot of sense (1) when it is clear what specific (temporary) gaps an external advisor is able to fill, (2) the issue at hand is extraordinary, as it falls outside the managerial expertise of the company, and (3) a recalibration of the family and business system is required. Additionally, it should be emphasized that consultancy in family businesses is a process of co-creation. Confidence that the expert will be able to obtain the situational knowledge is essential to successfully help the company. Together with a CPA, a banker, an attorney, and an investment specialist, a trusted consultant should be in your speed dial list of must-have advisors.[36]

Evelyn Micelotta is the Desmarais Associate Professor in Family Business at Telfer School of Management at the University of Ottawa. Dr. Micelotta's research explores questions about the longevity and success of family businesses around the world. She has studied family branding strategies of the oldest family businesses, multi-centenary family businesses in Japan, corporate philanthropy in Chinese family firms, and is participating in ongoing projects about family businesses in Saudi Arabia and the Netherlands. She has also led several consulting projects with family businesses. Her research has been published in international academic publications and she is associate editor of *Family Business Review*, a premier outlet publication for family business research.

Commentary by Drew Everett, U.S.

Our family business, Bush Brothers & Company, is a fourth- and fifth-generation food company (known most notably for Bush's Original Baked Beans and founded in 1908). My name is Drew Everett and I am the fourth-generation chairman of the board.

I suppose the short answer to the question "When does it make sense to engage family business consultants?" is "anytime" and "sooner rather than later." In our case, however, the guidance was extremely valuable during two generational transitions. We have continued the second engagement to assist with the ongoing efforts of our family council. This has added tremendous value as we developed several family policies and guidelines including family employment guidelines, a shareholder agreement (buy/sell), and a family constitution.

We faced many unknowns as we approached each generational transition. In the first transition, we needed to evaluate the business strategy and establish a more professional governance structure. As a result of our efforts in this transition, we established a board of directors with a majority of independent directors, developed our first strategic plan, and tendered a redemption offer to family members who chose to exit or diversify their assets. In the second transition, we needed to determine if the Next Gens were committed to the continuation of ownership and prepared to accept the responsibility of family governance to complement our majority, independent corporate governance. Regardless of the generation(s) in the business, there are many questions that need to be considered in each transition: ownership succession, leadership succession, broad family interest, and Next Gens' interest in continuing the business. There are many questions to answer, and each family has its own unique circumstances which create complexity in the decision-making process. It is beneficial to realize that you may not be as knowledgeable regarding the complexities of family business transitions. A good family business consultant that has experience and exposure to these challenges can help the family begin to navigate this journey in a proactive way, identify potential conflicts, and work toward mutually beneficial solutions for the family and the business. I recommend supplementing this engagement with a family education curriculum. The more the family understands the complexity of these decisions and the myriad of potential outcomes, the more comfort they can derive from the process, and the more opportunity there is to achieve an outcome that is agreeable and beneficial to all parties.

All of this planning takes time. It is hard to imagine that it is ever too early to start. Engagement of a good consultant is important, but what is equally important is that your consultant knows your family and develops a rapport with its members. The search for the right consultant should be thoughtful and considerate so that you find someone who appreciates the family's challenges, develops trust, provides objectivity, and through their knowledge and experience facilitates a process to achieve a good outcome. Most comforting to note is there are many resources to help family businesses succeed today. There are formal education programs that have been developed to educate family regarding the breadth and complexity associated with family business. There are also many family consultants and practitioners who are available with the experience to assist families in navigating their own unique situations. Looking back, we are grateful that we recognized that we could benefit from outside help and were willing to commit to the engagement and effort required to achieve the right outcome.

Questions for Further Reflection ————————————

- Do you have a most trusted advisor in your family and/or your family business? If yes, how well do you know her/him?
- What could a family do to be better prepared for hiring a family business advisor?
- Do you know advisors specializing in family firms? Where do you get to know them?
- What would be the criteria to select and, later, evaluate a family business advisor?

Your Notes | Your Action Items ————————————

Endnotes: Part 3

1. Peter Jaskiewicz and James G. Combs, "How to Keep a Family Business Alive for Generations," *The Wall Street Journal*, Nov. 20, 2015. https://www.wsj.com/articles/how-to-keep-a-family-business-alive-for-generations-1448045760.

3.1 Why Do Many Next Generation Members Fail to Succeed With the Family Business?

2. Denise H. Kenyon-Rouvinez and Anne-Catrin Glemser, "To Be, or Not to Be, the Next-Generation Family Business Leader," *IMD*, accessed January 29, 2021. https://www.imd.org/research-knowledge/articles/to-be-or-not-to-be-the-next-generation-family-business-leader/.
   Sabine B. Rau, Peter Jaskiewicz and Jim Combs, "How to Keep a Business Family Alive: Families That Fuel Next Generation Family Business Leaders," *FFI Practitioner*, October 22, 2019. https://ffipractitioner.org/how-to-keep-a-business-family-alive-families-that-fuel-next-generation-family-business-leaders/.
3. "Agents of Change: Earning Your Licence to Operate," *PwC's Global NextGen Survey* (Germany: PwC, 2019), 1–26.

3.2 How Can Next Generation Members Prepare Themselves in the Long-Run Before Joining the Family Business?

4. Andrea Calabrò, Alessandro Minichilli, Mario Daniele Amore and Marina Brogi, "The Courage to Choose! Primogeniture and Leadership Succession in Family Firms," *Strategic Management Journal* 39, no. 7 (July 2018): 2014–2035.
5. Cheryl Winokur Monk, "How to Get Children Interested in the Family Business," *The Wall Street Journal*, May 10, 2020. https://www.wsj.com/articles/how-to-get-children-interested-in-the-family-business-11588986481.
6. "Empowering the Future of Family Business," *KPMG Private Enterprise & STEP Project Global Consortium* (website), 2020, https://home.kpmg/xx/en/home/insights/2020/11/empowering-the-future-of-family-business.html.

3.3 How Can Next Generation Members Make an Informed Decision on Whether to Join the Family Business?

7. Thomas Zellweger, Phillip Sieger and Marnix Van Rij, "Coming Home or Breaking Free? A Closer Look at the Succession Intentions of Next-Generation Family Business Members," *Family Business Center of Excellence* (St Gallen: Ernst & Young, 2017).
8. Greg McCann, *When Your Parents Sign the Paychecks: Finding Career Success Inside or Outside the Family Business* (Indianapolis: JIST Works, 2007), 1–256.
9. Drew Smith, *Organize Your Genealogy: Strategies and Solutions for Every Researcher* (Cincinnati: Family Tree Books, 2016), 1–377.
10. Andrew Keyt, *Myths and Mortals: Family Business Leadership and Succession Planning* (Hoboken: John Wiley & Sons Inc., 2015), 1–224.
11. Michael Hyatt and Daniel Harkavy, *Living Forward: A Proven Plan to Stop Drifting and Get the Life You Want* (Grand Rapids: Baker Books, 2016), 1–208.
12. Francesco Barbera, Fabian Bernhard, Joshua Nacht, and Greg McCann, "The Relevance of a Whole-Person Learning Approach to Family Business Education: Concepts, Evidence, and Implications," *Academy of Management Learning & Education* 14, no. 3 (September 2015): 322–346.

13. Nick Di Loreto and Omar Romman, "Does Your Family Business Have a Succession Plan," *Harvard Business Review,* January 30, 2020. https://hbr.org/2020/01/does-your-family-business-have-a-succession-plan.

14. Dennis T. Jaffe, *Working with the Ones You Love: Strategies for a Successful Family Business* (Scotts Valley: CreateSpace Independent Publishing, 2014).

3.4 What Are the Ground Rules Between nonfamily Executives and Family Members Joining the Family Business?

15. Carolee Belkin Walker, "Why Running Slow Can Eventually Help You Run Faster," *The Washington Post*, August 7, 2018. https://www.washingtonpost.com/lifestyle/wellness/why-running-slow-can-eventually-help-you-run-faster/2018/08/02/83d8a546-8ac0-11e8-a345-a1bf7847b375_story.html.

16. Justin B. Craig and Ken Moores, *Leading a Family Business: Best Practices for Long-Term Stewardship* (Santa Barbara: Praeger, 2017), 1–181.
John L. Ward, *Perpetuating the Family Business: 50 Lessons Learnt from Long Lasting, Successful Families in Business* (New York: Palgrave MacMillan, 2004), 1–189.

17. Pramodita Sharma and Sanjay Sharma eds., *Pioneering Family Firms' Sustainable Development Strategies* (Northampton: Edward Elgar Publishing Inc., 2021), 1–384.

18. Allan R. Cohen and Pramodita Sharma, *Entrepreneurs in Every Generation: How Successful Family Businesses Develop Their Next Leaders* (San Francisco: Berrett-Koehler Publishers, 2016), 1–256.

3.5 When and How Should Family Members and Their Partners Be Hired in the Family Business?

19. John L. Ward, *Keeping the Family Business Healthy: How to Plan for Continuing Growth, Profitability, and Family Leadership* (San Francisco: Jossey-Bass, 1987), 1–304.

20. Jim Collins, *Good to Great* (New York: HarperCollins Inc., 2001), 1–320.

21. Peter Jaskiewicz, Klaus Uhlenbruck, David B. Balkin and Trish Reay, "Is Nepotism Good or Bad? Types of Nepotism and Implications for Knowledge Management," *Family Business Review* 26, no. 2 (June 2013): 121–139.

22. Renato Tagiuri and John Davis, "Bivalent Attributes of the Family Firm," *Family Business Review* 9, no. 2 (June 2006): 199–208.

23. Jack Mitchell, "How to Decide Who Can Join the Family Business," *Harvard Business Review*, January 28, 2020. https://hbr.org/2020/01/how-to-decide-who-can-join-the-family-business.

3.6 Who Should Decide Whether a Family Member and/or Their Partner Is Qualified to Work in the Family Business?

24. Claudio Fernandez-Araoz, Sonny Iqbal and Jorg Ritter, "Leadership Lessons from Great Family Businesses: A New Study Points to Four Best Practices," *Harvard Business Review* 96, no. 4 (April 2015): 82–88.

25. Nicole Bettinger Zeidler, "Family Business Employment Policies: Evening the Playing Field for the Next-Generation," *Compoundings Magazine* 67, no. 10 (October 2017).

26. Ivan Lansberg, "The Tests of a Prince," *Harvard Business Review* 85, no. 9 (September 2007): 92–101.

3.7 When and How Should Family Members Be Promoted in the Family Business?

27. Peter Jaskiewicz, Katharina Heinrichs, Sabine B. Rau and Trish Reay, "To Be or Not to Be: How Family Firms Manage Family and Commercial Logics in Succession," *Entrepreneurship Theory and Practice* 40, no. 4 (July 2016): 781–813.

28. Pramodita Sharma and Irving P. Gregory, "Four Bases of Family Business Successor Commitment: Antecedents and Consequences," *Entrepreneurship Theory and Practice* 29, no. 1 (January 2005): 13–33.

29. Sabrina Schell, Julia K. de Groote, Petra Moog and Andreas Hack, "Successor Selection in Family Business—A Signaling Game," *Journal of Family Business Strategy* 11, no. 3 (September 2019): 100286.

30. Alexandra Dawson and Daniel Hjorth, "Advancing Family Business Research Through Narrative Analysis," *Family Business Review* 25, no. 3 (September 2012): 339–355.

31. Elena Dalpiaz, Paul Tracey and Nelson Phillips, "Succession Narratives in Family Business: The Case of Alessi," *Entrepreneurship Theory and Practice* 38, no. 6 (November 2014): 1375–1394.

3.8 When and How Should Family Members Be Let Go From the Family Business?

32. Greg McCann, *When Your Parents Sign the Paychecks: Finding Career Success Inside or Outside the Family Business* (Scotts Valley: CreateSpace Independent Publishing, 2013), 1–266.
Andrew Keyt, *Myths and Mortals: Family Business Leadership and Succession Planning* (Hoboken: John Wiley & Sons Inc., 2015), 1–224.
Craig E. Aronoff, Stephen L. McClure and John L. Ward, *Family Business Compensation* (New York: Palgrave Macmillian, 2011), 1–128.

3.9 When Does It Make Sense to Engage Family Business Consultants?

33. "Size of Global Management Consulting Market from 2011 to 2020," Statista (website), 2021, https://www.statista.com/statistics/466460/global-management-consulting-market-size-by-sector/.

34. Kelin E. Davis, John A. Davis, Marion McCollom Hampton and Ivan Lansberg, *Generation to Generation: Life Cycles of the Family Business* (Boston: Harvard Business School Press, 1997), 1–320.

35. Alaric Bourgoin and Jean-Francois Harvey, "How Consultants Project Expertise and Learn at the Same Time," *Harvard Business Review,* July 27, 2018. https://hbr.org/2018/07/how-consultants-project-expertise-and-learn-at-the-same-time.

36. Wayne Rivers, "The Five Advisors You MUST Have In Your Family Business," *Family Business Institute,* July 16, 2019. Video, 6:17. https://www.familybusinessinstitute.com/five-advisors-you-must-have-in-family-business/.

PART 4: WEALTH

Overview by Peter Jaskiewicz and Sabine B. Rau

At its core, a family's wealth is the sum of its financial and non-financial assets. When speaking of family wealth, most think of financial wealth invested in a business, stocks, bonds, private equity, real estate, or stuffed in the safe at home. Few, however, realize that the family's wealth also includes non-financial wealth, such as the family's personal network (social capital), family members' knowledge and competencies (human capital), and family members' intellect, communication style, and education (cultural capital). Financial wealth is ultimately the result of the family's non-financial assets deployed over time. Prior generations of family members used their capabilities, networks, time, and effort to generate today's financial wealth. The norms that are commonly associated with financial and non-financial wealth are preservation, growth, and impact. To maintain wealth and create more for future generations and society, the family's focus should include non-financial wealth. Unfortunately, many families are preoccupied with the transfer of financial wealth while neglecting to nurture and transfer non-financial wealth.

Family offices (FOs) are privately held firms focused on the effective investment and transfer of a single family's wealth across generations. FOs experienced rapid growth; 35 percent were founded between 2010 and 2018. Two out of three existing FOs will be passed on by 2033, and Next Gens are expected to inherit about

$2,000 billion in financial wealth, marking one of the largest transfers of wealth in human history.[1] FOs offer a structure to manage and invest family wealth across generations. Unfortunately, surveys reveal that more than 50 percent of designated family heirs lack the necessary education and experience to understand the work of the FO. To make matters worse, many FOs do not nurture the social, human, and cultural capital of Next Gens, and they are often unable to inspire Next Gens to participate in the educational activities they offer.

This inability of some families and their FOs to nurture Next Gens' development does not bode well for the future of families and their wealth—both financial and non-financial. For instance, many of the questions shown in this book reveal that Next Gens long for more knowledge to chart their personal development paths including their future involvement in the family and its enterprises. Next Gens wonder about the meaning of their heritage, their ability to pursue careers outside of the family enterprise, start something entirely new, stay true to their personal values, and have impact. The answers to these questions are not straightforward and families could fare better if they were able to support Next Gens in finding answers to these questions rather than expecting them to adopt the parents' or the family's answers. The many interactions with enterprising families, FOs, and Next Gens allow us to share a few more nuanced observations about the differences between successful and less successful families when protecting and growing transgenerational wealth and ensuring that it is has impact.

Financial wealth without purpose has little value. Financial wealth needs a purpose. Purpose helps family members identify with their investment and its cause (e.g., building a portfolio of biotech investments to heal cancer). If the goal is only to generate a certain return annually, identification is not given. In families that identify a clear purpose, derived from their unique values, Next Gens are more likely to become stewards of the family's wealth and build upon the family's legacy. They are also more likely to be inspired, rather than burdened, by the family's financial wealth. Financial wealth with a clear purpose is valuable.

Building non-financial wealth across generations. Some families are only together because they share in the financial wealth of prior generations. They lack a vision to build for future generations and society. Some are in supermarket tabloids because they spend the family's financial wealth on extravagances rather than channeling their energy and wealth toward particular causes where they can make a difference. Those families that make a difference, however, build not only future financial wealth, but they also inspire and help their Next Gens develop their human, social, and cultural capital. In our experience, families whose Next Gens have comparatively better education, knowledge, and networks are truly rich and well equipped to lead meaningful and impactful lives.

Being independent to invest wisely. Next Gens that have a career and are able to take care of their day-to-day expenses independent of their family's financial wealth are better equipped to use their family's wealth to make a difference. Their intentions are directed toward a cause rather than satisfying their own consumption needs. Financial wealth is a token that can be exchanged into almost anything else, so it can become a catalyst that helps Next Gens and families make a difference and grow along the way. In other words, financial wealth offers value when put to use. It is often most impactful when leveraged in combination with the family's non-financial wealth (e.g., networks, human capital). In these cases, families not only invest wisely and build transgenerational wealth but also build legacies.

To conclude, families with wealth have an opportunity to pursue family, business, and societal causes with the aim to have an impact and make a difference. Those who do not share a purpose run the risk of entitling rather than inspiring Next Gens. Their financial wealth will isolate Next Gens rather than opening doors and helping them realize their potential. In this case, Next Gens are more likely to distance themselves from the family and exit its enterprises. Financial wealth, in itself, is a poor glue to keep the family united and happy. We can only hope that families and Next Gens alike will nurture their financial and non-financial wealth and invest it toward new beginnings rather than unhappy endings. The following chapter addresses nine questions from Next Gens about how to react to wealth, how to manage it, and how to put it to have impact.

4.1
Do I Have the Freedom to Leave the Family Business (Entirely) Behind and Do Something Else?

Response by Marleen Dieleman, Singapore

Blessing or Burden

Being born into a business family is often seen as a blessing by society—especially when the family possesses considerable wealth. Yet many young people who find themselves in this position perceive it as a burden as well. In fact, a survey by EY suggested that less than 5 percent of students from business families intended to become a successor in it, instead opting for large companies or for starting their own.[2]

There are several reasons young people feel apprehensive about the family business. The business may dominate family life, and young people may perceive it as a negative influence. They may not want to lead the kind of lives their parents have, nor give their own children a similar upbringing. Sometimes expectations are high or incompatible with one's own dreams. Occasionally, young people resent what they perceive as unethical business practices or negative impact, especially in family businesses carrying a stigma, such as plastics or coal mining.

It is not surprising that young people ask whether they can ignore the family business and pursue an entirely different path without feeling guilty about it. The question is not one that comes with a simple yes or no. What people often overlook is that there are many middle paths that may be more satisfying.

Deciding on the Degree of Involvement

A decision to join the family firm does not mean someone cannot do anything else with their lives at all, nor is it necessarily a decision for life. The level and type of commitment Next Gens feel toward the business varies.[3] As such, this decision may be more fruitfully seen as a matter of degree, which involves a few trade-offs.

Most Next Gens think of joining the family firm as a life-filling occupation that dominates everything else. It does not have to be. For instance, even those Next Gens who join the family firm full time may continue to pursue their passions by finding ways to do what they desire under the umbrella of the family business, or even by changing the business to match their interests. This path is especially valuable for those growing up in families that fully expect their Next Gens to join the business. If changing the business itself is not possible, they may pursue their dreams through volunteering, directorships elsewhere, or through other activities outside the family firm. Some may prefer even looser connections, such as being mostly engaged outside the family firm but remaining committed as a shareholder or having an oversight role (e.g., as a non-executive director) that does not take up a substantial chunk of one's time.[4] Of course, even if a Next Gen decides not to be part of the family business at all, there can be many ways to engage with the family. One can still be proud of the family values. It is feasible to participate in certain family activities or occasionally contribute one's skills to the company when required (as an artist or lawyer, for instance). Thus, one way of thinking about this decision is to decide on the degree of involvement, rather than seeing it as a yes-or-no question.

Another way to view the question is to think of it as something that may be part of someone's life, but perhaps not a permanent feature. For instance, some Next Gens may wish to build up a professional career outside before joining the family business, or would agree to serve the family business only for a limited time, thereby opening up opportunities to other meaningful ways to explore one's talents and one's impact on the world. I know of various millennials who decided to work for the family business for a while under the condition that they would be able to take a year off for a life-changing world tour or volunteering opportunity. Others growing up in an international business family resented the absence of their parents and may suggest not to join the business before their children are older due to the extensive travel required. Other successors I know insist on retiring at age fifty, working on a transfer of their responsibilities to professional managers before that time comes. Thus, the family business may offer many opportunities to lead, but these do not necessarily have to occupy one's entire life. Instead, in certain phases of life there may be less (or more) involvement to allow for other priorities as well.

Lastly, it is important to realize that people can change their minds. I often find that young people tend to envision their careers as a straight line from education to retirement with a clear goal. But most people discover only later what they want, what they are good at, and what makes them passionate—often through trial and error. Perhaps a Next Gen never wanted to join the family business, but they reconsider later. Or some family members have joined but now realize that they are not the best qualified, or that the business does not motivate them sufficiently. Or they did not like the business before, but after a business transformation they find it more attractive. Things can change. The decision whether to leave the family business may not be a single decision after all, especially not if communicated carefully so that the outcome does not cause irreparable damage to interpersonal relations in the family.[5] Joining the family firm may be better conceived as multiple stages of decision-making. Even if you get it wrong today, it is not too late to get it right later.

No Zero-or-One Decision

Can Next Gens leave the family business behind and do something entirely different? Of course, the answer is yes. However, is this the best way of asking the question? Framing the question as positioning oneself on a scale ranging from totally "married" to the family business to entirely separate from it may generate more optimal choices. Moreover, these choices do not have to be forever. There may be more than one decision moment. Many students in my family business classes feel greatly burdened by the choice of whether or not to join the family business. But looking at it as a matter of degree that can vary with time helps them see more opportunities and feel less burdened by their choices.

Marleen Dieleman is an associate professor at NUS Business School in Singapore. She holds a PhD from Leiden University in the Netherlands. Marleen teaches and researches on the strategy and governance of Asian family business groups. She has published widely on these topics, including books, articles in academic journals, book chapters, cases, and reports. Her work is featured regularly in international media and she is a frequent invited speaker. Marleen has worked with large Asian family business groups as a consultant, family meeting facilitator, or board member.

Commentary by Shalabh Mittal, India

Our family business is a diversified portfolio of businesses in shipping and in manufacturing of chemicals. My father comes from a business family but started the current business on his own. His first business was in the trade of chemicals and soon grew into the manufacturing of chemicals. Later, he bought into the ownership of a shipping business and focused on its growth. The shipping company eventually went public and later diversified into coal mining, oil and gas services, and exploration. The listed entity has gone through a rough time since 2012, due to a downturn in shipping and commodity prices, and is now almost closed. Our focus has therefore shifted to growing our chemical business and starting afresh in the shipping business with a new "asset-light" business model. Over the last two decades, I mainly worked in the shipping business. I am also actively involved in the strategy development of all other portfolio businesses and responsible for the treasury management of all businesses' funds.

Next Gens are unlikely to leave the family business behind because such a decision would be viewed in our culture as being disrespectful to the family—especially the father. Instead of discussing whether to leave the family business, I believe that Next Gens should turn the table and reflect upon their amount of involvement. Surely most Next Gens experience many kinds of pressures that can take away their joy in joining the family business. These might include performance pressure, conflicts with other family members working in the family business, and non-aligned interests of family and nonfamily members to name a few. Moreover, the decision to join the family business involves strong emotions, and once made, has long-term consequences: Once one joins the family business, it's not always easy to exit again. If the business is growing too fast, you are expected to be around to handle the growth pressures. If the business is going through a rough patch, you are expected to stick around until pressures ease. And if the business is growing stably, most organisations neither have the appropriate structures nor are they managed well enough to hand over the job to professional, nonfamily managers. Therefore, once they join, family members usually end up staying in the family business, which is not without costs. In a business where many family members are involved, there is not only a focus on growth but there is also politics to take care of your immediate family's interests. Despite all of these hurdles, joining the family business in some capacity earlier or later might be without alternative.

How Next Gens think about the family business vastly depends on how the previous generation raised them and how open both generations talk about being part of the business. Open and free conversations about joining or not joining the business ease, to some extent, the stress that many Next Gens feel.

Clear "you have to work from the bottom-up" plans help Next Gens to get to know all aspects of the business and earn the respect of family and nonfamily managers before critical decision-making roles are handed to them. Finally, working their way up helps Next Gens to understand their own skills, strengths, and weaknesses, enabling them to identify the role in the business they are most suited for, excited about, and can make a difference in.

Next Gens who are not clear about whether to join the business in the first place should work outside the business for a few years. Outside work experiences greatly helps in understanding oneself, enables one to see how other organizations work and helps soften the rough edges of one's ego. Equipped with such experience Next Gens can re-evaluate if the family business excites them. If it does, joining the family business at this later career stage should be temporary at first to test waters before committing oneself for the long term.

To conclude, I agree with Prof. Dielemann that leaving the family business doesn't have to be a zero-or-one decision. Instead, it is a continuous reflection upon the time and amount of involvement a Next Gen wants to commit to. Being on the board of directors, for instance, can ensure the business is run with the values and goals of the family. If the business is a major contributor to the family's finances, being on the board of directors might also be critical for preserving both the family's wealth and legacy. By understanding what it entails to be involved in a family business and having an open dialogue about it with one's family, one can decide whether to join the business immediately or in the future and in what capacity. Next Gens should therefore reflect upon their desired amount of involvement instead of considering leaving the family business completely behind.

Questions for Further Reflection

- What is the history of your family in terms of family members joining, not joining, and exiting the family business?
- Has a family member left the family business? If so, how did this process unfold and end?
- If family members have previously sold their respective ownership in the family business, has their relationship with fellow family members remained the same or changed? Why?
- If one of the active family members wants to leave, what would be the reaction of other family members?
- What would it mean, in terms of reputation of your family business, if prominent family members would leave the top management team, the board of directors, or sell their shares in the business?

Your Notes | Your Action Items

Your Notes | *Your Action Items* ⎯⎯⎯⎯⎯⎯⎯⎯⎯

4.2
Do I Deserve the Business and/ or Wealth I Will Inherit?

Response by Nava Michael-Tsabari, Israel

Like Hamlet's contemplation reflecting his own self-doubt ("to be or not to be"), this is the question most Next Gens of a family firm ask themselves. Wealth is defined as the total assets owned by a family at one time,[6] yet family firms have emotional value as well.[7] Even medium-sized family firms (businesses that generate about $13 million in revenues with some thirty employees) may create wealth which categorizes them among the wealthiest class in society.[8] However, Next Gens have mixed feelings about succession of firm and wealth, and when asked about it, their feelings of obligation are twice as high as their own desire to inherit.[9] I am a third-generation member of a multi-billion-dollar family firm, as well as an academic. Here is my answer taking into account my life experience. Scholars describe different attitudes that Next Gens have toward the family firm, however, these mainly refer to pursuing "a *career* in their family business,"[10] and not to the dilemma stated above. Scholars refer to employment in the firm, and not to the question of entitlement of the business and/or the wealth.

I Was Not the "Chosen One"
Growing up, it was already decided for me that I did not deserve the firm. As in any family, individuals are shaped by their unique perspective. So am I, the eldest child of our third generation. My cousin

was the chosen one, expected to inherit the leading position being the daughter of the eldest son, while I was born to the younger sister. My uncle preferred his own daughter. He decided that I was not worthy of the firm, which was even more difficult to deal with because nothing was explicitly explained. Trying to figure out who I was in these circumstances was complicated, exacerbated by the question of whether I still deserved the wealth. The family wealth felt like a mixture of burdens, responsibilities, and callings from my ancestors, need to justify myself and a constant reason to worry. I was afraid of failure being measured up to past successes, which were created by others. I was worried I'd let everyone down. I have not yet read a study that describes a similar mixture of feelings— just a few anecdotes. Like, for example, Phil Knight, the founder and owner of Nike, describing how he had to fight wealth's trial "to define" him. In his initial search he bought a Porsche and wore sunglasses everywhere.[11] The good news is that finding purpose and meaning in later years helped me also enjoy and feel at ease with wealth. The bad news is, it is a long process that demands personal growth.

It Is a Long Journey

My late grandparents, who I loved and adored, had expectations. I felt the weight of tradition. I was born into the family firm and did not have an identity that was separate from it. Being a Next Gen is a huge part of how I define myself. This is probably true for most Next Gens. How can I feel that I deserve anything when I do not know who I am? Finding the balance between being the next link in a chain to being an independent particle is the result of a long journey, which began early for me. Being born to the family that is connected by shared mission, history, and identity, what they think and expect has an enormous influence. A Next Gen receives implicit and explicit messages regarding how they should feel, think, and behave, like "don't come to the business." It should be no surprise that many Next Gens who feel that they want to control their own lives have been found to prefer not working for the family firm.[12] My trajectory was first defined by family members from the outside. It took years to regain my control and define my identity from the inside. Finding the balance between listening to my inner voice and outside voices is the result of this long journey.

Interestingly, the mistakes I made along the way, the actual and psychological losses that I endured as I was stumbling while trying to find my path—all these felt like the cost I had to pay. I was rebellious, lost money, and did not speak with my mother for a year. It was as if the mistakes alleviated the weight of wealth and allowed for a more relaxed attitude towards it. I kind of "paid for it" myself, didn't I? Finding the balance between the price one pays and the rewards one earns helps finding a justification for one's own path and identity.

Looking Back—the Lessons I Learned

Looking back, finding my path has worked in mysterious ways. The less I searched for solutions outside, and the more I learned to give meaning to what I did, the more I felt peace of mind. Finding my own purpose, which resulted in transforming the beautiful phenomenon of the family firm into research and teaching to other scholars and members of family firms, helped me resolve the entitlement issues. Turns out that when one co-creates her own path, it gives a feeling of competence and increases a sense of self.[13] The feedback from listeners who tell me my insights heal them, fills up my heart. Knowing who I am made it possible to define what I deserve.

My three lessons were (1) finding out who I was as an individual, (2) not being afraid to make mistakes, and (3) learning what defines meaningful work for me.

After a long journey I realized that I am part of the family firm and its wealth, and it is part of me, regardless of what others think. I experienced the "paradox of choice,"[14] where having more opportunities actually led to confusion and dissatisfaction. I had to learn that the family firm is not the only thing that defines me. I am confident and happy with the heritage and the lessons I can share with others. It is the result of a search for how I could give meaning to my actual and emotional inheritance. There will always be outside voices ridiculing or criticizing; however, it is the answers one finds inside that pave the way to the balance. It requires time to mature, but the possibilities to leverage wealth into contributions to others is an outcome worthy living for.

Nava Michael-Tsabari, PhD, is the founder and director of the Raya Strauss Center for Family Firm Research at the Coller School of Management, Tel Aviv University. Her dissertation from the Technion—Israel Institute of Technology was the first one on family firms in Israel. Her research examines emotions, organizational culture, and employment in family firms. She is a third-generation member of the Strauss family firm, a publicly traded multinational food conglomerate.

Commentary by Ariel Ben Zaken, Israel

My parents, Eli and Monique Ben Zaken, founded an Italian restaurant after immigrating to Israel. Their three children—my siblings and I—regularly worked and helped in the restaurant. I was the first to share the passion of my father, Eli, for wine. After military service as an officer in the paratroopers, I travelled to Burgundy, France, where I worked for Michael Picard at the Domaine Emile Voarick Winery and learned the secrets of growing wine. I served as the Castel Winery CEO between 2003 and 2018 and now serve as the chairman and owner of the Castel Winery with my brother and sister.[15]

My Story

I do not feel that the issue of inheriting wealth applies to my siblings and me, because we have been part of the capital produced since the humble beginnings. As I grew up, I had to learn all business topics on the go. I am sometimes asked if I studied at a university, and I answer that I could have graduated from Harvard for the price of all the mistakes I have made. And so, I learned. I was a partner in all the processes at the winery and built an infrastructure for effective decision-making by working with external consultants like psychologists, marketers, sales, and organizational consultants from whom I learned and gained a lot of knowledge.

Our Story

The crystallizing core of a family business is always created from the founding generation's initiative and vision. It is important to know when the family business was formed, but we should also consider the dynamic of the family, not just the business of the family. For instance, what is the Next Gen's connection to the firm's geographical location? What is the history of the family? Finally, what are the roles affixed to each sibling by the parents and what is it that the parents expect of each child?

Our story is intertwined with my parents' experience. They immigrated to Israel in the 1970s without family support and tried to find their place as new immigrants who did not belong. With planting the first vineyard, they planted their first dream of creation and earlier in the 1980s, my parents opened an Italian restaurant in Jerusalem. This became the first source of the family's livelihood. Much of our personal growth and development was woven into our journey through the restaurant's pulsating life. It was the center of our lives, through which our family grew, developed, ached, and laughed. Life went on through and by the restaurant. The siblings' roles, each of our responsibilities, and the commitment to the family and the business have been shaped there since our young ages.

The restaurant opened when I was eight years old. I grew up in a restaurant that is still a part of who I am and who we all are. The people who went through it and the stories written through us are part of what I know and learned about life. I spent hours in the kitchen, inventing dishes, liking the kitchen's playfulness and rhythm, and the feeling of being behind the scenes. At the age of twelve, I took public transportation from school directly to the restaurant. In high school, I was already self-employed and worked in the restaurant's bar for a living. Sometimes it seems that the life of the restaurant was more central than home. Moreover, each brother's role in the family structure can be traced back to these early times. There is an attachment to family at all costs in a family business, especially when the firm is small, and one has little need for personal development outside of the family. And with the responsibility that is created for one in the business, sometimes it feels like sailing in a small boat: When there are no problems, and the sea is calm, you should not be under any pressure, but when the boat is in danger, you jump to help even into deep water, even if you are not the captain. As the Next Gens, our deep commitment to and partnership with our parents resulted from the family fabric and our all responsibility to contribute to the shared livelihood. Let me conclude by saying that the psychological story that built the soul of the family is the ground from which we emerge and from which the business is created and developed and into which we are woven.

Questions for Further Reflection

- What and how, as a Next Gen, do you know about the financial wealth of your family, in terms of its origin, current investment, and actual value?

- How do you feel about this wealth? What type of difference does it make to your life?
- How do you discuss your wealth and the duties and rights coming with it with your parents, siblings, and cousins?
- How does your family's wealth change how others treat you when you join new groups? How does it change the ways in which you approach new people?

Your Notes | Your Action Items ──────────────────

4.3
How Do I Talk to My Friends and Colleagues About Our Wealth/Business Worth?

Response by Marshall Jen, Kevin Au, and Jeremy Cheng, Hong Kong, China

"Is it possible to speak openly about wealth?" This is the challenging question in the book *Why Me? Wealth: Creating, Receiving and Passing It On*.[16] Most Next Gens may question whether this endowed advantage twists human relationships and creates an invisible gap between themselves and others. When asked, about 80 percent of our recent mentorship program participants said they did not want to disclose the sensitive information of their family wealth to others. About one-fifth to half of the group never talked about their family wealth and their business' worth in front of others. The irony is we can locate their family and/or business background on the internet.

In this chapter, family wealth includes a family's ownership in the operating businesses, other investment assets, collectibles, and philanthropic endowments. Business worth refers to the estimated market value of the operating business. Oftentimes families are more sensitive about disclosing their family wealth, but more willing to share their business worth, especially when presented with new business opportunities. It is important for the Next Gens to differentiate their authority when sharing the information about family wealth and business worth.

The family and/or business name may signal a certain level of wealth. Even though the Next Gens do not talk about this explicitly, people around them may be aware of it. Regardless of how people come to know about (and confuse) the family wealth and/or business worth, the exposure may create complexities because this can involve other family and nonfamily stakeholders. Although the disclosure may help build a legitimate image to new business acquaintances, it can hurt family relations if risks of such disclosure are not well managed. A real story (with names disguised) below illustrates why.

Jasmine: Crossing the Boundary

Jasmine grew up watching her father, Howard, build his billion-dollar medical empire from scratch in China. A major disappointment in her life was not having built a close relationship with Howard due to his hectic schedule. Even though Jasmine had been deprived of Howard's attention since childhood, she aspired to join the family fold early on. She always tried hard to demonstrate her achievements and sought recognition from her father, whether it was in school, sports, or internships.

She graduated from college in February 2020 when the COVID-19 pandemic stressed the local medical system. Jasmine wanted to see how she could help the company overcome this crisis. Naturally, she turned to her father and asked if there was a suitable position for her in the business. Howard hinted that she might be able to join the government relations team. Managing much highly sensitive information, this position was so important that Howard preferred to "keep it in the family."

Hearing this response, Jasmine anxiously wanted to know about the trade. Through her high-power mentor, Jasmine was invited to a chat group in which heads and professionals of government relations in many listed companies shared their views on evolving government policies. Bearing the same surname as the founder, Jasmine was quickly identified as a family member and was seen by many in the chat as representing her business. Indeed, in a few conversations when people prompted her view on key corporate directions, Jasmine did not rectify this impression, fearing that she would be kicked out of this prestigious group if she was not working for the business. As the medical field was highly regulated, a government agent immediately reached out to a group director and asked if they had hired a new government relations contact. Within minutes, the matter was reported to Howard, who was upset and decided not to pursue his initial idea.

The Three-Question Framework for Assessing Self-Disclosure Needs

Jasmine's story leads to three questions that Next Gens should consider before disclosing their family business identity, family wealth, and/or business worth.

1. **Under which capacity do Next Gens talk about the family wealth and/or business worth?**

   The Next Gens should be aware that they are seen as a representative of the family and/or the business even though they do not carry an official title. The family name can bring access to different networks, but this comes with great responsibilities. Even though Jasmine had a good intention, she was never formally invited to join the company and she should have been vigilant of this boundary. A premature or even false representation can destroy the long-term legitimacy as senior generations put much emphasis on this issue.

2. **Under what circumstances is talking about family wealth and/ or business worth necessary?**

   The Next Gens should be transparent with the senior generation on how to leverage the family name. The embarrassment Jasmine created to Howard could possibly have been saved if she properly let her father know that her mentor introduced her to the prestigious network. This is not the same as seeking permission, which many Next Gens try to avoid, but showing courtesy to the current generation and their ability to exercise sharp judgments in managing sensitive relationships.

3. **Who are the Next Gens speaking to?**

While this question seems obvious, the prevalence of social media where people can mask their real identity can make this less straightforward. Unlike physical meetings where identities can be readily ascertained, oftentimes when people are introduced via virtual networks, they share much information without knowing the identity of the others and where they stand in relation to the company. If due diligence before the meeting is not possible, Next Gens should use discretion with everyone. In hindsight, Jasmine should have done her due diligence on the chat group and asked her mentor who was in the group. She might have then been able to know that the group consisted of not only professionals but also government agents. From that information, she can then make an informed decision.

Key Takeaways

Should the Next Gens be frank in talking about wealth? Genuine and enduring relationships are built on an appropriate level of self-disclosure.[17] Yet the Next Gens should be able to see this as a double-edged sword, especially at the start of any relationship. While Jasmine's case focuses mainly on the interaction with business associates, the Next Gens should be cautious of those who may take advantage of the disclosure and secure necessary planning.[18] The three-question framework is useful (but non-specific) in assessing the appropriateness of self-disclosure. In a nutshell, the Next Gens should:

- Know their official role in the business and their implied authority behind the family name.

- Understand that outsiders may confuse the roles of business executive and family member. Clarify any role ambiguity as it arises.
- Properly communicate intended representations and engagements with senior-generation leaders before taking any action.
- Assess the identity of parties in the dialogue and rethink what type of information should be disclosed, especially in a new virtual group.

Marshall Jen is an honorary project director of the Center for family business at The Chinese University of Hong Kong. His research focuses on leadership development and mentorship in families in business. A Next Gen of a listed family firm in Hong Kong himself, Marshall designs and teaches educational programs, and trains mentors for growing Next Gen power.

Kevin Au is an associate professor in management and directs both the Center for Family Business and the Center for Entrepreneurship that he founded at The Chinese University of Hong Kong. In addition to his academic roles, Kevin advises families in business and start-ups, serves formerly or currently as director of FFI and the STEP Project, and is a member of government committees in small businesses and social innovation in Hong Kong.

Jeremy Cheng, FFI Fellow, ACFBA, ACFWA, is a PhD student and member of the Center for Family Business at The Chinese University of Hong Kong. He is founder of GEN+ Family Business Advisory & Research, founding chair of the FFI Asian Circle, GEN faculty member, case committee member of the STEP Project, and a member of the research applied board of *Family Business Review*.

Commentary by Patricia Saputo, Canada
(with the help of Francesco, Lorenzo, and Tommaso Saputo Maltoni)

Our family enterprise is an investment holding company that derived from an international cheese manufacturing business founded together by G1 and G2, upon immigrating to Canada from Sicily after WWII. My role as the G3 is that of the CFO of the family office managing the investments, accounting, taxes, estate planning, and wealth transition of the holding company, which owns 10 percent of the publicly traded cheese operating company. The G4's helping to answer this question are my three sons who range from ages twenty-four to fifteen who currently don't have any role in the company (both operating and holding companies).

Being in my 50s I have previously held a board position in the operating company for eighteen years, but never had a formal job at the operating company after graduating and becoming a CPA. It became clear that there was a distinction between the "family" and the "Inc." As a board member, discussions about the operating company were confidential and it was understood that the communications department would disclose to the public any information the company thought necessary. I would never discuss the operations as that was not my daily business, so I made sure I prefaced to those I met that I was in the family office space. As my name was eponymous to the operating company's name, people made many assumptions about who I was. I was uncomfortable at first to correct them, but in time I felt it was necessary. You have to be comfortable with who you are as a person before you summon the courage to do so. I felt I had every right to speak about my "family" as I was in the family office space, but not the "Inc," where the wealth derived. At times, there are fine lines that could be accidentally crossed, but understanding your audience, the position with which you are speaking to that audience and the topic of conversation, you have a sense of what should and should not be shared. The reputation of the family has always been important to me.

The G4 response to the question is different, mainly due to their age. Their initial response is to stay humble, be well-grounded, and stay quiet about the wealth and the business, especially with people you don't know. This conversation has not come up for them and they feel if it does, it is better to say nothing, especially if you have nothing to gain from the situation. More particularly, Lorenzo has added the following:

> As a 22 year old, I am not expected to be fully qualified to speak about the family business and wealth. At most, I am asked surface level questions that can easily be answered by Google. I have never felt the 'need' to talk about the family wealth/business at all. I find it to be a choice and you should gauge whether you derive more value from remaining silent. If asked directly, I can still choose to give a vague yet factual answer that signals I wish to say no more while remaining respectful and polite. Nobody is forcing you to reveal all the intricacies of the family wealth, so always remember that you are in charge of where the conversation starts, goes, and ends. I keep a low profile, so even with friends in my circle, it is uncommon to strike a conversation regarding my family's wealth. People my age and in my network know about my family's wealth and my relation to it before they have had a conversation with me. A common assumption is that I will mention my family's wealth and success when meeting someone for the first time, but when they see that I haven't brought it up during any of our early encounters, they understand that it is something that I have chosen to keep to myself. It is only my closest friends who feel comfortable enough to talk about it with me, which I am okay with given that we have built trust.

Questions for Further Reflection ————————————————

- Do you believe that the family's wealth has an influence on how others behave toward you? If so, how?
- Do your siblings and/or cousins discuss their "family" in public although you prefer not to do so? When and where would be a good place to discuss this topic in the family?
- What would be the reaction of your classmates, fellow students, or colleagues if you revealed your family's wealth?
- How can you balance the need for privacy concerning your family's wealth and the need for openness and trust within your relationships?

Your Notes | Your Action Items ————————————————

4.4
We Have Wealth. When Should We Set Up a Family Office to Organize It?

Response by Kirby Rosplock and Dianne H. B. Welsh, U.S.

Families who have goals to perpetuate, grow, or sustain significant family wealth over generations are often motivated to set up a single-family office (SFO). But first, what is a single-family office? A family office is simply a business designed to manage wealth and other business interests for one or multiple family members. Family office origins date back centuries, and a family enterprise is often at its inception.[19] It may provide various services such as tax, estate planning, accounting, investing, compliance, recordkeeping, IT, reporting, trust administration, financial planning, governance, and security.[20] A family office's mandate is not fixed and often evolves—requiring updating and strategic planning.

The wealth creator(s) often set(s) up a family office, and subsequent generations monitor and maintain it. A study estimates that there are 7,300 family offices globally, managing $5.9 trillion collectively, with 42 percent (3,100) in North America alone.[21] To justify the expense of operating a full-service SFO, most experts advise that a family should have a minimum of $250 million.[22] Some may set up an office for less but typically set up a virtual family office and outsource to third parties. Family offices are an entrepreneurial endeavor and require a stewardship ethos in the family.[23] Many times, they are often an extension of a family enterprise.[24] The following are four best practices when establishing and evolving a family office:

1. **Scope**: Assess the family's current state, wealth, and answer: Is there enough wealth to justify the expense? Do we need to build it or buy family office services from providers? Do we have to buy-in and support from the family to set up the office? What services should be offered now or in the future?

2. **Purpose**: Understand the goals, mission, and vision of the family office by answering the questions: Why do we want a family office? What are its goals? What is its mission, values, and vision?

3. **Strategic plan**: Craft a strategic plan for the family office. Devising both a business and a financial plan is critical to its success. Who will create and design the family office strategic plan? What services will the office perform? Which personnel are essential to be inside the family versus outsourced? What risk controls and measures will be taken for security, safekeeping, and protection of the family's assets and well-being? What is our contingency plan when/if certain things do not go as planned?

4. **Process**: Build process for the ongoing oversight, maintenance, and management of the family office. How will we document how the office operates? How will we formalize family governance protocols? How will we monitor the performance of both family office employees as well as the management of our wealth?

The following case study illustrates the setup, management, and evolution of a noteworthy family office.

Mathile Case Study

From a single-family office's inception, strategic planning is a critical function. The Mathiles' story begins fifty years ago, in 1970, when Clay Mathile accepted a leadership role at Iams Food Company, then a small pet food manufacturer. He became its sole owner and CEO by 1982. By 1999, Iams commanded a 5.7 percent share of the

U.S. pet food market and sold one hundred different products in seventy-five countries. Mathile then decided to sell the company to Procter & Gamble for $2.3 billion.

Operating company sales often trigger the setup of a family office. In the Mathiles' case, they created their family office in 1997 and did initial wealth planning. The first eighteen months after the sale was consumed with work that involved merely investing the sale proceeds. But then, the family office asked, "Who do we really want to be?" This sale signaled the start of outlining the vision and goals for the family office. They considered, what we wanted to do? Why were we there? Why did we exist? What were our services? The outcome was a full-service family office focused on the first generation.

Not long after creating the first strategic plan, the family office realized it was time to focus on two adult generations' needs and goals coming up the ranks. While encouraging the second-generation family members' voices, this strategic planning cycle improved family office efficiencies, risk management protocols, and scoping appropriate service levels to different generations. Currently, assets are dispersed across the generations, with half of the family's third-generation family members coming of age. The office now serves three generations with varying client services and needs. The fourth strategic planning cycle focused on developing a flexible wealth advisory platform, providing visibility about family office activities, and engaging the third generation.[25]

Summary

Family offices are set up and operated, having different mandates and purposes. Recognizing they are entrepreneurial endeavors, it is essential to (1) evaluate the services and operations rendered, (2) clarify its purpose, (3) craft a family office strategic plan, and (4) and adhere to a process to administer the office. Some key family office takeaways from the Mathile's case include: (1) action, (2) alignment, (3) fluidity and order, and (4) knowing that involving outside experts and facilitators is required when starting and managing change in a family office. Strategic planning is continuous and informed by new information triggering the need to reassess and seek alignment. The twenty-year-old Mathiles' family office is exemplary in its efforts to support strategic planning as a method to embrace change.

In conclusion, pathways to a family office are all unique, as shared in *The Complete Family Office Handbook*,[26] which provides expanded foundational reading. There is never a perfect time to start your family's office strategic planning. Identifying family office consultants during the inception, and the planning and evolution of a family office are keys to its ongoing success. More insights on family office setup and planning may be found in *Setting Up a Family Office*[27] and *Effective Family Office: Best Practices and Beyond*.[28]

Kirby Rosplock is the founder/CEO of Tamarind Learning, a wealth education firm, and Tamarind Partners, a family office consultancy named 2019 Best Family Office Consultancy and Best Family Wealth Counseling by the Family Wealth Report. Kirby is ranked among the 100 Family Enterprise Influencers by Family Capital (2020). Kirby was honored with the Family Wealth Alliance's Family Wealth Industry Thought Leadership award (2018) and FFI's Richard Beckhard Practice award (2018). Kirby is dean of Family Office at PPI, and a Fellow/Faculty of FFI's GEN Program. Kirby authored *The Complete Family Office Handbook* (first and second editions) and *The Complete Direct Investing Handbook*.

Dianne H. B. Welsh is the Hayes Distinguished Professor of Entrepreneurship and founding director of Entrepreneurship at the University of North Carolina Greensboro. Dianne has held three endowed chairs. A recognized scholar in family businesses, international entrepreneurship, women-owned businesses, and franchising, she is the author of seven books and over 150 publications. She is a Certified Family Business Advisor and fellow with the Family Firm Institute. She received the Barbara Hollander Award (lifelong contributions) from the Family Firm Institute and the Legacy Award (lifetime contributions) from the Global Consortium of Entrepreneurship Centers. Dianne is writing on the eighteenth-oldest family business in the world and serves on the Tamarind Learning Council.

Commentary by David Hewitt, Canada

The Hewitt Group and Hewitt Foundation were both established in 2017 following the sale of my family's Caterpillar machinery dealership based in Montreal, Canada. However, we do not use the term family office, because we feel that this term gives the impression of something that exists to serve the family's needs. Both my grandfather and father, however, operated with a philosophy of putting first a focus on responsibilities to community, business, and philanthropic endeavors, ahead of their personal interests. Hewitt Group was, therefore, established along similar principals, which is why my role as president is best described as a stewardship mandate, with responsibilities to internal and external stakeholders.

I would say the initial impulse for creating an office stemmed from the interest both my father and I had in continuing to invest in Eastern Canada, growing dynamic businesses, creating jobs and general economic development in a region where our family has prospered. It was also important to build the capabilities to manage the family's growing philanthropic activities.

1. **Reflecting: What do we want and what are we good at?**

    Spending the greater part of a year following the sale of our business to meet with other business families, we started identifying some of the broad types of investments that would be useful to us and ways we might organize ourselves to operate effectively. Through these extremely beneficial meetings we realized that in addition to direct investments in companies, we were also interested in making direct investments in real estate and that we would be wise to establish a diversified portfolio of investments through money managers. Other families also helped us think about what activities we would best do ourselves (where we had unique competence and interest) and which would require outside expertise (where we lacked competence or interest).

2. **Building: Which structures do we need? Where do we need external help?**

    In our case, we decided to build in-house capabilities to invest directly in companies in industries where we already have knowledge. We, nonetheless, connected with a veteran private equity investor who has helped us think more strategically as we look at potential acquisitions. For real estate investments, we had experience owning and managing an extensive portfolio of properties for our company and so believed that, with some work, we could become smart investors. We, therefore, took the direction to build an internal real estate team, while also collaborating with established investors/developers. For the third broad investment area—a diversified portfolio of money managers—we realized that, despite our interest, we did not have the skills and the time to build adequate internal capabilities. Therefore, we created an investment committee (IC) that included one outside professional. The IC then ran an extensive process to identify a research firm that had deep expertise and global awareness of money managers across asset classes. To maintain some control and to build knowledge so that we would have the option to insource this activity one day, we established a non-discretionary mandate with the selected firm, whereby our IC interviews all money managers before making final recommendations to our advisory board.

At the same time that we identified what we wanted to invest in, we spent a great deal of time in the first eighteen months designing the governance of our group. We wanted to ensure we could properly substantiate that the decisions taken by management were in the long-term interests of the group and aligned with our mission and vision. A few of the members from the advisory board at our operating company joined my father on the new advisory board of the Hewitt Group, overseeing the strategic direction and all major decisions. It is a very engaged board, and I am learning more and more how to draw value from it as we refine strategy, execute our plans, and evolve our capabilities.

Conclusion

So why set up a family office? For us it made sense because we as a family had certain enduring objectives that were specific to us, including being actively involved in growing our regional economy and being highly effective in our philanthropy. We recognized areas where we lacked expertise and needed outside help, but at the core we wanted to be driving the bus because we like to be active in things that are important to us and this was going to be the best way to actualize our unique mission and vision as a family.

Questions for Further Reflection ─────────────

- What vision and mission do you and your family have concerning your joint wealth (outside of the family business)?
- What are some of the reasons for family members to manage their wealth together vs. separately?

- What are the pros and cons of a family office versus other alternatives to organize the family's wealth management?
- If you are considering setting up a family office, where can you go, prior to starting the family office, to talk to experts and other families who have already done so?

Your Notes | Your Action Items ———————————————

4.5
Should We Engage in Philanthropy and/or in Impact Investing? If So, How Would We Get Started?

Response by Isabel C. Botero, U.S.

Individuals and organizations today are likely to use more than $500 billion in philanthropy and charitable giving every year.[29] Similarly, it is estimated that the impact investment market around the world also surpasses the $500 billion.[30] Many of these funds are provided by business families through their individual or family combined practices. However, there are no clear tools that help business families select which approach may be better for them as they start thinking about engaging with their community. With this in mind, I provide some ideas of how to approach this question, and how to get started with the choice you select.

Defining Philanthropy and Impact Investing

To be able to select between these two practices we first need to clearly understand what philanthropy is and how it differs from impact investing. In its broadest sense, philanthropy encompasses the voluntary donation of resources (i.e., time, money, effort, or knowledge) to support causes that are primarily intended to promote the betterment of society with no direct expectation of economic returns.'[31] On the other hand, impact investment describes the investments made into companies, organizations, and/or funds with the intention of addressing social and environmental challenges while pursuing financial returns.[32] Therefore, the difference in these two practices rests on the goals and expected returns that the business family has about their money.

Important Questions to Drive Decision-Making

To be able to select between these two practices, individuals in business families need to initially consider three questions. First, how do Next Gens want to work with their family? Is it as whole unit (i.e., the whole family)? Or is it in smaller units (e.g., group of siblings, group of cousins, or a smaller nuclear family)? Second, after determining who is working together, Next Gens need to consider what the family or family group wants to do. And what can the family do? It is important to understand what the goal of the group is, and what resources are available to achieve the goal. For example, a family may want to make a difference in the community. However, they may not have the money necessary to give or invest to achieve everything they want. Thus, the family may choose to volunteer as a way to help. In this case, they have chosen to engage in a form of philanthropy. However, when the family group has the capability of pulling sufficient financial resources together, they can move to the third set of questions. These include: What does the family/group expect in return? Does the business family expect change? Do they expect financial continuity? Do they expect both? If a family is interested primarily in helping others without any financial return, they may consider engaging in philanthropy. However, if the family is interested in helping others, creating a legacy, and maintaining their financial capability to help others in the future, they may want to consider impact investing.[33]

Additional Considerations

There are two additional factors that are important to highlight. First, the choice between philanthropy and impact investing may change over time. For example, it may be that a family firm that is in the early generations or that is going through a difficult time may not have the financial resources to engage in philanthropic giving or in impact investing. Thus, they may start by engaging in volunteer work as the way to fulfill their giving goal. However, after some time the family may start to have the financial resources to begin donating to a specific cause. They may move from volunteering to engaging in financial giving for a cause without any clear expectations of results. Later on, they may decide that as a group the family is interested in obtaining blended value (i.e., integrating financial, social, and environmental domains), thus they will move to impact investment as a way to obtain these benefits. In this sense, an important part to answering whether the family should use philanthropy or impact investing may be to explore when to engage in these practices, instead of focusing on which practice to follow. Second, families may also consider engaging in both approaches. Instead of focusing on an either-or approach, the focus may be on better capturing which types of goals may be fulfilled with one approach versus the other. By thinking this way, business families may find that they can approach a wider range of family goals using different approaches. For example, it may be that family members are interested in a diverse set of causes. The number of causes may be greater than the financial resources available to the group. Thus, the family can redefine their way of engaging with the community so that each of the causes are supported through either volunteering activities, financial support without clear expectations of return, and impact investing opportunities to both help the community and help the family increase their resources to help in the future.

Getting Started

How can the Next Gens get started in determining what to do? These are my suggestions for the first three steps to take:

1. Identify the goals for the family and for the Next Gens (i.e., What does the family/the Next Gens hope to achieve?).
2. Outline the different resources available to the family and the Next Gens (i.e., time, knowledge, financial resources).
3. Determine how the family and the Next Gens would like to work to achieve these goals:
   - Do the Next Gens want to involve all of the family or just some parts of the family?
   - Do the Next Gens and the family want to work with other families or by themselves?

These three steps can help the family and Next Gens develop a plan for engaging in philanthropy and or impact investing.

Isabel C. Botero, PhD, is the director of the Family Business Center and an associate professor of entrepreneurship at the University of Louisville. She is a fellow for the Family Firm Institute and has an Advanced Certificate in Family Wealth Advising. Her research focuses on strategic communication processes and next generation issues in family enterprises. She is an associate editor for the *Journal of Family Business Strategy*. She is a past FOBI Scholar and has over forty publications in journals such as *Family Business Review, Journal of Family Business Strategy, Journal of Family Business Management, Journal of Management Studies,* and *Management Communication Quarterly*.

Commentary by Nathalie Marcoux, Canada

I am the eldest of a G2 of three children. My father, Remi Marcoux, founded TC Transcontinental (TC) almost fifty years ago, a business that is now involved in printing and packaging in Canada, the U.S., and Central and South America. Two family members work in the business and four sit on the board of the publicly listed company. I am in charge of our family office. TC is an important corporate donor. My sister, Isabelle Marcoux, the chair of TC, oversees the donations made through the company. She is also involved in soliciting donations to Centraide—a large not-for-profit organization involved in building communities in Quebec and across Canada. She put in place programs to solicit our employees to donate and opened her network to solicit major donors from outside TC. It is one way that we give back to the community—a priority since community is one of our core family values.

Our Philanthropy

Ten years ago, we asked ourselves if we should create a foundation to bundle our philanthropic efforts. As we already made many decisions together in the business, we decided to be active in philanthropy on a more individual manner. Therefore, we also voted that every member of the shareholders' circle receives an annual philanthropic budget that is taken from our family investment assets. Everyone is free to use their philanthropic budget to support those causes that are dear to their heart. For example, my sister-in-law, Caroline Bougie, is involved as chair of a Social Development Investment Committee for Centraide. Other members of my family are involved at different levels of other not-for-profit organizations. However, where our areas of interest intersect, we do engage together in philanthropy. For instance, our family made a major donation to the business school of the University of Montreal, the HEC (École des hautes études commerciales), for the school to create a program that incubates start-ups and helps young entre-preneurs develop their entrepreneurial abilities. For my father, it was important to contribute to the growth of our economy by help-ing new businesses emerge, like he did fifty years ago. As it was a major donation that was beyond our annual allocated amount, my father discussed it with my mother, my brother, my sister, and me. He wanted our buy-in even if, ultimately, he was the one making the decision. As the representative of my family, I was very much involved in the start-up of the program. We were creating a start-up to help start-ups! Now that the program is in its eighth year, I am involved in the selection of our cohorts, in the mentoring of entre-preneurs, and in opening my network of business people to them. It has been a rewarding experience to help these young entrepreneurs develop and grow their businesses, to see the ideas that they have, and the way they see the world of today. And most of them are quite successful.

Our Lessons Learned

I think the most important thing when being involved in philan-thropy is to identify the area that interests you (e.g., education, health, or environment). Next, you need to find a group of people you like to do philanthropy with, whether they are family members or outsiders. In our case, some activities are individual efforts while others are family-based and run through TC. What matters is that when you pursue philanthropy, you need to share the vision of how you can make a difference. For me, for example, it is important to have fun while engaging in philanthropy and to learn and grow. Like my mom, Carmelle, used to say when she did community work, "I end up receiving a lot more than I give!" Finally, we realized that it is important to be invested in philanthropy in ways that go beyond our financial means (e.g., by assuming board or committee posi-tions, by setting up programs in person, and by opening up our social network to make a larger difference).

Impact Investing

About impact investing, we are beginning in the family office to educate ourselves. We need to determine what the values we want to express are and through which vehicles. And we will do it like we usually do when starting in a new field, by taking small steps and allocating a predetermined percentage of our assets and learning throughout the process. And hopefully, creating meaning and having fun along the way!

Questions for Further Reflection

- What are your reasons for investing with your family members in philanthropy or impact investment?
- As a Next Gen, do you have to join your parents/aunts/uncles/siblings in investment projects? What would happen if you decided not to do so?
- When you look at the world, is there something you are passionate about and believe that it could be changed for the better? In what ways could this passion give you a direction for your philanthropic initiatives and/or impact investing?
- How much time have you spent engaging in a passion project that is dear to you?

Your Notes | Your Action Items

Your Notes | *Your Action Items* ——————————————

4.6
If We (the Next Generation) Want to Sell the Family Business, How Do We Start this Process?

Response by Heinrich Liechtenstein, Spain, and Tarek el Sehity, Austria

The intention to sell the family business decreases with each generation of family ownership: about 30 percent of business families intend to sell their family business in its first generation against 14 percent in the second and less than 10 percent in the generations beyond.[34] But how do those who want to sell the business go about it? To answer this question, we need to distinguish the intentions for selling. Before we do that, let us define two important terms: The shared family purpose is family members' shared intention to dedicate family resources to a greater cause transcending the immediate family interests. A dialogical process is a discourse whereby the listener adopts the words of the speaker with the aim of grasping their validity, avoid misunderstandings, and promote a reflective process.

Begin with the End in Mind[35]
Markets change rapidly, so that not becoming too attached to one business may be wise. Selling a family business brings about multifaceted challenges because it is not just about the sale of a business by individuals but by members of the family collective. Consequently, the stakes are not just financial, but social and even more so psychological. A two-stage process needs to be thoroughly considered. First, all the involved family members gain a clear understanding of why the family needs to sell its business. The sale should

be recognized as the unique opportunity it is to understand and experience what the family stands for beyond its common financial interests, and even more so, beyond its affective bonds. Also, we argue for a better understanding of the why of selling. Once this understanding is accomplished, the second stage is the necessary know-how of the first-time seller needs to be endowed with the skills and insights required to deal with highly experienced veteran buyers in the market. We start with three interpretations typical to family business sales in the hope of demonstrating the immense value of a holistic mindset.

The shareholder mindset: "We want to sell the family business out of a financial opportunity" (maybe: the once-in-a-lifetime-offer).

Family businesses sold for financial opportunity only do not provide a conclusive reason for the sale. Financial means are a means to as many goals as there are family members and tend to inflate individual goals to a level that renders shared family intentions and compromises unlikely. On the other hand, dysfunctional family situations (often caused by a lack of communication skills) may render it impossible to consider common goals so that separating through the sale of the business may be for the best of all concerned parties, including the business itself.

The stakeholder mindset: "We sell the family business to better adapt to family members' preferences and needs."

Family collectives are prone to having overly protective attitudes. Suppose a family business does not fit or suit the interests and capabilities of the Next Gens. In that case, the family may decide to sell the company (rather than bringing in professional management) and buy a business more suited to the Next Gens' interest. Business families with such a family stakeholder perspective are characterized by nepotism, which becomes unsustainable in the long run given the family system's growing complexity. If well-advised by professionals, the sale of a family business with such a perspective leads to establishing a family office managing the family wealth which allows family members to invest in businesses they feel more enthusiastic about.

The holistic mindset: "We sell the family business to align our family resources and activities to our purpose."

This third perspective unites the family behind a joint commitment that reaches beyond the family members' immediate interests. The family will sell its business whenever the business does not fit the family's shared purpose even if its members are emotionally invested. At the same time, the family may recognize that selling the business may be a way of securing the business's survival, although without its control. However, and different from the two prior perspectives, the resources generated will be reinvested in alignment with their purpose. As a consequence, responsibilities and leadership in the family are fully shared by the family members in a we-the-family spirit. Further, even significant family conflicts may be overcome due to the inherent value of the purpose such families share.

Roadmap to sale: Identify and develop with the help of experienced advisors the mindsets from which the sales of a family business may be intended

Consider trained facilitators to foster open dialogue and discussions removing disputes among family members. Embark on a dialogical journey to create and define one shared or multiple aligned purpose. Use the potential of sale of the family business to inquire about what it is that unites and matters to the family and fosters empathy among its members both *now* and *after* the potential sale.

Avoid accessing the potential money before you have sorted out your purpose—be it a personal or a shared family purpose.

"There is no favorable wind for the sailor who doesn't know where to go." — Seneca

The decision to sell your family business may often be a reasonable business decision. However, there is much more than business to a family business. We have emphasized the role of unique family perspectives motivating such sales and believe that the key to such important processes lies in the thorough understanding of what drives the question to sell.[36] Once the *why* of the decisions is clarified, we warmly advise reading about the *how* of selling strategies for family businesses in Jonathan Pellegrini's (2017) excellent book on the question.[37]

Heinrich Liechtenstein received an MBA from IESE Business School and a doctoral degree in business and economic sciences from the University of Vienna. He works as a professor of financial management at the IESE Business School in Barcelona, Spain. He is active in several supervisory and advisory boards of family holdings or foundations and of one private equity firm. Prof. Liechtenstein worked in wealth management and family owner strategy development. He also worked for the Boston Consulting Group and has founded and sold two companies.

Dr. Tarek el Sehity is a researcher and lecturer at the Sigmund Freud University in Vienna. He studied psychology at the Universities René Descartes Paris, Private Universität in the principality of Liechtenstein, Università La Sapienza in Rome, and obtained his PhD at the University of Vienna. His latest works concentrate on the role of shared purpose in business families as well as the psychological significance of philanthropy for donors.

Commentary by Simon Ebert and Jessica Ebert, Germany

In 2003, when we were Next Gens of a business family, the antecedent generation sold our family business. Wella AG was a fifth-generation family business, founded in 1880 by our great-great-grandfather Franz Ströher. At the end there were four family tribes with eleven core families altogether. What started as a hairdresser business later became an international hair and cosmetic enterprise.

Regarding Wella AG: During the sale process we were young Next Gens and watched the sale of the antecedent generation inactively. With reference to Heinrich Liechtenstein's and Tarek el Sehity's *why* and *how* dimensions of selling a family business, we are sure that there was no shared *why* in the group of family owners. There were different owner mindsets, ranging from the pure stakeholder mindset to the shareholder mindset. Next, the *how* was complex, costly, and time consuming, but with the help of experienced consultants and lawyers, the sale succeeded. After the sale to a U.S. company, our parents founded a family office to invest in diverse assets. Because selling a family business is not only selling business but also losing a part of family identity, we tried to build up new ventures not only to invest but to regain business family identity.

Air Hamburg Luftverkehrsgesellschaft was one of these new investments. The company is based in Hamburg, Germany, and was founded in 2006 by two friends. In 2012, our family stepped in to support firm growth and management. Almost ten years after we started to invest into the company, Air Hamburg is one of the biggest business jet operators in Europe with more than 500 employees and operating a fleet of currently forty-two aircraft. In 2020, the turnover was 185 million Euros. Our goal is to constantly grow the fleet by six to eight aircrafts per year now. Our family holds a 50 percent share of Air Hamburg. We have been active in the management since we started to invest into the company, with one of the managing directors being part of our family office. Besides this, we, as a family, are fully involved in the business, especially when it comes to aircraft and aircraft owner acquisitions.

Moreover, we see no need to sell the business at this time. We have been approached by competitors numerous times but have always turned them down immediately. We are in our mid- forties with young kids and are eager to grow the business in the upcoming years. However, we are all aligned with the idea that if one shareholder wants to step out, we all have to and will pull in the same direction to find a solution. There could be different scenarios on how to resolve such a situation. Selling the company as a whole, selling parts of the company to a financial investor, or merging with another company. However, whatever the potential outcomes, the discussion about whether to sell all or a part of the family business should always start with the family owners.

Having experienced that our antecedent generation lacked the shared or aligned *whys* when selling the family business, we recognize the immense value of a holistic mindset in the process of selling a family business as described by Liechtenstein and Sehity. We would, therefore, invest in the dialogue between all family members to ensure that we make important decisions together. In fact, we are already working on this with regular off-site meetings to keep up with each other and ensure that we all share in the same vision.

Questions for Further Reflection

- How does the family business help or hinder your family members' ability to get along?
- Are you and all of your family members engaged and passionate about your family business? Why or why not?
- If you are constantly fighting with your siblings, or other family members, would leaving the family business be a possible route

to re-establish a better relationship with them, or would you break off all ties?

- Is your business model well-positioned for the future, or would it make sense to sell the family business and re-invest the proceeds in a field with a brighter future that you are passionate about?

Your Notes | *Your Action Items* ———————————

4.7
I Am Not Sure My Personal Values Align with Those of Other Family Owners. How Can I Exit the Family Business (or Family Office) Gracefully?

Response by Maximilian A. Werkmüller, Germany

The DNA of Family Businesses

Family-owned businesses are a sustainable pillar of a stable economy. As family-owned businesses accrue the experiences in family business entrepreneurship and entrepreneurial responsibility since the generation of their founders, they focus on quality and high-level client satisfaction and define respective global standards. Business successes overarching several generations are based on strong and sustainable (ethical) values and require strong rules, attributed to these values, which serve as the family's "DNA."[38] Basically these values apply to each family member without exemption, including spouses. The desire of a family member to exit the business will hit the overwhelming majority of families as unexpected and meet them unprepared for such a crisis.[39]

The Toxic Impact of Disputes and Emotions

In many cases the motivation for leaving arises from a family dispute and its poor outcomes. Resignation after a lost battle with other family members may turn into the wish for leaving, especially if the dispute is about the compliance with the family's rules and values.[40] Disputes between family members or family branches are not an exception.[41] Without referring to specific data one must assume that at least every second family has to administer a family member's withdrawal from the business and—even worse—maybe even its exit from the family and their rules. The question implied in this chapter—How can I exit the family business gracefully?—deserves particular attention due to so many cases going horribly wrong.

Thorough Preparation Is Key

If a family member intends to withdraw from the family business, a thorough evaluation of the agenda for the leave is mandatory. Undoubtedly, there were and still are situations where an exit is the only possible way to solve a major dispute and lead a wounded family member into resilience. On the other hand, the loss of a family member always entails the danger that other family members feel blamed and publicly disgraced. For that reason, the preparation for the leave must start with a thorough signal in advance to the right person.

Appoint a Scout

Withdrawal from the family's institutions requires strong and thorough support by a person within or around the family who is trustworthy and regarded as accountable by the family member who wants to leave and all other family members. This person may be an elderly family member or a retired former external advisor. This person should be addressed first by the potential leaver and should comprehensively understand their motivation. This trusted family member acts as trusted advisor for the family member who wants to leave (the leaver). The advisor's job is to form a secure base for the family member who is leaving.[42] On the one hand, the advisor will help to forward the message to the others and negotiate the leaver's exit package, if applicable. On the other hand, the advisor operates as a sounding board and assures appropriate communication in all directions. The latter is of major importance as a wrongfully operated communication may trigger severely negative emotions which may lead, in turn, to an inappropriate and disappointing result.

Elaborate Your Agenda and Ensure Appropriate Documentation of Agreements

In order to ensure appropriate processing, the agreement should be documented and followed by a legal framework which covers all legal aspects of the intended leave. There is no leave without legal aspects. If a leave attracts public attention, a thorough preparation and the execution of the agenda is even more important. Confidentiality until the end is key.

Tell a "Good Story"

Whatever the reason for the leave is—the story being told to family members and the public must be positive. A prominent example of an exit which was not performed well is the example of the Duke and the Duchess of Sussex, Harry and Meghan, leaving the royal family. Without any doubt this exit was public. Apparently, things were not thoroughly prepared. Shortly after the couple left the country, members of the royal family allegedly started to complain to the media about the way the exit was executed. This turns to be the worst thing that could happen as negative headlines cause damage to both parties, to the leavers and to the rest of the family. However, even if no member of the royalty applies, such cases may even end at court. In order to avoid such public failure, the story being told needs to enable other family members to align with the leaver's motivation. The scout has a major function in that respect.

Keep the Door Open

If you think about leaving the family's business as a project, you should also prepare for the possibility that you could change your mind and remain in the family business. Whatever the reason may have been, the door shall never be slammed and completely locked.

The way a family member performs his leave will give direction to the question of whether restitution is possible. So, the leaver should act prudently, exit gently, and still keep "a key in his pocket." This key may be invisible from a legal perspective and not be consented to in written. If all these steps are taken, the mission can be successfully accomplished. After leaving, a peaceful coexistence should be the goal for all parties involved.

Conclusion

Withdrawal from a family business and from a family's governance is not unusual. The stronger a family governance limits family members regarding pursuing their own interests or lives the more likely it is that single family members will quit with the family's institutions and history. Three important steps to leaving include the following:

1. Appoint a trustworthy scout and elaborate your project agenda.
2. Grant confidentiality, perform your agenda, and negotiate the issues step by step.
3. Conclude with your family on a level which enables you to "keep a key" in your pocket.

Maximilian A. Werkmüller is an associated professor for economics, finance and family office management at Allensbach University in Konstanz, Germany. He pursued his legal education at the universities of Trier, Bonn, and Münster before passing Germany's second legal bar exam in 1998. He then started his career at HSBC Germany as a specialist for estate planning until he was asked to become responsible for an international family's German single-family office in 2011. Since 2019, he has had his own legal consulting business in Düsseldorf and established a second one in Zurich.

In 2020 he joined a family business consulting firm as an associated partner.

Commentary by Peder and Felix Bonnier, Sweden

We are seventh-generation members of a Swedish-based family business bearing our last name, the Bonnier Group. Bonnier was started in 1804 as a publisher and book retailer and in over 200 years has evolved to a diversified northern European media and publishing conglomerate as well as a real estate company. We are still fully private, with the significant majority of our operations fully owned and controlled, and with ownership spread out across more than one hundred owners who in turn are spread out all over the world. A small minority of the family is involved operationally in parts of the business, but around twenty of us have board seats, seats on our family council, or act as governing owners in other capacities within our corporate structure. The majority of our owners take a more passive role and pursue a wide variety of professional careers outside of the family enterprise.

With so many owners, in such differing capacities, it is only natural that preferences vary. Some shareholders may have a dramatically higher appetite for risk and as a result seek higher returns on their capital than what the family business offers. Some may need capital to pursue businesses on their own or to finance lifestyle choices. And some may feel that, as the question posits, their values are drifting apart from those of the family business at large. We have been lucky enough not to see a lot of this divergence of preference and values, in part due to a constantly active and evolving organized discussion around our common values, not the least through our ownership directive and shared value statement. Even so, we believe that it is essential for a business of our scope to give members of the family the opportunity to exit the business in an unstigmatized way. We do this through allowing transactions between family members, as well as allowing family members to offer their shares in a buy-back scheme, where the business simply buys back and cancels their shares at a predetermined, but dynamic price.

The caveat is that a family member wishing to participate in the buy-back scheme has to sell all of her or his equity. Thus, in order to get liquidity, a shareholder has to leave the ownership collective in full. The glue that ties us together are our common values, the sense of identity that is closely linked to the business and our history, as well as the pride and community that the family business provides. Selling your shares does in no way mean leaving the family, but it does mean leaving a large proportion of the common activities and community that we share. It also comes with a pricing mechanism that yields a significant liquidity discount to the implicit market value of the shares.

These two factors—the sense of identity that comes with being a family owner, and the liquidity discount on the share price—put together have led to minimal transactions in the last twenty years, though there have been a few. But if one should wish to leave, the idea is that that there is a structured method for how to do it, and that the terms and conditions that apply are determined fairly and beforehand. For us this has been instrumental in reducing the sense of "lock-in" and the issues that may arise from that, issues we believe could easily have occurred if such methods were missing.

Questions for Further Reflection

- On a scale from 0 (not at all) to 10 (very much), how much do you want to get out of your family's business? And what emotional and financial price are you prepared to pay for it?

- Who in your family will be most hurt when you leave? And which story could you tell to help this person and others to better cope with your decision?
- How can you phrase your wish to leave in a way that is not insulting to anyone in the family (even if you feel tempted to tell them everything) and would allow the family not to "lose face"?
- Who has the trust of the most powerful coalition in the family and, at the same time, your trust so that you could ask this person to act as a guide throughout this process?

Your Notes | *Your Action Items* ———————————

4.8
I Want to Start My Own Business. Can I Ask Our Firm or Family for Help?

Response by Denise Fletcher, Luxembourg

It is often said that the entrepreneurs of today are the family businesses of tomorrow. This assertion is supported by findings in a Global Entrepreneurship Monitor (2019–2020) Report on Family Entrepreneurship that cites that 75 percent of respondent entrepreneurs across forty-eight economies indicate that their family was actively involved in either starting or developing a new business.[43] In spite of this, and the fact that it is becoming more popular for family firms to encourage entrepreneurialism within the younger generation, it is often challenging for Next Gens to carve out an entrepreneurial identity for themselves. This is even more so the case if the intention is to pursue new ideas that are not central to the core business and which might disturb long-planned succession strategies or expectations held by senior family members. Making the decision to get on board the entrepreneur(ship) is an important career decision that has huge implications not only for the Next Gens who are planning this, but also for current members of the family business who might have to adjust their expectations.

Can I Ask Our Firm or Family for Help?

To answer this question, it is important to acknowledge that although there are prominent images about how entrepreneurs operate as lone heroes single-mindedly heading off into the marketplace, finding success in an early-stage venture is very much dependent on having the right team and resources in place. Despite popular conceptions, it can be difficult for new start-up ventures, even if they have a good idea, to find financing, develop a prototype, build a team, and evaluate the range of market opportunities. This is especially the case if the business is disruptive in its business model or technology. Here then, the stakes are high, market information is uncertain, access to information and market research is not evenly distributed, and feedback from customers is unreliable.

If the Next Gen is fortunate enough to have access to a rich pool of knowledge, resources, and competences (whether financial, social, relational, or emotional), this can only be of benefit as the venture gets off the ground. These resources, and the social capital they generate, will help to build the chunks of learning (i.e., concepts, experiences, and practices, including failure) that are essential. This is especially true as the Next Gen perfects their competencies and leadership, first as an entrepreneur and hopefully, later as a future family business leader.

The answer to the question: "Can I ask our firm for family for help as I start my own business?" is an unequivocal "yes." What is more complex, however, is the context that has given rise to the decision to launch a new business? It is possible to imagine three scenarios that could be driving the motivation to start a new venture—motivations which are possibly more emotionally motivated and related to issue of self-identity. These scenarios are typical of the situations that young family members find themselves in early in their career, but each has different implications for how the approach to the family business should be made.

Scenario 1: Under the umbrella.

Here, the Next Gen already works within the family firm but is dissatisfied with their role and work. They see opportunities to break away from the main business to do their own thing. However, their preference is to work in a related industry which in some way extends or complements the core economic activity of the family's business. In this scenario, the new venturing activities would come under the umbrella of the parent business as a related legal entity in which the parent company invests, but the new venture is given the freedom to explore new markets. In this scenario, given that the goal is to achieve more freedom and space for the Next Gen to grow, they would retain leadership, independence of decision-making, and emotional responsibility for the venture. In this scenario, however, the ultimate goal would be to contribute to the regenerative capabilities of the success of the parent company,[44] either by prospecting for a new line of business or mentoring a future heir/successor.

Scenario 2: Cutting loose.

The Next Gen already works within the family firm but is not motivated by their role and work, leading to the decision to start their own business in a topic or industry that is closer to their (rather than their family's) heart. For some time, this member has tried to communicate to the family owners about the need for the company to be more intrapreneurial[45] and they have struggled with the management and leadership styles dominating the company. In spite of this, they are continually thwarted when trying to demonstrate creativity and innovation. For this reason, it is likely that the would-be entrepreneur might be unwilling to ask the family business for support. It would be sensible, however, not to break all ties with the family and, instead, to stay in touch with the family business not as investors or full partners, but as a useful resource. As a useful resource, Next Gens can help try out new ideas in the family business and provide mentoring, business knowledge, introductions, and invaluable social capital.

Scenario 3: Buying in with new talent.

The Next Gen does not currently work within the family firm, but the wider family is associated with a business and there is an opportunity to approach the business for knowledge, mentors, resources, or possible investment. In pitching the new business idea to the parent business, it would be important to stress how the new venture could bring future financial returns, new markets to exploit, as well as fresh talents and experiences that would be useful for the future of the parent company. The member could emphasize how their venture would ensure a future supply of entrepreneurial talents.[46] It would also be important to gain the buy-in of one or two senior figures in the family who could champion the business case to skeptical members.

Conclusion

Reflecting on these scenarios will encourage a probing of (1) the motivations for becoming an entrepreneur and (2) the current state of relations with the family business. Reflections about one's entrepreneurial intentions center on preferences for independence, autonomy, and achievement outside of the dominant family group. Reflections on relationships with the dominant family group depend on whether the relations are generally good and there is a future succession expectation, or whether relations have become so strained that the only way forward is to break away to pursue different interests. Either way, to make a new venture as successful as possible, it is essential to be clear on the motivations driving the new venture and to be open to feedback. Remember that family businesses need entrepreneurs and their talents because that is the only way they can secure tomorrow!

Denise Fletcher is professor of entrepreneurship and innovation at the University of Luxembourg. Her principal research interests include entrepreneurship and family business, especially theories and methodologies that enable detailed process-minded understandings of how entrepreneurs of family business owners design social structures, discourses, and artifacts to mediate the problems they encounter as they engage in purposive market or value creating ventures. Dr. Fletcher has published widely in the small business and entrepreneurship journals. She is editor of the monograph "Understanding the Small Family Business," London: Routledge, and senior editor for *Organization Studies*.

Commentary by Charles Wates, United Kingdom

I am a fourth-generation governing owner of Wates Group and founder and managing director of Needspace? Limited—a wholly owned subsidiary of the Wates Group.

The Wates Group, established in 1897, is one of the leading privately owned construction, development, and property services businesses in the UK. We employ approximately 4,000 people and together, we inspire better ways of creating the places, communities, and businesses of tomorrow. The third generation of ownership oversaw a process through which family members stepped back from executive roles and moved towards a model of engaged ownership. The fourth-generation owners are closely involved in the company, all adding value in different ways according to their unique and complementary interests and skills.

Needspace? Limited was founded in 2006 and provides quality managed workspace to the growing number of small businesses in Greater London and the South East. We offer a range of office, workshop, and studio units on flexible licence arrangements to small businesses looking to grow in an entrepreneurial environment.

For four generations, the Wates Family has encouraged family entrepreneurship broadly aligned to the property and construction sectors. Examples include Wates City of London, a publicly listed office developer, Pinnacle, a leisure complex operator and developer, Gambado, a children's play center operator, and Myriad, a renewable energy installation and service contractor. The family has picked up several key learnings from our entrepreneurial pursuits.

Family Entrepreneurialism

The core of our family enterprise is construction and development, reflected in the Wates Group. Family entrepreneurialism is seen as a non-core but an important part of keeping the entrepreneurial flame alive. This is especially relevant in the fourth generation as the day-to-day management of the Wates Group is handled by nonfamily executives, allowing the family members the freedom to explore opportunities. Our preference is to support entrepreneurialism outside of the group so it does not become a distraction for group executives; accordingly, these entrepreneurial activities report directly to the family office.

Our preference is to seed fund family entrepreneurs through co-investment by other family members. Each business should have its own governance structure, and our expectation is that the director of the family office be on the board. We believe that it is important for the family entrepreneur to have skin in the game through personal investment, and ideally the family would wish to have a majority shareholding in the venture (51 percent).

Given the change in role of family members from owner-managers to governing owners, family entrepreneurialism has become an important activity for family members alongside the governance of the Group. In addition, we have been able to use third-party capital either through funds or co-investment to leverage and grow the ventures. Some of the learnings from these professional investors have also been useful in driving greater performance from the Group.

Challenges and Conclusion

Given the reputation of the core business and its robust policies, procedures, and governance, there is a real temptation to smother small business dynamism in a large business bureaucracy in order to try to de-risk the investment. The trouble with this is that it dampens the entrepreneurial flame and removes entrepreneurial agility. I was asked to comment on the question: "I want to start my own business. Can I ask my family for help?" In short, my answer to this is a resounding "yes." The family is a great resource of knowledge and business experience. A well-run family office can be a good source of seed capital, knowledge, and useful support to help you build a business. It can help you to turn an inspired business idea into a fabulous and sustainable business.

Questions for Further Reflection ———————————

- If you did not have a family business background, what steps would you have to take to ask your family for financing for your start-up?
- If you ask your family for financial investment in your start-up and it goes bust, what would be the worst possible consequences? What could you do to prevent them?
- If you ask your family to become co-investors of your start-up, which would make them co-owners? If it is highly successful, what could be some conflicts down the road? How could you prevent them in the first place?
- Are there any non-financial resources like networks, advice, or access to experts that your family could offer you? What could be an upside and/or a downside of asking for them?

Your Notes | *Your Action Items* ———————————————

4.9
I Will Leave the Family Business Behind, Which Other (Career) Path Should I Pursue in My Life?

Response by Mattias Nordqvist, Sweden

The Need for a New Career Path

Growing up in a family that owns a business is often seen as a privilege. The meaning of this privilege tends to be associated with opportunity, security, and community. Opportunity because growing up in a business family means to have access to a job and to learn how to run a business. Security because the link to a family business many times means access to financial wealth. Community because the family business connection offers access to a variety of internal and external networks. While growing up in a family that owns a business certainly can be a privilege for some, it is not a privilege for all.

Many are those who have suffered from what they perceived as an expectation, or even obligation, to take over the family business regardless of whether they wanted to do it or not. Opportunity is then replaced with contretemps. Security is replaced with constraints. Community is replaced with restriction. Here, growing up in a family business is not a privilege; it is a burden. Regardless of whether a Next Gen of a business family sees the link to a family business as a privilege or as a burden, there might be a day when they leave the family business behind. For instance, according to the 2019 US Family Business Survey published by the professional service firm PricewaterhouseCoopers, 62 percent of family business owners expect their Next Gens to gain outside work experience. Leaving the family business might be an independent choice, or triggered by the choice of others to, for instance, sell the family business or close the business. Whether voluntary or non-voluntary, a Next Gen's exit from business will create a need to pursue a new path in your life.

What Should the New Career Path Be?

It is difficult to find a simple answer to this question. The career path that suits one former family business member might not fit another. There are probably as many possible career paths as there are people who leave their family business behind. My belief, however, is that it is possible to address this question with a general attitude. An attitude towards life in general and towards the new career path in particular. I suggest that this attitude builds on two essential ingredients: *courage* and *purpose.*

Whatever path to pursue after leaving the family business behind, pursue it with courage. The narrator of South African Nobel Laureate J.M. Coetzee's novel *Youth* is a young student who is plotting his exit—not from a family business—but from his native country of South Africa. He seeks to pursue a new path, outside the familiar and outside the customary. Once embarked on his new path—a life as computer programmer in London—he eventually finds himself constrained by his lack of courage to make the most out of his new path. He does not dare to act on the opportunities that he is confronted with, mostly because of a fear of failure. Reflecting in the novel's wonderful ending, the young man assigns his perceived misery and bitterness to exactly this lack of courage to act and fear of failure. With envy, he compares his disappointing life with those who dare, and those who are not afraid of failure, and if they fail, they have courage to try again—until they succeed at whatever path they are pursuing. "What more is required than a kind of stupid, insensitive doggedness, as lover, as writer, together with a readiness to fail and fail again" (Coetzee, 2002:167), the narrator concludes.[47]

If a courage to act, and a courage to fail, is the first essential ingredient of the attitude needed after leaving the family business behind and pursuing a new path. Purpose is the second. Purpose in the context of a new career path to pursue in life is less about *what* one does, and more about *why* one does it. Whatever the choice of career or enterprise after leaving the family business behind, it is important to make sure to do something that one cares about, something that has a personal meaning. Remember that we only have one life. It is more likely that we find purpose and meaning in a new path if we pursue an activity or a career path that is in line with our values—that is, what is important to us personally. It is also more likely to find purpose and meaning in a new career path if pursuing an activity or a career path that is meaningful and has a purpose for other people as well.

For some Next Gens leaving the business behind and finding an activity and career that is in line with personal values, that offers meaning and a purpose in life, entails building further on the family's entrepreneurial legacy, and starting new businesses. For others it means leaving the business as the principal realm of activity behind altogether, and to pursue a path in the social and philanthropic realm, building a new legacy that focuses mainly on the social rather than the economic.

Creating a Career Path that Becomes a Privilege

Circling back to the question asked in the title of this chapter, there is an answer that is simple. Whatever path one decides to choose, and regardless of whether it is mainly with the aim to build economic value, or mainly with the aim to build social value, or a combination of the two, act with courage and act with purpose. Then the next career path pursued in life will not be a burden. It will be a privilege.[48]

Mattias Nordqvist is professor of business administration with a focus on entrepreneurship at the House of Innovation, Stockholm School of Economics, Sweden. He is also affiliated with Jönköping International Business School and its Center for Family Entrepreneurship and Ownership. His research focuses on entrepreneurship, strategy, and ownership/governance in different types of family firms and other firms. He has published widely in these areas and was a founding associate editor of the *Journal of Family Business Strategy*. He is an associate editor of *Family Business Review*. Mattias is also active as keynote speaker, guest lecturer, advisor, and coach to business leaders.

Commentary by Abdullah Adib AlZamil, Bahrain

In 1920, my grandfather Abdullah Hamad AlZamil (died in 1961) started his trading and real estate business in Bahrain, the country he moved to from his hometown of Onaizah in central Saudi Arabia. Zamil Group was transformed in the 1970s into a predominantly industrial conglomerate with global presence and had since been headquartered in Khobar, Saudi Arabia. I am one of over eighty members of my family's third generation and I run the Zamil Private office, our single-family office responsible for investing family members' wealth outside of Zamil Group.

At the risk of repeating what you have just read in Prof. Nordqvist's response to the question of leaving the family business behind, I want to focus my commentary on the angles of *privilege* and *attitude* upon which he built his response. Indeed, being born into a business family often provides job opportunities, the security of wealth, and the protection and belonging that come with the family's status in its community. However, you could also inherit the weight of the legacy of the founder and the leaders that came after. Narratives that are so useful to encourage and build pride and brand could turn into unrealistic expectations, and a rigid frame within which individualism seldom finds room to express itself. One could feel trapped in a gilded cage. Attitude is obviously key in addressing such mental challenges, to continuously have the *courage* to try different roles—economic or otherwise, and to do it with a clear sense of *purpose*. And if I may, I would like to add a third ingredient to Prof. Nordqvist's *attitude*, and that is *self-worth*.

Growing up in a family business environment could lead the person to define their self-worth only through the narrow lens of their role within that business. If all of a sudden that role disappears, an existential crisis could settle in its place. One could worry about public perception of the circumstances surrounding their leaving the business: "What would people say?" The person may also feel limited in their experience to the narrow nature of the business, or of the loss of income, perks or even work flexibility. However, there are times when leaving the family business and branching out is the right decision to make, for the person, the business or perhaps both.

One of my younger cousins excelled in finance beyond the learning and challenges that his role within the family business provided him with and decided to move to a job at an investment bank. In his view, he will be able to pursue his passion—the thing he knows how to do best in an environment that will provide him growth and satisfaction. However, his is a story of an ambitious young person seeking career fulfilment, and that's not always the case.

At times a family may feel the need to terminate the employment of one or more family members due to incompetence, redundancy, or behavioural issues and this will always be an awkward and tricky process. Leaders within the family have to be acutely aware of the impact this will have on the life of the member leaving the business as well as the relationships within the family overall. There's a lot more at stake here than in the case of terminating the employment of someone with no family links. Having governance bodies, such as a family council, can help manage the termination process in a way that addresses the sensitivity of the situation and provides resources to the departing family member in their new endeavours. It could also maintain the link to the business and benefit the family from a wider range of knowledge expertise of those family members outside the business while continuing to provide them with the benefits of belonging as previously discussed. When family members know they will be supported if they leave the family business, then leaving will be much less of a thorny subject. Such support could be in helping find them more suitable employment, helping provide or source funding for new projects, allowing access to business development, research resources, and so on. It won't feel as if they were cut off, but rather helped to move on. Therefore, the bond between the exiting family members and the family, instead of being damaged or even cut, will be preserved. And if these family members find their calling in these new projects, their personal bonds with the family as well as their individual self-worth will be strengthened. This could be the *individual's* time to shine, an opportunity for them to pursue purposes close to their heart, be it in business, philanthropy, arts, or academia. The fulfilment derived from pursuing those passions will likely replace any separation anxiety caused by leaving the family business.

Questions for Further Reflection

- What are you passionate about? What are you good at?
- When you lose track of time, what is it that you are doing in these moments?

- Where would you want to be in ten years from now? How do you see yourself living your life? And what role does your family play in your vision?
- How do you want others to remember you, and for what?

Your Notes | Your Action Items ————————————

Endnotes: Part 4

1. *The Economist*, Dec 15th 2018: "Super-help for the super-rich—Family offices become financial titans https://www.economist.com/briefing/2018/12/15/family-offices-become-financial-titans.

4.1 Do I Have the Freedom to Leave the Family Business (Entirely) Behind and Do Something Else?

2. Thomas Zellweger, Phillip Sieger and Marnix Van Rij, "Coming Home or Breaking Free? A Closer Look at the Succession Intentions of Next-Generation Family Business Members," *Family Business Center of Excellence* (St Gallen: Ernst & Young, 2017).

3. Thomas Zellweger, "Succession in the Family Business," in *Managing the Family Business*. (Cheltenham: Edward Elgar, 2017), 220–327.

4. Craig E. Aronoff and John L. Ward, *Family Business Governance: Maximizing Family Business Potential* (New York: Pelgrave Macmillan, 2011), VIII-96.

5. Judy Lin Walsh and Aline Porto, "Is It Time to Leave the Family Business?," *Harvard Business Review*, January 24, 2020. https://hbr.org/2020/01/is-it-time-to-leave-the-family-business.

4.2 Do I Deserve the Business and/or Wealth I Will Inherit?

6. Lisa A. Keister, "The One Percent," *Annual Review of Sociology* 40, no. 1 (January 2014): 347–367.

7. Thomas M. Zellweger and Joseph H. Astrachan, "On the Emotional Value of Owning a Firm," *Family Business Review* 21, no. 4 (December 2008): 347–363.

8. Michael Carney and Robert S. Nason, "Family Business and the 1%," *Business & Society* 57, no. 6 (July 2018): 1191–1215.

9. Bill Noye, Dominic Pelligana, Michelle De Lucia and Greg Griffith, "Family Business—The Balance for Success: Colliding Generational Perspectives, Reinvigorating Successful Family Businesses," *The 2018 KPMG Enterprise and Family Business Australia survey report* (Australia: KPMG Enterprise, 2018).

10. Pramodita Sharma and Irving P. Gregory, "Four Bases of Family Business Successor Commitment: Antecedents and Consequences," *Entrepreneurship Theory and Practice* 29, no. 1 (January 2005): 13–33.

11. Phil Knight, *Shoe Dog: A Memoir by the Creator of Nike* (New York: Scribner, 2016), 1–400.

12. Thomas Zellweger, Philipp Sieger and Frank Halter, "Should I Stay or Should I Go? Career Choice Intentions of Students with Family Business Background," *Journal of Business Venturing* 26, no. 5 (September 2011): 521–536.

13. Daniel Mochon, Michael I. Norton and Dan Ariely, "Bolstering and Restoring Feelings of Competence via the IKEA Effect," *International Journal of Research in Marketing* 29, no. 4 (2012): 363–369.

14. Barry Schwartz and Andrew Ward, "Doing Better but Feeling Worse: The Paradox of Choice," in *Positive Psychology in Practice*, eds. Alex Linley and Stephen Joseph (Hoboken: John Wiley & Sons, 2004), 86–104.

15. Castel Winery Mentioned in: Michel Bettane and Thierry Desseauve, *The World's Greatest Wines: 365 Fine Wines For Every Day* (New York: Stewart, Tabori & Change, 2006), 1–576.

4.3 How Do I Talk to My Friends and Colleagues about Our Wealth/Business Worth?

16. Denise Kenyon-Rouvinez, Thierry Lombard, Matthieu Ricard and John L. Ward, *Why me? Wealth: Creating, Receiving and Passing It On* (Marietta: Family Enterprise Publishers, 2007), 124.

17. David H. Olson, "Circumplex Model of Martial and Family Systems," *Journal of Family Therapy* 22, no. 2 (May 2000): 144–167.

18. Philip Marcovici, *The Destructive Power of Family Wealth: A Guide to Succession Planning, Asset Protection, Taxation and Wealth Management* (New York: John Wiley & Sons, 2016), 1–296.

4.4 We Have Wealth. When Should We Set Up a Family Office to Organize It?

19. Kirby Rosplock and Dianne H.B. Welsh, "Sustaining Family Wealth: The Impact of the Family Office on the Family Enterprise," in *Understanding Family Businesses: Undiscovered Approaches, Unique Perspectives, and Neglected Topics*, eds. Alan L. Carsrud and Malin Brännback (New York: Springer, 2012), 289–312.

20. Kirby Rosplock, *The Complete Family Office Handbook: A Guide for Affluent Families and the Advisors Who Serve Them* (Hoboken: John Wiley & Sons, 2021), 1–480.

21. James Beech, "Global Family Office Growth Soars, Manages $5.9 Trillion," *Campden FB*, July 18, 2019. https://www.campdenfb.com/article/global-family-office-growth-soars-manages-59-trillion.

22. Kirby Rosplock, *The Complete Family Office Handbook: A Guide for Affluent Families and the Advisors Who Serve Them* (Hoboken: John Wiley & Sons, 2021), 1–480.

23. Dianne H.B. Welsh, Esra Memili, Kirby Rosplock, Juan Roure and Juan Luis Segurado, "Perceptions of Entrepreneurship Across Generations in Family Offices: a Stewardship Theory Perspective," *Journal of Family Business Strategy* 4, no. 3 (September 2013): 213–226.

24. Juan Roure, Juan Luis Segurado, Dianne H.B. Welsh and Kirby Rosplock, "Toward a Conceptual Model of the Role of Entrepreneurship in the Family Office," *The Journal of Applied Management and Entrepreneurship* 18, no. 4 (October 2013): 42.

25. Kirby Rosplock, *The Complete Family Office Handbook: A Guide for Affluent Families and the Advisors Who Serve Them* (Hoboken: John Wiley & Sons, 2021), 1–480.

26. Rosplock, *The Complete Family Office Handbook: A Guide for Affluent Families and the Advisors Who Serve Them.*

27. Barbara R. Hauser and Keith Drewery, *Setting Up a Family Office* (London: Global Law and Business, 2020): 1–80.

28. Angelo Robles, *Effective Family Office: Best Practices and Beyond* (Greenwich: Family Office Press, 2017): 1–114.

4.5 Should We Engage in Philanthropy and/or in Impact Investing? And, How Would We Get Started?

29. "Charitable Giving Statistics," *National Philanthropic Trust* (website), 2020, https://www.nptrust.org/philanthropic-resources/charitable-giving-statistics/. Andrew Milner, "The Global Landscape of Philanthropy," *WINGS Global Philanthropy Report* (Brazil: WINGS, 2018): 1–72.

30. Abhilash Mudaliar and Hannah Dithrich, "Sizing the Impact of Investing Market," *Global Impact Investing Network,* April 1, 2019. https://thegiin.org/research/publication/impinv-market-size#:~:text=The%20GIIN%20estimates%20the%20current,market%20to%20be%20%24502%20billion.

31. Neus Feliu and Isabel C. Botero, "Philanthropy in Family Firms: A Review of the Literature," *Family Business Review* 29, no. 1 (March 2016): 121–141.

32. Antony Bugg-Levine and Jed Emerson, "Impact Investing: Transforming How We Make Money while Making a Difference," *Innovations: Technology, Governance, Globalization* 6, no. 3 (July 2011): 9–18.

33. Chris Addy, Maya Chorengel, Mariah Collins and Michael Etzel, "Calculating the Value of Impact Investing," *Harvard Business Review* 97, no. 1 (January 2019): 102. Paul Brest and Kelly Born, "When Can Impact Investing Create Real Impact?," *Standford Social Innovation Review,* Fall 2013, https://community-wealth.org/sites/clone.community-wealth.org/files/downloads/article-brest-born.pdf.

4.6 If We (the Next Generation) Want to Sell the Family Business, How Do We Start This Process?

34. Jonathan Pellegrin, *The Art of Selling the Family Business: Responsible Stewardship of Family Wealth* (North Charleston: CreateSpace Independent Publishing, 2017), 34f.

35. Stephen R. Covey, *Seven Habits of Highly Effective People* (New York: Free Press, 1989), 1–384.

36. Viktor E. Frankl, *Man's Search for Meaning* (Boston: Beacon Press, 2006), 1–192.

37. Jonathan Pellegrin, *The Art of Selling the Family Business: Responsible Stewardship of Family Wealth* (North Charleston: CreateSpace Independent Publishing, 2017).

4.7 I Am Not Sure My Personal Values Align With Those of Other Family Owners. How Can I Exit the Family Business (or Family Office) Gracefully?

38. Lucia Ceja, Remei Agulles and Josep Tàpies, "The Importance of Values in Family-Owned Firms," *IESE Business School Working Paper,* no. 875 (July 2010). https://ssrn.com/abstract=1701642.

39. Dawn R. DeTienne and Francesco Chirico, "Exist Strategies in Family Firms: How Socioemotional Wealth Drives the Threshold of Performance," *Entrepreneurship Theory and Practice* 37, no. 6 (November 2013): 1297–1318.

40. Matthias Blaum, "Das "streitige" Ausscheiden," in *Governance im Familienunternehmen,* eds. Peter May, and Peter Bartels (Köln: Bundesanzeiger Verlag GmbH, 2017), 237–256.

41. Nigel Finch, "Identifying and Addressing the Causes of Conflict in Family Business," *SSRN* (May 2005): 1–23.

42. Alexandra Michel and Nadine Kammerlander, "Trusted Advisors in a Family Business's Succession-planning Process—An Agency Perspective," *Journal of Family Business Strategy,* 6, no. 1 (March 2015): 45–57.

4.8 I Want to Start My Own Business. Can I Ask Our Firm or Family For Help?

43. Donna Kelley, William B. Gartner and Mathew Allen, "Family Entrepreneurship," *A Global Entrepreneurship Monitor* (Boston: Babson College, 2020). https://www.gemconsortium.org/report/20192020-global-entrepreneurship-monitor-gem-family-entrepreneurship-report-2.

44. Shaker A. Zahra, "Entrepreneurial Risk Taking in Family Firms: The Wellspring of the Regenerative Capability," *Family Business Review* 31, no. 2 (June 2018): 216–226.

45. "Fostering Intrapreneurship," *Family Enterprise Foundation* (Website). Accessed January 6, 2021, https://familyenterprisefoundation.org/learning-community/relate-by-themes/fostering-intrapreneurship/.

46. Judy Lin Walsh, Sam Bruehl and Nick Di Loerto, "Is the Next Generation of Your Family Business Entrepreneurial Enough," *Harvard Business Review,* May 8, 2020. https://hbr.org/2020/05/is-the-next-generation-of-your-family-business-entrepreneurial-enough.

4.9 I Will Leave the Family Business Behind, Which Other (Career) Path Should I Pursue in My Life?

47. John M. Coetzee, *Youth: Scenes from a Provincial Life* (London: Penguin Books, 2003), 1–176.

48. Judy Lin Walsh and Rob Lachenauer, "Should You Join the Family Business?," *Harvard Business Review,* June 4, 2018. https://hbr.org/2018/06/should-you-join-the-family-business. Marcela Ramírez-Pasillas, Hans Lundberg and Mattias Nordqvist, "Next Generation External Venturing Practices in Family Owned Businesses," *Journal of Management Studies* 58, no. 1 (January 2021).
Thomas M. Zellweger, Robert S. Nason, Mattias Nordqvist and Candida G. Brush, "Why Do Family Firms Strive for Nonfinancial Goals? An Organizational Identity Perspective," *Entrepreneurship Theory and Practice* 37, no. 2 (March 2013): 229–248.

SYNTHESIS AND TAKEAWAYS

by Sabine B. Rau and Peter Jaskiewicz

Asking Questions

Questions are not only starting points on the journey of self-discovery, they are also opportunities to learn and incubate new ideas about how things work. Asking questions provides the opportunity to understand complex phenomena. These opportunities also help us gather data and either reject or support our ideas about reality, enabling us to better understand, predict, and adapt to the contexts in which we live, work, and play.

For Next Gens of enterprising families, asking questions is even more important because there is a lot at stake—the family, ownership, business, wealth, and one's place inside (or outside) of them. Looking at the different norms from these four circles that Next Gens confront, we realize the potential conflicts arising across them: Whereas the family expects unconditional support and love, ownership is based upon the power and responsibility from voting rights; the business works well in case of merit and performance; and wealth demands preservation, growth, and impact. Many of the questions raised by Next Gens in this book mirror the inherent conflicts that they sense when looking at their future roles straddling the four circles.

We began this book by introducing our Four-Circle Model because Next Gens' thirty-five questions highlight their desire to understand and manage the inherent complexity within the four circles and where the family interacts with nonfamily members outside of them. Both leading academic-practitioners and members of enterprising families from twenty-seven countries briefly responded to these questions, offering intriguing food for thought about the inherent norms within each circle and how to address competing expectations at the intersection of the circles and beyond them. It is our hope that reflecting upon the responses and setting up one's own action plan will provide Next Gens with the opportunity to connect with partners, friends, siblings, parents, aunts and uncles, cousins, nonfamily executives, and other stakeholders to better understand themselves, their families, and their families' enterprises. However, like most opportunities worth pursuing, asking questions and finding relevant answers is not without risk.

First, there is the risk that Next Gens wait too long to ask questions and find answers. Some questions reveal a lack of basic understanding that could undermine the legitimacy and acceptance of Next Gens. Therefore, it is essential for Next Gens to raise these questions early in life and pose them to people who are discrete and trustworthy. Put differently, Next Gens should ask questions and look for their answers as early as possible and from there onwards, learn continuously.

Second, asking questions to understand the different concepts, processes, and activities of the family and the family enterprise grants Next Gens a level of autonomy, making it harder for other family and nonfamily members to manipulate or control them. Such proactivity is valuable and meaningful. However, proactive Next Gens also risk being labeled as demanding or as "activist family members," akin to activist shareholders in corporations. It is therefore important for Next Gens to strike a balance between proactivity (e.g., tabling well-grounded requests for insights) and diplomacy (e.g., being humble and empathetic). Otherwise, Next

Gens run the risk of fueling tensions within the family and the larger team of executives.

Third, asking questions and searching for tailored answers, like becoming a responsible owner, leader, or steward of wealth, requires considerable investment of time and effort. While all investments carry a certain level of risk, this is a worthwhile investment that any Next Gen should be aware of, and any Senior Gen should support. That said, both family and nonfamily members must realize that the required investments take time and involve many interactions and dialogues over many years. Put differently, such investments are not a sprint or a marathon but rather an ultra-triathlon. It is not about starting fast but making it to the finish line.

Starting the Journey

Beyond these general insights, we have learned about a number of starting points for the Next Gens' learning journey: We found that each family is unique. They are different across countries and within the same culture. Each of us should understand how our own family is unique by asking questions about our core norms and beliefs, our structure, our patterns of interaction, and our level of unity. Even if family is of lesser importance to some Next Gens, it has usually left a lasting mark on their values, identity, and thinking. Business and wealth, like family, are founded and grow. Unlike family, business and wealth can disappear. Because the family has an enduring influence on our lives, it is important to care for it. Otherwise, the family will not empower but burden us. In the worst case, families become entrenched in enduring conflicts that severely limit Next Gens and threaten everything that the family achieved in its more glorious past.

We also learned that being an owner means to be responsible for what we own. This responsibility, at its core, is to determine which individuals to entrust with decisions and to monitor them. This is a responsibility that cannot be delegated to others, so the only way to relinquish it is to give up ownership. In this context, we also learned that ignoring this responsibility is in itself a choice, though a poor one. Conversely, those who embrace their ownership responsibilities have an opportunity to shape the future of their family, its enterprises, their community, and society.

Building on knowledge about ownership, we saw how Next Gens joining the family business can shape the future of their families, enterprises, and wealth. Taking an active leadership role or selecting, onboarding, and supervising a leadership team is the right of owners. Being able to grow into a leadership role depends upon one's upbringing, education, and experience, but is foremost a matter of motivation and maturity. Maybe more importantly, it is not about having to grow into a leadership role in the family business but being accepted in one's chosen role in the family business by other family members, owners, and executives. When Next Gens are widely accepted in their role in the family business—whether on the shop floor or the top floor—they will not only be more satisfied about their work but tensions with other family members will be low.

Finally, we learned that wealth needs a purpose. Without a purpose, financial wealth is just money, and money will be spent. Moreover, non-financial wealth, without a purpose, will dissipate. The family, as a unified group, can give wealth a purpose. Equipped with a purpose, the family can decide what they want to achieve, the strategies they want to follow, and the structures they want to implement. If financial wealth is tied up in a family business, it is often not the topic of discussion, but when a family has accumulated considerable financial wealth that is independent of the business, or, if such wealth is freed through the sale of the business, then questions about how to repurpose financial wealth become pressing. Although the family's wealth is often measured in terms of money, it is the non-financial wealth—the networks, education credentials, work experiences, and personalities—of Next Gens that usually determine whether a family will be able to deal with its own challenges, build transgenerational wealth, and make a difference to their enterprises and society.

Asking questions as a Next Gen is not only the beginning of a learning journey, it's an opportunity to become intellectually, emotionally, and financially independent. No matter where Next Gens are in the world, what they are passionate about, and which sector they work in, being a Next Gen who is both truly independent and equipped to understand their family, makes them a most valuable family member, a responsible incoming owner, a competent potential employee, and a potential steward of the family's wealth and legacy.

We wish all Next Gens (and their families) a challenging yet satisfying learning journey.

Your Notes | *Your Action Items* ———————————————

ABOUT THE AUTHORS

Peter Jaskiewicz was born into a business family in Poland and grew up in Germany. Wanting to understand why succession failed in his family's business, Peter researched family businesses during both his doctoral studies at the European Business School in Oestrich-Winkel, and while visiting INSEAD, Fontainebleau, and IESE Business School, Barcelona. Today, he is a full professor of family business at the Telfer School of Management in Ottawa, where he holds a University Research Chair in Enduring Entrepreneurship and leads Telfer's family enterprise initiative. His findings have received numerous awards and were considered among the most globally influential scholarship on family business in 2013, 2015, and 2017. Peter has presented his research insights to members of the European Parliament, the European Commission, and to employees of the United Nations. In addition, he has also worked with the federal government in Canada. He is an associate editor of the leading journal in the family business field—the *Family Business Review*—and of the pioneering knowledge-sharing platform—familybusiness.org. He has been a visiting professor at Zhejiang University (China), Sorbonne Business School and University de Nanterre (both France), and King's College (United Kingdom), and is a frequent keynote speaker at both academic and practitioner conferences. He trains family business professionals on succession planning and, in his advising practice, provides support to the development of responsible Next Gen owners and effective

Next Gen teams. He lives with his wife, Lidiane Cunha, and their two children, Anna and Leon, in Ottawa, Canada.

Sabine B. Rau is one of the most renowned experts on moderating succession processes and co-creating family constitutions (also called family protocols) in Germany, as well as abroad. Born into a family with a family business, she was inspired to study management. During her management studies, she realized that family businesses, and their specific questions, were not part of the management curriculum. With the aim to teach family business at universities, Sabine drew from relevant and rigorous research to help her build a family business center at the European Business School (EBS) at Oestrich-Winkel—a leading business school in Germany. Following the development of the family business center at EBS, Sabine took over as the chair of family business at Otto Beisheim School of Business (WHU) in Vallendar, Germany. Currently, Sabine holds visiting professorships at the Telfer School of Management (University of Ottawa) at Berlin's European School of Management and Technology (ESMT), and she also teaches at the Université de Luxembourg. Until the beginning of 2017, Sabine was a full professor of Entrepreneurship at King's College London. Prior to starting her academic career in 2001, as a research fellow at INSEAD in Fontainebleau, Sabine founded her own business while working for her family's business. In 2003, Sabine took over the presidency of the International Family Enterprise Research Academy (www.ifera.org), which she led until 2007. She now serves on several boards as an independent director. Sabine is a mother of three adult children, and a grandmother of two children.

For A Better Canada and A Better World

Telfer's Focus on Family Enterprises and Next Gens

The Telfer School of Management at the University of Ottawa is located in the heart of the nation's capital and is the proud home of virtually 4,300 students, 200 faculty members, and over 30,000 alumni. At Telfer, everything we do—from teaching and research to policy advice—is firmly aligned with helping Canada reach its potential. We believe that the effects of better business practice means a better Canada and that a better Canada means a better world: https://telfer.uottawa.ca/en/

At Telfer, we are strong supporters of family enterprises and their impact on both the economy and the community. To make a difference to family enterprises and their communities in Canada and globally, we are:

- Building an institute to become a thought leader, training ground, and safe space for family enterprises and Next Gens.
- Supporting projects for Next Gens—including this book.
- Featuring new coursework on the family enterprise in many of our degree-granting undergraduate and graduate programs, such as our MBA and BCom programs.
- Developing a new executive education program that empowers Next Gens to become responsible owners, effective managers, family leaders, and stewards of their family's wealth.
- Providing leadership development and executive education programming for family enterprises through Telfer Executive Programs: http://tlfr.ca/telferexecutiveprograms.

INDEX